BUSINESS PROCESS MANAGEMENT SYSTEMS

OTHER AUERBACH PUBLICATIONS

Agent-Based Manufacturing and Control Systems: New Agile Manufacturing Solutions for Achieving Peak Performance
Massimo Paolucci and Roberto Sacile
ISBN: 1574443364

Curing the Patch Management Headache
Felicia M. Nicastro
ISBN: 0849328543

Cyber Crime Investigator's Field Guide, Second Edition
Bruce Middleton
ISBN: 0849327687

Disassembly Modeling for Assembly, Maintenance, Reuse and Recycling
A. J. D. Lambert and Surendra M. Gupta
ISBN: 1574443348

The Ethical Hack: A Framework for Business Value Penetration Testing
James S. Tiller
ISBN: 084931609X

Fundamentals of DSL Technology
Philip Golden, Herve Dedieu, and Krista Jacobsen
ISBN: 0849319137

The HIPAA Program Reference Handbook
Ross Leo
ISBN: 0849322111

Implementing the IT Balanced Scorecard: Aligning IT with Corporate Strategy
Jessica Keyes
ISBN: 0849326214

Information Security Fundamentals
Thomas R. Peltier, Justin Peltier, and John A. Blackley
ISBN: 0849319579

Information Security Management Handbook, Fifth Edition, Volume 2
Harold F. Tipton and Micki Krause
ISBN: 0849332109

Introduction to Management of Reverse Logistics and Closed Loop Supply Chain Processes
Donald F. Blumberg
ISBN: 1574443607

Maximizing ROI on Software Development
Vijay Sikka
ISBN: 0849323126

Mobile Computing Handbook
Imad Mahgoub and Mohammad Ilyas
ISBN: 0849319714

MPLS for Metropolitan Area Networks
Nam-Kee Tan
ISBN: 084932212X

Multimedia Security Handbook
Borko Furht and Darko Kirovski
ISBN: 0849327733

Network Design: Management and Technical Perspectives, Second Edition
Teresa C. Piliouras
ISBN: 0849316081

Network Security Technologies, Second Edition
Kwok T. Fung
ISBN: 0849330270

Outsourcing Software Development Offshore: Making It Work
Tandy Gold
ISBN: 0849319439

Quality Management Systems: A Handbook for Product Development Organizations
Vivek Nanda
ISBN: 1574443526

A Practical Guide to Security Assessments
Sudhanshu Kairab
ISBN: 0849317061

The Real-Time Enterprise
Dimitris N. Chorafas
ISBN: 0849327776

Software Testing and Continuous Quality Improvement, Second Edition
William E. Lewis
ISBN: 0849325242

Supply Chain Architecture: A Blueprint for Networking the Flow of Material, Information, and Cash
William T. Walker
ISBN: 1574443577

The Windows Serial Port Programming Handbook
Ying Bai
ISBN: 0849322138

AUERBACH PUBLICATIONS

www.auerbach-publications.com
To Order Call: 1-800-272-7737 • Fax: 1-800-374-3401
E-mail: orders@crcpress.com

BUSINESS PROCESS MANAGEMENT SYSTEMS

Strategy and Implementation

James F. Chang

Auerbach Publications
Taylor & Francis Group
Boca Raton   New York

Published in 2006 by
Auerbach Publications
Taylor & Francis Group
6000 Broken Sound Parkway NW, Suite 300
Boca Raton, FL 33487-2742

International Standard Book Number-10: 0-8493-2310-X (Hardcover)
International Standard Book Number-13: 978-0-8493-2310-2 (Hardcover)
Library of Congress Card Number 2005045248

Library of Congress Cataloging-in-Publication Data

Chang, James F.
  Business process management systems : strategy and implementation / James F. Chang.
       p. cm.
  Includes bibliographical reference and index.
  ISBN 0-8493-2310-X
  1. Reengineering (Management) 2. Workflow--Management. 3. Process control--Data processing--Management. 4. Business--Data processing--Management. 5. Management information systems. I. Title.

  HD58.87.C429 2005
  658.4'063--dc22   2005045248

Taylor & Francis Group
is the Academic Division of T&F Informa plc.

**Visit the Taylor & Francis Web site at
http://www.taylorandfrancis.com**

**and the Auerbach Publications Web site at
http://www.auerbach-publications.com**

Dedication

For my loving parents, Dr. Yeu-Wen Chang and Mrs. Lan-Fei Chang

Table of Contents

Acknowledgments

Prior to writing this book, I have written a few articles on Business Process Management (BPM) and Enterprise Application Integration (EAI) that appeared in trade journals. Stan Wakefield, who was working as a publishing agent, read my articles and asked whether I had any interest in writing a book. His suggestion piqued my interest, thus starting my journey into book writing. What I thought would take six months to complete has now taken almost two years. Despite having had no free time during weekends and nights for the past two years, I am glad I undertook this journey. The sense of accomplishment at the end of the journey has more than made up for the lost time.

This book would not have been possible without the help of a lot of people. My friend Jon Frierson deserves special mention for the numerous hours he spent proofreading my chapters and providing invaluable advice on how to make this book more readable. I want to thank Mark Evans, Chief Information Officer (CIO) of Tesoro Corporation, for giving me the opportunity to implement Business Process Management System (BPMS) solutions. Felix Racca provided my first education in BPMS technologies. I want to thank my editor, John Wyzalek of Auerbach Publications, for accommodating changes to the publication schedule. Finally, I want to thank my friends, Patrick Azria, David Rhys Davies, George Drupals, and Jeff Nguyen for the support and encouragement they have provided.

About the Author

James Chang is the founder and president of Ivy Consultants, Inc. He has extensive experience implementing Enterprise Resource Planning (ERP)–enabled business solutions and process-centric integration solutions for Fortune 500 companies. Mr. Chang has written several articles on BPM and EAI. He graduated cum laude with a Bachelor of Science degree in operations research and industrial engineering from Cornell University. He can be reached at jchang@ivyconsultants.com.

Chapter 1

Theories of Process Management

The business process reengineering (BPR) movement of the 1990s emphasized technology as a key enabler of process management and process change. As a result, information technology (IT) has steadily gained prominence in the management suites of large enterprises. No longer do companies view IT as a back-office burden that adds overhead but does not contribute to enterprise competitiveness. As a direct consequence of the reengineering movement and the rise of IT, large corporations flocked to implement Enterprise Resource Planning (ERP) software, such as Systems Analysis & Program Development (SAP), Oracle and Peoplesoft. Such was the demand for ERP systems that the number one ERP vendor, SAP, grew its revenue from €255 million in 1990 to €7.3 billion in 2001. These decisions were often dictated by corporate boardrooms. There are stories from the mid-1990s about customers seeking out SAP salespeople to buy SAP software. Despite its ubiquitous presence in the corporate world, ERP software was expensive to implement and difficult to change once implemented. ERP implementations often led to rigid, cookie-cutter business processes. However, they did accomplish the radical change concept espoused by the reengineering theorists. With the advent of new business process- and internet-based technologies, we have entered a new technological world with a new process-based design and implementation framework to employ business solutions. In this new technological world, business process designers are directly involved in systems design. The closer working relationship between business process designers and IT helps to reduce the gap between the business requirement and the final deployed solution.

The key concept of Business Process Management (BPM) is the convergence of technologies with process management theories. This convergence produces new process design and implementation approaches that enable what Michael Hammer terms the process enterprise.[1] The process enterprise is organized around core processes that traverse departmental and divisional lines, and these processes are standardized and measurable throughout the enterprise. Utilizing the BPM process design approach and technology (a new breed of technology that we will call Business Process Management Systems (BPMSs)), BPM solutions enable process enterprise to measure and standardize processes and provide reusable processes that can be networked. This new breed of technology eases the task of changing business processes by separating the underlying applications from the business processes. Processes are no longer etched in stone once they are conceived. That inflexibility to support changing business processes was the bane of many business applications. In this section, we will discuss the process management theories that led to BPM. Once we have described process management theories and have illustrated their benefits to corporations, we will dive into how to use technology and the implementation of BPM to reap these benefits.

What Is Process Management?

The effects of globalization and the technological advances of the last 20 years profoundly increased the pace of change and the severity of competition in the business environment compared to the previous five decades. In response to this rapidly changing business environment, management theorists and scholars are constantly putting forth new ideas to help corporations succeed in this turbulent world. These new ideas are like the flavor of the day. One idea after another would be put forth, generating excitement in the management press, only to fade away in a few years. The uninitiated outsider might perceive these management fads as unrelated concepts that arose independently. The truth is most of these management ideas often built on one another and shared central themes that have not changed through the years. Whether it is Total Quality Management (TQM) of the 1980s or BPR of the 1990s, the one central theme common to these management ideas is the concept of process management.

Before we discuss process management, a definition of process is warranted. In the systems engineering arena, a process is a sequence of events that uses inputs to produce outputs. This is a broad definition and can include sequences as mechanical as reading a file and transforming the file to a desired output format; to taking a customer order, filling that order, and issuing the customer invoice. From a business perspective, a process is a coordinated and standardized flow of activities performed by people or machines, which can traverse functional or departmental boundaries to achieve a business objective that creates value for internal or external customers. Not surprisingly, the business process ought to create value. This is only common sense — any activities that do not contribute value really should not be performed. Business processes should also be coordinated and standardized. Processes should not be haphazard sets of activities to accomplish a business objective. By coordinating and standardizing the activities, processes are reusable and maximize the value they create while lowering the costs when compared to a nonstandardized approach of executing activities. Standardization of processes entails measurability. If processes are not measurable, it is not possible to determine the value they create. This business definition of process is more familiar to business readers, and we will use this definition when referring to processes.

Every management theorist has a slightly different definition of process management. One definition that generically describes process management is from Professor Mary J. Benner of University of Pennsylvania and Professor Michael L. Tushman of Harvard University:

> Process management, based on a view of an organization as a system of interlinked processes, involves concerted efforts to map, improve, and adhere to organizational processes[2]

This definition of process management is succinct but encompassing. It also resonates with the process enterprise concept that Michael Hammer described. Whereas traditional organizations are composed of departments and functional silos, this definition views organizations as networks or systems of processes. To manage a process, the first task is to define it. This involves defining the steps (tasks) in the process and mapping the tasks to the roles involved in the process. Once the process is mapped and implemented, performance measures can be established. Establishing measurements creates a basis to improve the process. The last piece of the process management definition describes the organizational setup that enables the standardization of and adherence to the process throughout the organization. Assigning enterprise process owners and aligning employees' performance reviews and compensation to the value creation of the processes could accomplish this.

Early Process Concepts

The current theories of process management have their origins in the quality movement and business process reengineering movement of the past two decades. However, the genesis of process management and management in general, can be traced to the birth of the modern corporation. Adam Smith claimed that mass production required a new organizational form and new methods of work. In his seminal work, *The Wealth of Nations* (1776), Smith recognized that the division of labor was essential for increasing the productivity of workers. While observing workers at a pin factory in France, he noticed that workers performing single steps in pin manufacturing could produce far more pins than workers engaged in manufacturing whole pins. The productivity increase was orders of magnitude higher, 48,000 pins by 10 person teams compared to at most 20 per person working independently. Smith determined that the productivity increases were due to the dexterity each worker obtained by performing the assigned tasks and the time saved by not having to switch from one task to another. Smith's idea of specialization of labor established the foundation for the functional organizations in which corporations align themselves today.

Adam Smith introduced the idea of labor specialization. This necessitated defining roles and tasks performed by different individuals. This is the basis of business processes spanning multiple individuals. The next revolution in process management came from Frederick W. Taylor and Henry Ford. Spurred by the introduction of mass production, Frederick Winslow Taylor, an engineer also known for inventing carbon steel machine tools, expanded on Smith's labor specialization with the introduction of the scientific method and measurements to the manufacturing processes. In his book, *The Principles of Scientific Management* (1911), Taylor stressed that corporations needed to remove production inefficiencies and improve the division of labor.[3] He proposed to accomplish these with scientific management techniques. Theses techniques include the following:

- Time and motion studies to observe how different workers perform their jobs and standardize work activities on the most efficient work procedures
- Standardization of materials, equipment, and work methods for all activities in the manufacturing process
- Systematic methods for selecting the best workers suited for each job and provide them with training to perform tasks that are standardized
- Alignment of the workers' pay to their output

Taylor's scientific management and division of labor also applied to management ranks. In his view, managers served to coordinate the various jobs that individual workers performed. It was also the managers' responsibility to monitor and motivate the workers to perform their tasks. In the management hierarchy, Taylor espoused specialists for performing individual functions. Thus, there were accounting, recruiting, selling, and production functions within the organization. All of these functions reported to the chief executive, whose responsibility was to coordinate the work of the various functional groups and plan for the corporation's future. Taylor's organizational concepts were widely adopted by corporations and are still seen today. Taylor's contribution of scientific management led to the establishment of industrial engineering as an engineering discipline.

Henry Ford found practical uses for Taylor's scientific management theories. When he started the Ford Motor Company in 1913, Ford sought to bring the automobile to the masses by offering it at an affordable price. To accomplish this he offered one car model, the Model T, in one color, black. This approach, and the rigorous assembly line method, allowed Ford to offer automobiles the everyday man could afford to buy. In his assembly line concept, Ford viewed manufacturing of cars as a single process with sequenced activities. He extended Adam Smith's concept of labor specialization and added prescribed sequences to accomplish tasks. Each worker performed a single task in a prescribed and repeatable manner. The moving assembly line replaced the nodal assembly with flowline: products flowed to the workers instead of workers moving from one assembly station to another. Ford made profitable use of interchangeable parts, a concept already developed in handgun manufacturing. This feature enabled mass production and introduced specifications to the manufacturing process.[4] Not only was Ford successful at selling automobiles to middle-class Americans, he was able to pay his workers premium salaries because of the productivity gains from his manufacturing process.

Adam Smith's labor specialization, Henry Ford's assembly line, and Frederick Taylor's scientific management produced the functional corporations with specialized departments made up of specialized workers. This organizational setup optimized the tasks each department needed to perform. It enabled corporations to mass produce goods efficiently to satisfy the demand spurred by the economic expansion of the post-World War I era. According to productivity data published in 1961, annual factory productivity in the United States increased 1.2 percent from 1869 to 1878, 1.3 percent from 1889 to 1919, and 2.1 percent from 1919 to 1957.[5] The introduction of scientific management and moving assembly line concepts in the 1910s certainly contributed to the productivity increase in the period after 1919.

Modern Process Management Theories

The functional organization served corporations well from the beginning of the century to the post-war boom of the 1950s and 1960s. After the Second World War, the Marshall Plan established the United States as the sole economic superpower supplying goods and services for rebuilding Europe. On the domestic front, spending was skyrocketing for building new suburbs to house the G.I.s home from the war, and for government-sponsored urban renewal programs. Investment dollars diverted to military use during the war years were now redirected to civilian projects. Demand for American goods was so high that corporations' main concern was insufficient capacity. This meant there was little concern for product quality or catering to customer requirements. Consumers, starved of goods during the Depression and war years, bought anything American companies were selling.

The happy days ended in the 1970s when the economic environment changed and corporate competition increased. Several economic factors contributed to the change in the economic environment. In 1971, faced with increased foreign deficits from war-induced inflation, the United States withdrew from the gold standard, ending the Bretton Woods world monetary system. Under the Bretton Woods system, the dollar was fixed at $35 per ounce of gold. Other currencies had fixed exchange rates against the United States dollar. The various central banks were obligated to buy/sell their currency to limit fluctuation to within 1 percent of the fixed parity. The collapse of the Bretton Woods monetary system ushered in an era of increased volatility in world currency markets. This translated into increased volatility in demand for products and services. This volatility in demand was detrimental to the mass production strategy that corporations were pursuing. Further adding volatility to demand, the world economy also experienced severe recessions due to the energy crisis. Around this time, Europe and Japan re-established their economic bases. As trade barriers lowered in the 1970s, United States corporations began to find competition from European and Japanese companies both in domestic and export markets. The increased competition led to consumer choice in purchases. Complicating matters further for American corporations was the maturation of the consumers. From 1949 to 1969, the average family income increased from $14,000 to $28,000 in the United States. Because of higher average income, consumers demanded more customized goods and services. They were no longer satisfied with whatever corporations sold them. All of these factors created challenges for corporations built for mass production. Instead of the supplier-driven economy that existed before, corporations were faced with a customer-driven economy. This set up our current environment in which customers demand quality products that cater to their needs. Customers are also now demanding a satisfactory purchasing experience and customer service. Corporations that do not provide an easy buying experience risk exclusion from future sales. This increased competition and the resulting shift from the supplier-driven economy to a customer-driven economy have forced corporations to rethink their organizations and business practices.

Total Quality Management Movement (TQM)

The turbulent business environment resulted in new management thinking and focus. One of the management initiatives to help corporations compete in this customer economy was total quality management (TQM). The ideas of TQM were not new. They were developed by William Edwards Deming, Joseph Juran, and Kaoru Ishikawa starting in the mid-1940s. Deming was perhaps the most prominent of the three. During the 1940s, Deming was an advisor of sampling for the Census Bureau. After he left the Census Bureau, Deming began to introduce the statistical quality control methods he developed at the Census Bureau to industrial corporations. However, he was not successful in convincing United States companies to adopt his ideas. When Douglas Macarthur called for American professionals to help rebuild Japan, Deming was among the 200 scientists and engineers who joined Macarthur. It was in Japan that Deming was able to influence corporations to employ his quality management ideas. Deming viewed quality management as more than the statistical quality control first introduced by American statistician W. A. Shewhart in the 1920s. In the course of his career, he gradually developed a prescriptive set of practices that have been labeled Deming's 14 points. These 14 points relate to statistical quality control and span from top-management obligations, to human resource practices, and organizational setup. In addition to Deming, Joseph Juran was another influential quality guru who had a significant impact on corporate Japan. While Deming focused on organizational practice and behavior to achieve quality with his 14 points, Juran focused on the importance of senior management in quality improvement, and he extended quality improvement to the business processes. Kaoru Ishikawa was the third founder of the quality management movement. He introduced the concept of the quality circle organization, continuous improvement philosophy, and bottom-up analytical methods such as cause and effect diagrams. Many scholars have credited them with the remarkable turnaround of corporate Japan into a strong global competitor from the rubble of World War II. We will discuss more about their ideas when we delve into TQM philosophy and practices.

Starting in the 1970s and continuing through the 1980s, American companies found increasing competition from Japanese firms. Japanese firms were often able to deliver higher quality products at lower prices to the marketplace. Stunned by lost market share, American corporations started to look for answers in their Japanese competitors. American companies began to embrace quality management practices three decades after Deming first proposed quality management concepts to American corporations.

What Is Total Quality Management (TQM)?

Now we have described the circumstance for the introduction of the quality management movement to the United States, the next question to answer is what is TQM? This is not an easy term to define and entire academic articles have been devoted to its definition.[6,7] Even though Deming started the quality movement, he never used the term TQM. In an article he published, Deming remarked:

> The trouble with total quality management — failure of TQM, you call it — is that there is no such thing. It is a buzzword. I have never used the term, as it carries no meaning (Deming, 1994).[8]

This is a confounding remark by one of the primary founders of TQM. If Deming did not recognize TQM, then what is TQM? In their widely cited 1995 article, J. Richard Hackman of Harvard University and Ruth Wageman of Columbia University investigated the conceptual core of TQM, and how the current practices of TQM as a social movement stacked up against the founders' values and prescriptions.[9] I will refer to their article to describe the concepts of TQM. Table 1.1 provides a summary of Hackman and Wageman's discussions on TQM's philosophy, assumptions, principles, and practices.

According to Hackman and Wageman's description of the TQM philosophy, all three founders of TQM share a more socialistic view of the corporation then the traditional capitalistic theorists. They place strong emphasis on the corporation's responsibility to the community, customers, and employees, rather than solely to shareholders. For the corporation to stay in business and pursue its goals, as outlined in the philosophy, TQM strategy relies on four assumptions. The first assumption is that the cost of poor quality is higher in the long-run than the cost of putting in place

Table 1.1 TQM Concepts

Philosophy	The purpose of an organization is to sustain itself so that it can contribute to the stability of the community, provide goods and services to customers and provide an environment for organization members to grow
Assumptions	The cost of poor quality is higher than the cost of doing it right the first time
	Workers innately care about the quality of work they are doing and they will take the initiative to enhance quality given the right managerial environment
	Problems are often cross-functional and require collective participation from all relevant functions to resolve these problems
	Senior management has the responsibility for quality management and their commitment is crucial to the success of quality improvement in an organization
Principles	Focus on work processes — quality problems are mostly dependent on the work processes that designed and manufactured the products and services
	Analysis of variability — uncontrolled variances are the primary causes of quality problems, and these variances should be analyzed and controlled by the front-line workers
	Management by fact — quality improvement programs should be based on systematic data collection, analysis and experimentation for solution implementation
	Learning and continuous improvement — quality improvement is never-ending and employee learning is a major part for carrying out quality improvements
Practices	Determine customer requirements
	Form supplier partnerships that are not based solely on price
	Create cross-functional teams to analyze and resolve quality problems
	Employ scientific methods to monitor quality and identify areas for quality improvement
	Use process management techniques to identify opportunities for improvement

processes to produce high quality products and services in the first place. TQM founders believed that organizations that produce quality goods would do better economically than organizations that do not focus on quality. The second assumption is people naturally want to do quality work. If workers are given the right information and supportive management, they will take the initiatives to improve their work. Given this assumption, it is counter-productive to have an environment that creates fear and assesses blame. The third assumption is the interconnectedness of functional organizations. Most of the critical problems faced by organizations exist along cross-functional lines. Cross-functional teams, with representation from the relevant functions, are required to resolve these problems. The last assumption addresses the role of senior management. Quality has to be driven top-down and is ultimately the responsibility of senior management.

Based on these four assumptions, Hackman and Wageman outline five practices (or interventions in their parlance) that Deming, Juran, and Ishikawa prescribed. The first practice is to identify customer requirements. Without customer requirements, it is hard to achieve the quality customers want. This sounds intuitive in today's customer economy; however, in the past customer focus was not as necessary as it is today. A customer can be external or internal. It is only after customer requirements are gathered that the information is available to tailor quality improvements to areas that customers care most about. The second practice is to form strategic supplier relationships. The lowest cost supplier may not be the ideal supplier. Companies should focus on total cost, which includes the cost of quality. Quality suppliers most likely will result in lower total cost than low-cost suppliers who do not focus on quality. The third practice is to use cross-functional teams to improve quality. There should be steering teams that focus on identifying the top vital problems of the organization. Once steering teams have identified problems, cross-functional diagnostic teams should analyze the root causes of the problems, and develop and test solutions to resolve these problems. Cross-functional teams are necessary because most central problems faced by organizations span multiple functions within organizations.

The fourth practice is to use scientific methods for monitoring quality and identifying areas for quality improvement. Scientific methods in this case refer mostly to statistical and probabilistic techniques. These techniques include control charts, Pareto analysis, and cost-of-quality analysis. Control charts are used to monitor quality through statistical sampling. All processes produce variances. A stable process is indicative of quality and fluctuates randomly within a range of what is considered normal. Control charts can monitor whether a process has become unstable and needs to be improved. Pareto analysis is referred to as 80/20 analysis, where 20 percent of the factors cause 80 percent of the result. It is used to determine the few factors that contribute significantly to quality problems. Different contributors are ranked according to their effects on a particular outcome. The contributors with the most impact on the outcome are the ones requiring priority attention. The third commonly used quality technique is cost-of-quality analysis. This analysis involves quantifying the costs related to quality improvements and costs incurred for substandard quality. The goal is to identify the quality improvements that can offer the most amount of cost savings.

The fifth practice the TQM founders advocated is using process management techniques that teams can employ to generate quality improvement ideas. These techniques include, process flowchart, brainstorming, and cause-and-effect diagrams. Process flowchart is a graphical representation of the activities involved in a particular work process. The exercise of defining the process flowchart helps organizations identify activities that do not add value and establish a baseline for process improvement. Brainstorming is a group exercise whereby participants are encouraged to generate ideas for improvement without inhibitions. It often helps stimulate creativity from the group. The ideas generated can be analyzed to identify the most promising candidates. A cause-and-effect diagram is also known as fishbone diagram. It links the problem to its potential causes. It is a good method for the group to understand the relationship between possible causes of a quality problem.

Aside from the practices prescribed by the TQM founders, a few practices developed by practitioners deserve mentioning. These include competitive benchmarking and employee involvement. These practices are consistent with the TQM founders' principles and philosophy. Benchmarking is the practice of gathering data about best practices from other organizations. With benchmarking, a corporation can get insights into competitor information, learn alternative methods of performing work, and guide the goals of quality improvement programs. Employee involvement is any mechanism that encourages employee participation in quality improvement. This can be a mechanism for employee suggestions, quality focus groups, and events to encourage and celebrate quality achievements.

In another study based on the Delphi method, scholars at the University of Minnesota identified seven core concepts of Deming's management method.[10] Because Deming is regarded as the primary founder of TQM, his ideas are relevant to the definition of TQM concepts. These seven concepts are:

1. Visionary leadership
2. Internal and external cooperation
3. Learning

4. Continuous improvement
5. Process management
6. Employee fulfillment
7. Customer satisfaction

The Delphi method, developed by the RAND Corporation in the 1950s, is an approach that uses an expert panel to understand a complex subject. Not surprisingly, several of the concepts in the RAND study are the same as ones discussed in Hackman and Wageman's article. Visionary leadership, according to the Delphi study, is the ability of senior management to articulate a long-term organizational vision that is driven by customer requirements. In the TQM world, there is strong emphasis on customer satisfaction. It is viewed as the driving force behind organizational changes and quality improvements. The second concept is an emphasis on cooperation. Functional groups should cooperate extensively because most central problems organizations face are cross-functional in nature. It is essential that an atmosphere of cooperation exists within an organization. This extends to the relationship with external partners (e.g., suppliers) as well. Corporations should find suppliers who are attentive and provide quality products and services. As defined previously, the vendor–supplier relationship should not be based solely on costs.

The third concept is focus on learning. Without proper training, workers are not able to perform quality work and they will not have the necessary understanding to improve their work processes. Furthermore, continuous learning is essential to continuous improvement. The latter implies continuous change. Without proper training, the workforce cannot be expected to keep up with changes and improvements. This brings us to the next concept, continuous improvement. Continuous improvement at an incremental pace is essential for the survival of the organization. Continuous improvement ensures the organization is constantly improving quality and productivity, thus lowering costs. As we will see later, Deming's and the TQM's concept of incremental improvement is fundamentally different from the more radical wholesale process change approach of the BPR movement.

The fifth concept is process management. Similar to the process management practice discussed in Hackman and Wageman's article, process management is a set of management and methodological practices to manage business processes. These management practices include a team-based approach to enhance quality (e.g., quality circles), elimination of merit-based rewards, and elimination of fear from the work environment. Methodological practices are an expansion of Taylor's scientific methods and include using statistical analysis and quality tools. These practices have expanded from their manufacturing origin to applications in design and to the deployment of products and services. It is interesting to note that the founders of TQM, especially Deming and Ishikawa, eschew the use of merit rewards for workers. They view merit rewards as denigrating to worker pride and undermining employee behavior and can damage continuous improvement. There is considerable on-going discussion in academic circles surrounding the right mix of intrinsic (e.g., workers' inherent pride in doing quality work) and extrinsic (e.g., merit-based rewards) motivations in the workplace.

The sixth concept is employee fulfillment. Satisfied employees are more likely to produce quality work. The organization should provide a working environment that is challenging and enjoyable for the workforce. This concept is closely related to learning and the intrinsic motivational forces that Deming recommends.

The last key concept of the Deming management method is customer satisfaction. This is perhaps the most important of the seven concepts. Satisfied customers perceive that products and services are of high quality. To keep the organization in business, it is necessary to have satisfied customers who will continue to purchase the products or services the organization is offering. It is also the driver behind several of the other concepts. In this competitive environment, the means to improve customer satisfaction are continuous improvement in quality and lower costs. Taken together, Hageman and Wageman's article and the University of Minnesota study provide a comprehensive overview of the concepts and contents of TQM.

Implications of Total Quality Management (TQM)

Because of the ambiguity surrounding the concepts of TQM, it is worthwhile to discuss what it is not. As expressed in Deming's 14 points, TQM is not management by objective. Management by objective is setting specific objectives for each manager to meet yearly. Deming opposes this concept because explicit goals are generally narrowly focused, and teams tend to lose motivation after the goals have been achieved. Other management practices that TQM opposes are bottom-line management and focus on short term gains. If management only cares about the bottom-line, they will likely make decisions that hurt the organization's long-term prospects. The TQM assumption that higher quality will ultimately enhance profitability and sustain the business is the driving force behind this. Similarly, a focus on short-term gains can hurt the continuous improvement focus that TQM organizations should pursue. Continuous improvement is long-term and even though the improvements it produces are incremental, it should not be confused with a focus on short-term one-time gains.

During the 1980s and 1990s, corporations rushed to implement TQM programs. It has been three decades since this bandwagon got started. Despite its popularity, TQM has not always experienced smooth sailing. Wallace Co., the winner of the Malcolm Baldrige National Quality Award of 1990, filed for bankruptcy protection shortly after winning the award in 1991. Analog Devices (ADI), an early adopter of TQM, witnessed a steep decline in its stock share price at the time of its TQM implementation. In 1987, ADI initiated a corporatewide TQM implementation. By 1990, it had cut the product defect rate by a factor of 100, doubled semiconductor yields, and halved manufacturing cycle time. However, in the same period, it saw its stock price drop from $18.75 to $6.25. In 2003, Global Metal-lurgical, winner of the Malcolm Baldrige National Quality Award in 1988, filed for bankruptcy. Stories like these led *The Economist* to publish "The Cracks in Quality" and "Straining of Quality" in 1992 and 1995, respectively. *The Economist* cited a survey by Arthur D. Little of 500 American companies. That survey found that only 36 percent of the companies responded that TQM was having a significant influence on its ability to compete. In another survey quoted by *The Economist*, A. T. Kearney surveyed 100 British manufacturing companies in 1992 and discovered that only 20 percent of the companies believed TQM had achieved tangible results.

These surveys raise the question of whether TQM is a legitimate management practice that offers benefits for organizations. It is worth noting that these survey results are not based on hard data from either financial or operational performance. They represent opinions and perceptions about TQM. As we know, perception does not always mirror reality. This is especially true in organizations that have undergone major changes. Implementation of major changes, whether they are process, cultural, or organizational, usually imparts stress on the organization, which could influence the participants' views of the change programs. Could the negative opinions be a case of divergence between perception and reality? After all, Japan witnessed extraordinary increases in competitiveness as a result of TQM, and major American corporations, such as Ford, are swearing by TQM as important to their competitiveness.

Several academic articles have been published to analyze the financial and operational results of successful TQM implementations. A recent research study by Kevin B. Hendricks of the University of Western Ontario and Vinod R. Singhal of the Georgia Institute of Technology found that quality award-winning corporations achieved 34 percent higher stock performance compared to the Standard & Poor's (S&P) 500 Index in the five-year period starting from one year prior to winning quality awards. Moreover, the same study discovered that quality award-winning companies achieved higher operating income growth (91 percent versus 43 percent), revenue growth (69 percent versus 32 percent), return on sales

(8 percent improvement versus no improvement), and return on assets (9 percent improvement compared to 6 percent improvement). This discovery was made over the same five-year period when compared to benchmark corporations from same industries with similar sizes.[11]

George S. Easton of Emory University and Sherry L. Jarrell of Georgia State University published a study in 1998 on the performance of 108 American companies that implemented TQM programs. These firms were selected based on their announcements of TQM programs and subsequent confirmation of evidence of adequate TQM programs. Interviews were conducted with these firms by a former senior examiner for Malcolm Baldrige National Quality Award. After the interview process, these sample firms were divided into two groups: one group is characterized as having advanced TQM programs and the second group is labeled as less advanced TQM firms. The group of advanced TQM firms had estimated Baldrige Quality assessment scores of at least 450 out of 1000, while the group of less advanced TQM firms had estimated scores of less than 450. Each of the sample companies were compared to their individual control group of three firms with no evidence of TQM programs in the same industry. The differences between the control groups and the sample firms in financial and operational performance were calculated after five years. Table 1.2 summarizes the Easton and Jarrell study results.

The results from Easton and Jarrell indicated that TQM firms had a median increase of at least $700 in net income per employee, a median operating income increase of at least $3,030 per employee, a median sales per employee decrease of $3,330, and a stock price increase of 21.02 percent when compared to non-TQM firms after five years TQM implementations.

Table 1.2 Performance Differences between TQM Firms and Control Firms Five Years after TQM Implementations

	Full TQM Sample	Less Advanced TQM Firms	Advanced TQM firms
Median Net Income Per Employee	$0.7K	-$0.7K	$0.84K
Median Operating Income Per Employee	$3.03K	$1.27K	$4.83K
Median Sales Per Employee	–$3.33K	–$12.18K	$2.63K
Stock Price	21.02 percent	14.20 percent	22.11 percent

Source: Easton, G. S. and Jarrell, S. L. 1998. The Effects of Total Quality Management on Corporate Performance: An Empirical Investigation. *Journal of Business.* 71.2: 253–307.

The results are more striking when examining only advanced TQM firms as shown on Table 1.2. It is worth noting that less advanced TQM firms actually have decreases in median net income per employee and median sales per employee when compared to non-TQM firms. These results indicate that TQM is not a program that should be implemented partially. Deming and the other TQM founders stressed the importance of commitment to TQM and continuous improvement. Especially important is the concept of driving out fear and persistence in TQM practices (or constancy of purpose in Deming's words). Several corporations have experienced the so-called quality paradox. TQM practices have been shown to improve productivity. In some cases, improvement in productivity leads to an increase in capacity at a faster rate than demand. During downturns in the economic environment, firms are under pressure to decrease capacity. This leads to layoffs. Downsizing is detrimental to TQM programs because it creates fear. The existence of fear negatively affects employees' participation in continuous improvement programs. In any event, the two broad-based studies discussed here illustrate that TQM programs do improve firm performance. This is especially true for the more entrenched TQM firms compared to firms that have implemented TQM partially.

Six Sigma

One recent TQM development worth mentioning is the Six Sigma methodology. Motorola developed Six Sigma in the 1980s as its implementation of TQM program. It has often been described as TQM on steroids. The use of Six Sigma became a management fad after Jack Welch adopted it for General Electric (GE) in 1996. Jack Welch often named Six Sigma as a key contributor to GE's financial success under his rein. Welch's endorsement of Six Sigma led many corporations to follow suit. It has been estimated that more than 25 percent of Fortune 200 companies have serious Six Sigma programs in place.[12] The use of Six Sigma is not limited to manufacturing companies. Many service companies have also successfully implemented Six Sigma programs. As an implementation methodology, Six Sigma provides a tool kit and a structured framework for companies to implement. The main premise behind Six Sigma is to use rigorous data analysis to pinpoint the source of errors that contribute to process variation. The path for Six Sigma to accomplish its goal is the Define, Measure, Analysis, Improve, and Control (DMAIC) methodology. Under this methodology, an improvement program starts with the definition of the problem. After the problem has been defined, measurements are taken to quantify the problem. This is followed by a detailed analysis of relevant processes to identify the root cause of the problem. Once the cause has been identified, solutions are put in place to resolve the problem, thereby improving the process. The last step is to put in controls to make sure the problem does not occur again.

In addition to prescribing an implementation approach, Six Sigma also requires that companies have a certain number of Six Sigma practitioners. There are three types of Six Sigma certifications: green belt, black belt, and master black belt. Green belt holders are familiar with the Six Sigma methodology and philosophy. They are typically the project leaders on Six Sigma projects. They serve to cascade the Six Sigma philosophy to the entire organization. Unlike black belts and master black belts, green belts are usually not involved fulltime with Six Sigma implementation. Black belt holders receive significant training in statistical techniques, DMAIC, interpersonal, and project management skills. They are the experts on Six Sigma projects and they spend significant amounts of time engaged in Six Sigma work. Black belts are usually high potential employees within the organization. Master black belts receive even more training than black belt holders. They know how to use statistical problem-solving techniques and the mathematical theories behind these techniques. In addition to implementation work, master black belt holders are involved heavily in training other belt levels. Corporations immersed in Six Sigma programs ideally have one percent of their employees trained as black belts. Each black belt engages in five to seven projects per year. There is usually one master black belt for every ten black belts in organizations. Six Sigma projects are focused and do not last for more than several months. The average project cost saving is $100,000 to $300,000. Projects seek to fix specific problems in existing processes, thus incrementally enhancing the process. This is in line with TQM practice in general and is different from business process reengineering projects, which redesign business processes. Aside from specific problem-solving tools (e.g., DMAIC) and dedicated employees, successful Six Sigma organizations also exhibit many practices espoused by traditional TQM. The focus on statistics mirrors TQM's practice of management by fact. Senior management of Six Sigma organizations are expected to be heavily involved in Six Sigma programs. Their roles are, to champion the programs, provide unwavering support to the Six Sigma practitioners, and articulate a clear vision and objectives to the organizations. In successful Six Sigma organizations, vision and objectives are executed throughout the organizations. As with TQM, Six Sigma is as much a corporate culture as it is a tool for process improvements.

Recently, another Six Sigma methodology, Design for Six Sigma (DFSS), has gained popularity. This methodology is still in the development stage and is aimed at designing or redesigning products and services. Instead of incrementally improving the process, this methodology provides a framework for designing the process or product as perfectly as possible from the beginning. In this regard, DFSS is allowing Six Sigma to expand into the process redesign arena. At a high level, DFSS is a multi-phase approach. The first phase is to identify the customers' requirements and the elements that are critical to quality (CTQ). These CTQ elements are prioritized and then trade-off analyses are performed on them using statistical methods. The next phase is to generate solution concepts that address all the key requirements. Using statistical methods and simulation, the best solution concept is selected. After the best solution concept is selected, it is time to formulate and tune the concept into a design. This phase utilizes several statistical design practices (e.g., experimental design, Monte-Carlo simulation) to determine how key inputs influence important performance measures. The result of this phase is a design that is optimized for the best performance given the key inputs. The last phase is to verify the design is ready for release through performance testing and formulation of control measures to monitor the design once it is in use. From this high-level description, we can see the extensive use of mathematical tools to formulate the best design. True to the focus on analysis of TQM philosophy, the main difference between DFSS and other design techniques (whether product or process) is precisely this heavy focus on analytics for arriving at the best solution.

The empirical results of Six Sigma programs have been impressive. GE announced in its 1999 annual report that it had realized cost savings from Six Sigma of $2 billion in 1999. Motorola attributed total cost savings of $16 billion from 1986 to 2001 to its Six Sigma program. Black & Decker reported in its 1999 annual report that it saved $30 million from its Six Sigma initiative in 1999 and it projected savings of $60 million for 2000. Another Six Sigma poster child, Honeywell, reported in its 2001 annual report of $3.5 billion in savings due to Six Sigma from 1995 to 2001. With cost-saving stories like these, Six Sigma is gaining popularity as one of the most widely deployed management practices. Except for the creation of the belt programs, Six Sigma is not much different from other TQM methodologies. However, its strong emphasis on management commitment, a clear implementation guide, and focus on cost savings have made Six Sigma the most well known TQM practice. Furthermore, with publicists like Jack Welch and Larry Bossidy, Six Sigma automatically enjoys high credibility among corporate executives. All of these factors are helping to create a tremendous buzz surrounding Six Sigma.

Business Process Reengineering (BPR)

Another management philosophy to enhance corporate competitiveness in this customer economy is BPR. The BPR movement arose with the publication of two academic articles in 1990. In the first article, Thomas H. Davenport and James R. Short argued that the combined use of IT and business process redesign could transform organizations and improve business processes to the degree Taylor's scientific management once did. They defined business process redesign as "… the analysis and design of work flows and processes within and between organizations."[13]

They prescribe a five-step methodology for achieving process redesign. The methodology starts with setting business vision and process objectives. Instead of rationalizing tasks to eliminate bottlenecks, as done in previous process redesign works, they suggest that process redesign should be performed on entire processes to achieve desired business vision and process objectives. The second step is to identify the processes to be redesigned. This is similar to the Pareto analysis practiced in TQM. Instead of redesigning all processes, key processes that offer the most impact should be redesigned. The next step is to understand and measure the existing processes. This is to understand the problems in the existing processes and to set baseline performance measurements to judge future improvements. The fourth step in their five-step methodology is to identify how IT can be leveraged in the process redesign. Instead of simply supporting process redesign, Davenport and Short argue that IT can actually create process redesign options. The last step is to implement a prototype of the process. This prototype should extend beyond IT applications and into business organization and serves as the base for iterative improvement before being phased into full implementation. The combination of IT and business process redesign creates what the authors term new industrial engineering. Just as scientific management created the original industrial engineering discipline, IT, and business process redesign would be essential tools in the new industrial engineering discipline.

About the same time that Davenport and Short published their ideas on business process redesign, Michael Hammer published his radical-sounding concept of BPR.[14] Hammer claims the process rationalization and automation efforts of the past have not improved productivity and performance significantly. He believes corporations were simply automating processes designed prior to the wide usage of computers. This type of automation does not address fundamental process limitations. He argues that corporations need to radically change business processes to take advantage of computers. The reengineering efforts need to be broad and encompassing. They should have cross-functional boundaries and utilize IT to enable the new processes that come out of the reengineering efforts. In *Reengineering the Corporation: A Manifesto for Business Revolution*, Hammer and co-author James Champy, further discuss the need for change. They debunk Adam Smith's labor specialization theory and the functional hierarchical organization that resulted from it. They state that the new post-industrial economy, started in the 1980s, is different from the mass production economy of the past. In this new economy, customers have the upper hand, competition has intensified, and constant changes are normal for the conduct of business. To compete in this new customer economy, companies need to reinvent how tasks are performed. Instead of incremental improvements to business processes, companies need to start from scratch and invent a better way of performing business processes. The goal of radical change is to achieve dramatic improvements in critical, contemporary measures of performance, such as cost, quality, service, and speed. [15] Hammer and Champy offer a set of prescriptions to reengineer business processes. The guiding principle is to organize around processes instead of tasks. Workers who share complementary tasks report to the same supervisor even though they do not share the same skills. In essence, the authors suggest that corporations should be grouped along process boundaries rather than functional boundaries. Every process should have a process owner. The role of the process owner is to attend to the performance of the process. They further state that workers should be trained to perform all the tasks in the process rather than only a single step. In other words, labor specialization, as espoused by Smith, Taylor, and Ford, should be dismantled. The key enabler for BPR is IT. IT serves as the disruptive technology that allows generalists to do the work traditionally performed by specialists, enables everyone to make decisions (as opposed to managers making all the decisions), and offers shared databases that allow direct access to the same information regardless of functions. In fact, shared databases are essential to BPR. Traditional IT infrastructures have often been designed to satisfy independent business. Various functions have their own information systems and databases. This created barriers to process performance because transactions had to be recreated in different applications and information replicated in different functional databases. Using a common database eliminates this barrier and presents an opportunity to reengineer the business processes without functional systemic limitations.

Implications of Business Process Reengineering (BPR)

Undoubtedly, Michael Hammer has garnered most of the BPR press because of the radical rhetoric with which he communicates. However, the ideas expressed by Hammer (and later Hammer and Champy) are similar to the new business process redesign concepts of Davenport and Short. They agree that the processes should be transformed holistically rather than by fixing bottlenecks in small increments. Furthermore, they agree on the essential role IT should play in business process transformation. Most importantly, their ideas point to a formulation of the process enterprise that is different from the functional hierarchical organization with which corporations had been aligned. In their writings, the founders of BPR have repeatedly demonstrated the poor coordination of functional organizations and the superiority of process organizations in coordination and in achieving performance gains. In its most radical form, the process enterprise is one that eliminates functional structure in favor of an exclusive process-based structure. The more realistic approach for becoming a process enterprise is to have a matrix structure of process-hierarchy and functional-hierarchy. Table 1.3 illustrates the differences between process organization versus functional organization.

As illustrated above, process enterprise holds the promise of being more responsive to market requirements, and it is suited for companies that offer differentiated products/services rather than competing on cost alone. However, organizational realignment by itself does not result in

Table 1.3   Functional versus Process Organization

	Functional Organization	*Process Organization*
Work Unit	*Department*	*Team*
Key Figure	*Functional Executive*	*Process Owner*
Benefits	Functional excellence Easier work balancing because workers have similar skills Clear management direction on how work should be performed	Responsive to market requirements Improved communication and collaboration between different functional tasks Performance measurements aligned with process goals
Weaknesses	Barrier to communication between different functions Poor handover between functions that affects customer service Lack of end-to-end focus to optimize organizational performance	Duplication of functional expertise Inconsistency of functional performance between processes Increased operational complexity
Strategic Value	Supports cost leadership strategy	Supports differentiation strategy

Sources: Silvestro, R. and Westley, C. 2002. Challenging the paradigm of the process enterprise: a case-study analysis of BPR implementation. *OMEGA: International Journal of Management Science.* 30:215–225. Rotemberg, J. J. 1999. Process- Versus Function-Based Hierarchies. *Journal of Economics and Management Strategy.* Winter: 453–487.

improvements. Organizational realignment has to be accompanied by change in management practices and mindsets. A 1996 *Harvard Business Review* article by Ann Majchrzak and Qianwei Wang of University of Southern California presents data supporting this viewpoint.[16] In their study, the cycle times of 86 printed circuit board assembling departments at electronic companies were analyzed. These departments performed the same manufacturing processes at large and small electronics companies. They labeled 31 of the 86 departments as process-complete, meaning these departments perform manufacturing processes, support tasks, and customer interfacing. The rest are traditional functional departments that do not perform most activities outside of the manufacturing processes. To the authors' surprise, they discovered process-complete departments did not have faster cycle times than functional departments. After more analysis, they found process-complete departments had faster cycle times when management practices were put in place to foster collective responsibility. These practices include jobs with overlapping tasks, group-based rewards, open workspaces, and collaborative work procedures. Analysis of the data, after taking into account these management practices, revealed that process-complete departments that implemented these practices achieve cycle times as much as 7.4 times faster than process-complete departments that have not implemented these practices. Furthermore, process-complete departments that operated on traditional functional mindsets have cycle times as much as 3.5 times longer than functional departments. The lesson of this study is the importance of managerial mindset and practices. Organizational restructuring alone does not inherently bring about forecasted improvements. Structural change has to be accompanied by changes in managerial practices and mindsets to reach the desired objectives. In fact, as we will discuss a little later, the lack of focus on the human side of change is one of the biggest drawbacks of traditional BPR practices.

What are the effects of BPR on corporate performance? Several success stories have been widely publicized. Ford was able to reduce 75 percent of its staff in its accounting department, Mutual Benefit Life achieved 60 percent productivity improvement in its insurance applications department, Hewlett-Packard improved on-time delivery performance by 150 percent in its purchasing department, and American Express was able to reduce average time for transaction processing by 25 percent. However, by Hammer's own admission, 50 percent to 70 percent of business process reengineering projects failed. In addition to Hammer's own assessment of the failure rate, one study indicated that only 16 percent of corporate executives were fully satisfied with their BPR implementations.[17]

The radical nature of BPR implementation has often been associated with its failure. Instead of building on what already existed, BPR implementations approached business process changes as blank slates. In the ideal world, this approach should bestow competitive advantage from innovative business process designs. The reality often turned out to be quite different. There was usually inadequate representation of the business users and decision makers on the project implementation teams. IT and outside consultants often comprised the majority of project team members. This resulted in solutions heavily influenced by best practices suggested by ERP systems being implemented. These best practice business processes are generic and usually do not represent innovative, differentiating processes. BPR has often been used to disguise restructuring. Thus, it often engendered resentment from the employees. Initial BPR prescriptions did not include recommendations on how to cope with organizational change and human resource issues. Change management on many BPR projects often served only training and communication roles. The combination of a top-down implementation approach and an inadequate change management function in BPR project methodologies resulted in strong resistance from front-line workers and middle managers. Furthermore, early BPR implementations were heavily technical and process-focused. Often, these changes were undertaken without corresponding changes in the organizational setup. This resulted in halfway measures of reengineering with redesigned cross-functional processes that were partly owned by various functional departments. The lack of identifiable process ownership often led to chaos. These various factors led to unsatisfactory opinions of BPR in the corporate world.

Do these explanations of failure and the high failure rate mean the fundamental approach of BPR is faulty? Studies that profile successful BPR projects do not come to this conclusion. A McKinsey study conducted in 1993, at the height of the BPR fad, discovered BPR projects that are broad-based and in-depth generate the highest business unit benefits.[18] This study analyzed the BPR implementation results of 20 companies. It found that 11 of the 20 projects achieved performance improvements of less than 5 percent. The performance measure evaluated was earnings before interest and taxes, or reduction in total business unit cost. These results hardly show the massive improvements BPR gurus had in mind. However, six of the 20 projects achieved an average of 18 percent in business unit cost reduction. The authors investigated these six projects and discovered these projects were more radical (in terms of breadth and depth) than the rest of the 20 projects. Breadth is defined as the number of key processes that have been reengineered. Depth is defined as the number of the six organizational elements (roles and responsibilities, measurements and incentives, organization structure, IT, shared values and skills) that are included in the reengineering projects. In their study, the six successful projects include all the key processes and organization elements in their BPR implementations. The authors conclude the degree of radical change is proportional to the business benefits that BPR projects generate. Perhaps it is important to remember that this study profiles successful implementations rather than all implementations and was published during the height of the BPR craze. Teng et al. published another study that profiled successful BPR projects in 1998. This was a broad-based survey of 105 firms that completed at least one BPR project. The authors discovered there is a strong correlation between the degree of radical change and the level of success at responding firms. The degree of radical change is determined by respondents' perceived level of change in seven aspects of reengineering. The seven aspects of reengineering are similar to those of the McKinsey study: process work flows, roles and responsibilities, performance measurements and incentives, organizational structure, IT, culture and skill requirements. Other interesting results from this study are, the importance of process evaluation, process transformation, and social design. Respondents rate these three stages as most important to success among the eight project stages. The eight stages in sequence are as follows:

1. Identification of BPR opportunities
2. Project preparation
3. Analysis of existing process
4. Development of process vision
5. Technical design
6. Social design
7. Process transformation
8. Process evaluation

Respondents rated analysis of existing process and technical design as least important to perceived success. The two studies discussed here illustrate that successful BPR projects share a high degree of radical change. We can also conclude from the second study that existing processes and technical designs are not important factors in BPR success. However, social design, execution of process transformation, and the ability to evaluate reengineered processes are important to the success of the BPR implementations. These results correlate to the contention that change management and the human side of implementations are more important than the solutions themselves.

Early BPR results led to the formulation of a new generation of BPR rhetoric from its founders. This revisionist BPR thinking increasingly focuses on the cultural context of the organization. The founders no longer stress the radical approach that was in the original BPR thinking. The new rhetoric of BPR emphasizes the importance of people and the change management aspects of implementation. Instead of dramatic and wide-ranging process changes, revised BPR thinking calls for a holistic approach to reengineering that involves business processes, technology, and social system issues (including culture). Revisionist BPR thinking looks to redesign critical business processes that will confer the most value through targeted changes to organization, processes, technology, and culture. The aim is no longer to change the organization's entire culture but only to target those aspects of culture that are critical to the success of reengineering implementation. An illustration of this is the case of instituting multi-skilled jobs and job rotations in a culture that values specialized trade skills. A blanket enforcement of this change will undoubtedly engender widespread resistance.[19] The recognition that wholesale change of the corporation is likely to fail led to changes in BPR thinking toward focusing on small leap improvement projects. It is often easier to achieve consensus among the affected parties in this type of project, which has been shown to significantly reduce implementation timeline. Although IT is still a key enabler, it has become less important in revisionist BPR thinking. People-led change, rather than system-led change, is increasingly viewed as critical to achieve project success. In short, the ideal of process enterprise is still the goal; however, the path to this goal is not in one gigantic step but a series of smaller steps.

Comparing Business Process Reengineering (BPR), Total Quality Management (TQM), and Six Sigma

The revisionist BPR thinking sounds strikingly similar to the TQM practices. Aside from the rhetoric, the theoretical differences between BPR, TQM, and Six Sigma have become minimal. Six Sigma is a derivative of TQM and thus they share the same philosophy. BPR has evolved from a radical start-from-scratch approach to a small leap improvement approach to process improvement. From a theoretical perspective, these three practices all aim to achieve process management and improve corporate performance through the institution of process improvements and monitoring. Under the process management umbrella, BPR, TQM, and Six Sigma all represent tools that corporations can utilize to achieve process management. Process management is the desired outcome, and the various practices are the means to achieve this outcome.

While sharing the same theoretical base, BPR, TQM and Six Sigma differ tactically in implementing process management and achieving their goals. Table 1.4 compares aspects of BPR, revisionist BPR, TQM, and Six Sigma.

Table 1.4 Comparison of BPR, TQM, and Six Sigma

	Radical BPR	Revisionist BPR	TQM	Six Sigma
Level of change	Radical	Small leap	Incremental	Incremental
Scope	Organization	Processes	Processes	Single process
Focus	Start from scratch	Redesign current processes	Redesign current processes	Improve current processes
Participation	Top-down	Top-down/ Bottom-up	Bottom-up	Bottom-up
Role of IT	Essential enabler	Primary enabler	Key enabler	Key enabler
Other Enablers	Process owners	Process owners	Statistical tools	Statistical tools
Risk	High	Moderate	Moderate	Moderate
Principle goal	Cost reduction	Cost reduction	Quality improvement	Quality improvement

Sources: Valentine, R. and Knights D. 1998. TQM and BPR — can you spot the difference? *Personnel Review.* 27.1: 78–85. Simpson, M., Kondouli, D., and Wai, P. H. 1999. From benchmarking to business process re-engineering: a case study. *Total Quality Management.* July: 717–716.

The scope of radical BPR is to reshape how the entire organization does business. This has proven to be too risky. Revisionist BPR thinking is to focus on a smaller scope of change under a process management framework. Under this framework, process owners would be the main drivers of process improvement initiatives. The ultimate goal of BPR is the establishment of the process enterprise. TQM also shares similar incremental process improvement approach. It aims to achieve process improvement using cross-functional teams. Even though process enterprise is not a stated goal of TQM, its cross-functional approach and focus on processes would lead to the enterprise being process-centric. In contrast, Six Sigma projects are even smaller in scope than TQM and revisionist BPR projects. The Six Sigma methodology is very good at identifying defects and coming up with solutions to improve the process. Its forte is in analyzing many factors that could contribute to an observed defect, finding the exact factor that causes the problem, and coming up with a solution that fixes the problem. Some solutions that result might be: maintaining temperature at certain level, changing the speed at which a machine should be operated for maximum result, or identifying a worker has not followed standard operating procedure. However, its DMAIC methodology is not suited to remedy processes that significantly under perform. In this type of scenario, the processes are performing as designed. This situation calls for end-to-end process creation or a major redesign of the process. The maturation of Design for Six Sigma (DSS) in business process design will help Six Sigma address this shortcoming. Regardless of how these process management practices evolve, they represent different tools in the toolkit that corporations can use to achieve process management. In a 2002 article, Michael Hammer commented:

> "Process management is the culmination of the movement to transform business operations. It provides a unifying theme for initiatives directed at improving organizational performance."[12]

As process management movements evolved, the process enterprise is the natural next step. In fact, this has always been the goal of the BPR movement. Despite its past failures, the ideal of process enterprise is still appealing. It promises to enable corporations to react faster to changes and allow for tighter process executions. These characteristics over functional organizations are important to organizations that need to offer differentiated products and services rather than commoditized products and services. The process enterprise has the means to measure the performance of every step of its processes. This information allows deficiencies to be identified and provides a baseline for the processes to be improved. From a business perspective, philosophical origins and theoretical novelties are meaningless. While academics argue about the legitimacy of BPR as a management theory or the orthodox meaning of TQM, corporate executives are much more interested in implementing improvement programs that improve the bottom-line. There is no prescription that will apply to all corporations. Process management is the framework that unifies BPR, TQM, and Six Sigma. It is the toolkit while BPR, TQM, and Six Sigma are the tools. Even if the organization is not prepared for, or does not aspire to be, a process enterprise with a process organizational hierarchy, there is a tool in the process management toolkit that it can use to improve its process.

Notes

1. Hammer, M., and Stanton, S. 1999. How Process Enterprises Really Work. *Harvard Business Review*, 77(6): 108–118.
2. Benner, M. J., and Tushman, M. L. 2003. Exploitation, Exploration, and Process Management: The Productivity Dilemma Revisited. *Academy of Management Review*, 28: 238–256.

3. Taylor, F. W. 1911. *The Principles of Scientific Management*. Reprinted (1967) W. W. Norton & Co. New York.
4. Norcliffe, G. 1997. Popeism and Fordism: Examining the Roots of Mass Production. *Regional Studies*. 31.3: 267–280.
5. Kendrick, J. W. 1961. *Productivity Trends in the United States*. Princeton University Press, Princeton, New Jersey.
6. Boaden, R. J. 1997. What is Total Quality Management … And Does it Matter? *Total Quality Management*. 8.4:153–171.
7. Yong, J. and Wilkinson, A. 2001. Rethinking Total Quality Management. *Total Quality Management*. 12.2:247–258.
8. Deming, W. E. 1994. Report Card on TQM. *Management Review,* January: 22–25.
9. Hackman, J. R. and Wageman, R. 1995. Total Quality Management: Empirical, Conceptual, and Practical Issues. *Administrative Science Quarterly,* 40: 309–342.
10. Anderson, J. C., Rungtusanatham, M. and Schroeder, R. G. 1994. A Theory of Quality Management Underlying the Deming Management Method. *Academy of Management Review*, 19: 472–509.
11. Hendricks, K. B., and Singhal, V. R. The Impact of Total Quality Management (TQM) on Financial Performance, Evidence from Quality Award Winners. Forthcoming in *Quality Progress*.
12. Hammer, M. 2002. Process Management and the Future of Six Sigma. *MIT Sloan Management Review*. Winter: 26–32.
13. Davenport, T. H. and Short, J. E. 1990. The New Industrial Engineering: Information Technology and Business Process Redesign. *Sloan Management Review*. Summer: 11–27.
14. Hammer, M. 1990. Reengineering work: don't automate, obliterate. *Harvard Business Review*. July–August: 104–12.
15. Hammer, M. and Champy, J. 1993. *Reengineering the Corporation: A Manifesto for Business Revolution*. Harper Business, New York City, New York.
16. Majchrzak, A. and Wang, W. 1996. Breaking the Functional Mind-set in Process Organizations. *Harvard Business Review*. September–October: 93–99.
17. Peltu, M. 1996. Death of cuts. *Computing*. May 9: 34.
18. Hall, E. A., Rosenthal, J. and Wade, J. 1993. How to Make Reengineering Really Work. *Harvard Business Review*. November/December: 119–131.
19. Lathin, D. 1995. In the midst of the re-engineering forest. *Journal for Quality and Participation*. January: 56–65.

Chapter 2

Business Process Management

In Chapter 1, we discussed the various process-focused business improvement practices. We concluded that these process-focused business improvement approaches, such as Six Sigma, Business Process Reengineering (BPR) and Total Quality Management (TQM), are tools under the process management framework. Both TQM and BPR see the need for process management. Process management was identified as one of seven core concepts of Deming's management method by a Delphi study.[1] In his recent writings, Hammer proposed viewing process management as an umbrella under which BPR, Six Sigma and TQM can work together.[2] Davenport also pointed to this outcome when he talked about the potential future of BPR in a 1994 article. The outcome he prefers is for reengineering to be combined with quality and other process-oriented improvement approaches into an integrated process management approach.[3] This brings us to the management approach of Business Process Management (BPM). The concepts of BPM first arose in the mid-1990s. By that time, many companies had already implemented TQM and BPR, or other business improvement programs. The challenge faced by these companies was how to continuously improve their business processes. The answer came in the form of BPM. According to Elzinga et al. of University of Florida, BPM is:

> a systemic, structured approach to analyze, improve, control, and manage processes with the aim of improving the quality of products and services. ... BPM is thereby the method by

which an enterprise's 'Quality' program (e.g., TQM, TQC, CQI) is carried out.[4]

From this definition, BPM has evolved into a management approach. One article calls it "the strategic business approach to achieve break-through results in process performance and external customer satisfaction."[5] Because of its focus on business processes, BPM can work with diverse process-focused management practices such as TQM and BPR. The technology supporting BPM, which some have referred to as Business Process Management System (BPMS), also provides capabilities that fit nicely with TQM and BPR. The convergence of process-focused business improvement practices is inevitable. Organizations and management experts have increasingly come to realize that advocating a particular process improvement practice over others and employing that practice as a management strategy could be risky.[6] Management fads come and go. Organizations are advised to employ all the management tools and approaches that are available to them. If we accept Hammer's definition of process management as a structured approach to performance improvement that centers on the disciplined design and careful execution of a company's end-to-end business processes, we can see it is very similar to Elzinga et al.'s definition for BPM. Comparing BPR and TQM literature, we can see that process management is a theme shared by both. This has led many management experts to consider BPM as the convergence of TQM and BPR. BPM provides the foundation on which process improvements are made. Whereas BPR is a leap approach toward improving business processes or creating new business processes, TQM, and Six Sigma are incremental approaches toward improving business processes.

Business Process Management (BPM) Concepts

BPM as a management philosophy has only been discussed since the mid-1990s. Still no definitive set of prescriptions defines BPM. After canvassing the existing literature on BPM, we found several management principles and practices that are associated with it. Not surprisingly, most of these concepts are identical to BPR and TQM concepts. Figure 2.1 summarizes these principles and practices.

Business Process Management (BPM) Principles

Processes Are Assets

BPM's first principle is processes are assets that create value for customers. One of the two characteristics Davenport and Short assigned to processes

BPM Principles and Practices

Goal	Improve products and services through structured approach to performance improvement that centers on systematic design and management of a company's business processes.
Principles	1. Business processes are organizational assets that are central to creating value for processes are organizational assets that are central to creating value for customers 2. By measuring, monitoring, controlling, and analyzing business processes, a company can deliver consistent value to customers and has the basis for process improvement 3. Business processes should be continuously improved 4. Information technology is an essential enabler for BPM
Practices	1. Strive for process-oriented organizational structure 2. Appoint process owners 3. Senior management needs to commit and drive BPM and execution of BPM process improvements should take a bottom-up approach 4. Put in place information technology systems to monitor, control, analyze, and improve processes 5. Work collaboratively with business partners on cross-organizational business processes 6. Continuously train the workforce and continuously improve business processes 7. Align employee bonuses and rewards to business process performance 8. Utilize both incremental (e.g., Six Sigma) and more radical (e.g., BPR) methodologies to implement process improvement

Figure 2.1 BPM principles and practices.

is processes have customers. The customers, internal or external, are the recipients of the results created by the processes.[7] Functions or individuals do not produce value for customers. They might be responsible for part of the overall work, but customers will not perceive value from standalone functions. An example is the sales function. Salespeople consider themselves revenue generators, and they might have an inflated view of their importance in the organization. However, without the customer service, accounting, manufacturing, and order fulfillment functions, customers will not receive value from the sales function. Processes are actually responsible for the end-to-end work of delivering value to the customer. Organizations should invest in their processes as they do in other assets. This does not mean that all processes are core to an organization. Different organizations have different objectives. Thus, their core processes differ. For instance, Dell Computer's core competence is in their efficient configure-to-order online sales process. They differentiate themselves from their competitors by offering customized products that are relatively inexpensive. They are able to accomplish this by having a world-class order fulfillment process their competitors cannot match. In Dell's case, their core process would be the order fulfillment. Another differentiator is Dell's customer service process. Dell's customers enjoy prompt services on the equipment they purchase. This allows Dell to price at a premium to smaller competitors who might have lower fixed cost base. We can also consider the customer service process to be core to Dell. For pharmaceutical companies the core process would be the drug discovery process. Large drug companies often invest billions of dollars into research and development. Out of thousands of compounds, only one or two would launch as a new drug. The company with the best drug discovery/development process for determining which projects to undertake and when to terminate a dud would gain competitive advantage.

Processes Should Be Managed and Continuously Improved

Because processes are assets, core processes and processes that generate the most value to customers, should be carefully managed. A managed process produces consistent value to customers and has the foundation for the process to be improved. Management of processes entails the tasks of measuring, monitoring, controlling, and analyzing business processes. These three tasks go hand in hand. Measuring of business processes provides information regarding these business processes. Process information allows organizations to predict, recognize, and diagnose process deficiencies, and it suggests the direction of future improvements.[8] Monitoring of processes is akin to statistical process control (SPC) in industrial engineering and quality management. When processes are monitored, variances can be detected. A process that has high variability is a process that produces inconsistent results to the customers and high variance indicates there is a problem in the process. Once a process displays high variability, there should be a mechanism allowing the process to be controlled. This mechanism might be adding more resources (people, machinery, etc.), shutting down the process if the situation is dire, or activating an alternative process for some of the demand to flow through. Analysiing process information is an essential step to identifying what process needs improvement, and which improvements are most likely to yield the most value.

The third principle is continuous improvement of processes. This is a natural result of process management. Process improvement is facilitated by the availability of process information. Process improvement is not a one-shot deal. One of the complaints against BPR is it is a one-time improvement effort.[9] The business environment usually dictates that organizations need to improve to stay competitive. Business processes are central to an organization's value creation. It follows that processes should be continuously improved. Under the BPM framework, BPR and incremental process improvement methodologies (i.e., Six Sigma, TQM, etc.) are tools that organizations can use to implement process improvement. With a focus on continuous improvement, an organization is better prepared to face change, which is constant in our customer-oriented economy. This helps to develop a corporate culture that is process-oriented and ready to adapt to changes.

Information Technology (IT) Is an Essential Enabler

The focus on processes has its origin in the industrial engineering discipline. Originally conceived to improve manufacturing and logistics functions, Industrial Engineering (IE) focuses on processes and utilizes statistics as the enabling tool for monitoring process variances. Davenport and Short first proposed using information technology (IT) as an essential tool for the new industrial engineering discipline. In the new industrial engineering, business processes are the focus for improvement, and IT is the key enabling tool.[10] Though TQM does not specifically emphasize IT as a key enabler; it emphasizes the need for information and management by fact. IT is the key information provider for corporations. It is implicitly an important component for TQM. With BPM, the role for IT is even greater than with BPR and TQM. IT can provide real-time process information that is very important for BPM to accomplish its tasks of monitoring and controlling business processes. It is not feasible to measure business processes real time without an automated measurement mechanism. IT provides this mechanism. When Computer-Aided Design/Computer-Aided Manufacturing (CAD/CAM) arrived on the manufacturing scene, it revolutionized the whole design to the production process. In the past, design systems were not integrated with production systems. After designs are completed, lab machineries have to be customized to allow the building of prototypes. The prototyping process could be time consuming. Once the prototype has been constructed it is tested, and feedbacks are sent to the design team for revisions to the original design. The design and prototyping process undergoes several iterations before the product is ready for production. Then the complex task of setting up the production process is undertaken. With CAD/CAM, designs are done using the system that can immediately take the design to construct the prototype. This automated integration dramatically speeds up the development process. Furthermore, when it is time to implement the production process, the information from CAD/CAM is passed to manufacturing equipment to expedite setting up the manufacturing process. Just as CAD/CAM plays an essential role in enabling design changes to quickly move to production, IT will allow BPM to integrate process design, development, and implementation.

Business Process Management (BPM) Practices

Process-Oriented Organizational Structure

The core concept of BPM is a relentless focus on processes. Processes are the core assets of an organization, and they produce the values that justify an organization's existence. In order for processes to be effectively managed and improved, BPM, like other process-focused business improvement practices, espouses a process-oriented organizational structure. Three types of process-oriented structures have been identified:

- Process organization
- Case management organization
- Horizontal process management organization

The first organizational option is the process organization, which aligns the organizational structure along process lines. Each process unit would contain various functions that support the process. The advantage of process organization is it optimizes the performance of the process. However, it does this at the cost of duplicating functions for the processes. This could result in functional work not performed consistently and rising cost due to function duplications.

In *Total Improvement Management,* quality experts H. James Harrington and James S. Harrington raise two different models of what they termed network organizational structures.[11] The network organization is derived from the matrix organization of the past. In the matrix organization, employees report to functional heads. Project managers, product line managers or regional managers would also have reporting relationships with employees in the functional departments. The goal is for the organization to have multidimensional (usually two) alignments to enhance customer focus. Harrington and Harrington referred to the first network organization structure as case management structure. In this organizational structure, employees would still report to functional heads. In addition, they would report to case managers. The case manager has the responsibility to oversee the end-to-end process of an individual case. The case could be a patient (this structure was pioneered in the health care industry to provide better patient service from admission to discharge) or any kind of project (e.g., engineering or construction).

The second type of network organization is the horizontal process management structure. Here the functional departments would still exist as the first dimension. The second dimension is the process dimension. The organization would create process owners who are responsible for core processes. The core processes could be order-to-cash, product development, purchase-to-pay, etc. Harrington and Harrington made the point that, in horizontal process management structure, an employee's solid line reporting would be to the process head, while the functional head would have a dotted line relationship. However, this is not necessary for process management organization to work. Hammer described the success of process management structure at Duke Power where the process managers do not have direct reporting relationships with the employees involved in their processes.[12] This organizational setup reduces duplication of functions but still allows the organization to benefit from process-focus. The downside is it is difficult to implement. Organizations looking to adopt network organizational structure should have a sophisticated level of management expertise because matrix organizations often lead to confusion among the employees about roles and responsibilities. The important point is not which organizational structure to adopt but that the organization should have a culture of being process-focused. When the business environment presents new market opportunities, process-focused organizations would promptly seize the opportunity to create new processes for exploiting those new markets. BPM organizations would be better equipped to exploit these new opportunities than organizations that are not process-focused. In other organizations, the amount of communication and coordination between functions to implement the new processes needed to access these new market opportunities may present serious challenges to organizations that are not process-focused.

Appoint Process Owners

In a process network organization or a functional organization that is proceeding to be process-focused, the role of the process owner is vital. In these organizations, the core processes that are essential to producing customer value and confer competitive advantage have been identified, and process owners are assigned to these processes. Because these processes are strategic to the organization's success in the marketplace, successful management of these processes is vital. A process owner is responsible for the performance of the process assigned. The process owner designs, deploys, and improves the process. He or she would have employees performing functional tasks directly reporting to him or her. If the organization is aligned with functional employees having solid line reporting relationships to functional heads, the process owner would be responsible for influencing functional workers and functional heads on how best to perform functions associated with the process. The process owner should be a senior member of the organization who has the clout to influence other senior managers. As Hammer succinctly puts it, "there is no such thing as a successful junior process owner."[13]

In any matrix organization, the roles and responsibilities are always a point of confusion for employees. For process management organization to work, the process owners should have good communication skills to clearly delineate the roles and responsibilities to employees working with them. A poorly performing process owner could jeopardize the performance of a core process, which might be more harmful to an organization than the effects of the ineffectual functional manager.

Top-Down Commitment, Bottom-Up Execution

In order for BPM to work, top management needs to commit to it and support the process-focused management approach it requires. Undoubtedly, organizations adopting BPM will go through difficulties and oppositions. There have been many discussions in the management literature about resistance from managers toward business process improvement programs. This resistance is due to uncertainties of the change programs in the managers' domain of responsibility. The natural tendency of management is toward empire building. Process-focused organizations are known to require only half as many managers as functional organizations.[14] In face of uncertainty, middle managers are likely to passively resist BPM. Top management commitment to BPM is critical to overcome this resistance. Top management should not embark on BPM simply because it is fashionable or as a show to the board of directors that business improvement programs are been implemented. They have to take an active role and commit to BPM. Without top management commitment, BPM will likely disappear because of internal organizational resistance.

Practitioners have found the best way to implement BPM is to align it with the strategic goals of the organization. Once the organizational goals are promulgated, it becomes possible to determine the business processes that are essential to accomplish the organizational goals. Once these processes have been identified, BPM would be the enabler to manage these processes. This is a natural consequence that processes are organizational assets to enable the organization to produce value. In a survey of European companies, Pritchard and Armistad found that linking BPM to strategic programs like Business Excellence strategies or linking BPM to evaluation of organizational performance increase the staying power of BPM in an organization.[15] Executing process improvement should use a bottom-up approach. The benefit of a bottom-up approach is it encounters less resistance from the employees most directly affected by the change. Bottom-up design has received blessing even from BPR founders who originally advocated top-down design help from external consultants. Davenport acknowledges that internal process design, which pretty much amounts to design that tolerate process variations, has a greater chance of internal acceptance and is thus worth the trouble.[16] The employees who are performing the business processes have the most knowledge about it thus making them natural agents for effecting the changes. However, the process owner has the responsibility for the final process design. External consultants should probably be used because, as the BPR founders contended, it is unlikely innovative designs will come from inside the organization. Using external consultants will help bring new ideas and help with innovation. The challenge is how to retain internal employees' pride of ownership of the final designs. That is one key criterion in choosing the right external consultants.

Use Information Technology (IT) to Manage Processes

Adoption of BPM and process management techniques by organizations has led to a strong interest in the technology world to develop products and solutions to support BPM. The BPM technology has matured to the point where real-time process management is possible. BPMS represents a breakthrough in the use and implementation of information systems. Traditional systems implementation methodology is focused on functions and objects. Processes are relegated to workflow, which usually does not receive major attention during the implementation. BPMS breaks the object design mentality, which is more like Lego building blocks with limited process design capability. It puts the process at the central focus of solution design. This aligns the IT solution to be more in line with the process-focused reality for BPM organizations. Process designs could be performed and simulations conducted in the BPMS. This capability is akin to CAD/CAM, which helps with design work and speeds up design-to-prototyping process. Aside from the design functions, BPMS, once implemented, allows organizations to measure, monitor, control, and analyze processes real time. In a nutshell, (much more will be discussed in future chapters), BPMS serves as the control center over people, enterprise applications, and data. As the control center, BPMS receives real-time data from all tasks that are performed in the processes it controls. Monitoring of processes is possible with the real-time process information. Like statistical process control (SPC) in manufacturing, BPMS could note variations in the processes. Once a variation has been detected, BPMS has the ability to resolve the variation. For instance, if a process were overwhelmed because of strong customer demand, the organization would know through monitoring the business process that it is potentially in disarray. With the ability to control business process, the organization has the mechanism to respond to the problem. This mechanism might be adding more resources (people, machine, etc.), shutting down the process if the situation is dire, or activating an alternative process for some of the demand to flow through. Measuring the business process provides process data that can be analyzed. The analysis of process data is an essential step to identifying what process needs improvement and improvements to which areas are most likely to yield the most value. BPMS provides the BPM organization with a powerful tool in its process design–implement–analyze–improve cycle. In the BPM organization, BPMS is an essential tool for success. Much of this book will be devoted to discussing to BPMS and its implementation.

Collaborate with Business Partners

The management of business processes should not stop at the edge of the organization. Increasingly companies are getting more and more focused on what they want to perform in house. Areas where a company does not have core competence are most likely to be outsourced. An example is the rise of contract manufacturing companies. Companies like Dell, Hewlett-Packard, and many companies in the chip design industry do not manufacture any or a majority of the products they sell. The tasks of manufacturing are outsourced to contract manufacturing companies like Solectron and Taiwan Semiconductor Manufacturing Company. Companies that have outsourced manufacturing require very close collaboration with the manufacturing companies. A contract manufacturer might have to participate in the product design, order fulfillment, and inventory management processes. In other instances, companies might have to collaborate with totally unrelated companies or even competitors because of the added value created for the customers.[17] Thus, it is necessary to extend process management outside the enterprise. This involves sharing information with business partners and helping business partners with their business processes.

Continuous Learning and Process Improvement

In the BPM world, employees will be introduced to new technologies and work activities. In a process-focused environment, workers belong to processes and they can be expected to perform broader sets of tasks than in traditional functional organizations. The broadening of tasks workers are expected to perform and new technologies that are implemented to support BPM require workers to be up to date on their skills and knowledge. BPM organizations thrive on continuous improvement. This concept has its origin in TQM. In one of his 14 points, Deming admonished companies to "Improve constantly and forever the system of production and service, to improve quality and productivity, and thus constantly decrease costs."[18] In the customer-centric economy, competition is fierce and customers will choose suppliers who can provide the best quality for the lowest price. Organizations have no choice but to continuously improve their current offerings and introduce innovative new offerings. To achieve continuous improvement, workers need leading edge knowledge to achieve innovation. Workers who are constantly upgraded in their knowledge base are also more likely to accept new ideas and concepts and less likely to be set in traditional ways of performing work. Continuous improvement also implies that changes are being made to processes and work activities constantly. Employee training needs to accompany these changes if the improvements are to be executed effectively. The cycle of learning and improvement enhances employee morale and helps to institute an adaptive organizational culture. In the adaptive organization, workers embrace changes. This helps create a culture that strives for excellence.

Align Employee Rewards to Process Performance

Things that are rewarded get accomplished and behaviors that are rewarded are repeated. This is one of the principles of employee incentives. In the BPM organization, the goal is to maximize the value from the business processes. It follows that employee rewards should be aligned to the performance of the business processes. In the functional organization, employees are most often rewarded on functional performance. This creates the situation where workers only want to maximize their functional performance at the cost of collaboration with other functions. Customers who demand customized service can also be affected because the customization could impair functional performance. The result is process performance is not optimized and customers do not perceive as much value as they want. In the customer-centric economy, this could lead to customer defection to competitors. In the BPM organization, delivering customer value and optimizing process performance are two central goals. When employee rewards are aligned to process performance, they foster collaboration among workers who are engaged in the same process. The functional walls no longer separate workers. This discourages the "not my problem" mentality and the practice of throwing issues over the functional wall. TQM founders frowned on work incentives. They believed that intrinsic motivation, i.e., workers' pride of doing quality work, is more important than extrinsic motivation, i.e., financial-based rewards. They might have been overly optimistic in their belief. Given most Fortune 500 chief executives have financial rewards, the importance of extrinsic motivation over intrinsic motivation is especially true in the individualistic American culture.

Utilize BPR, TQM, and Other Process Improvement Tools

Many business process experts have described BPM as the convergence of business process improvement approaches. Under the BPM approach, the previous process-focused business improvement approaches could be seen as tools for improving the processes. With these tools in its armory, BPM organizations can choose the proper tool for the appropriate situation. For incremental improvements, Six Sigma Define, Measure, Analysis, Improve, and Control (DMAIC) could be deployed. When a process is underperforming the business needs, a more radical tool like BPR or Design for Six Sigma (DFSS) could be employed. BPMS is also a potent tool in the BPM armory. Used in conjunction with the process improvement tools, it expedites the process improvement projects. In BPM organizations that have employed BPMS for process management, BPMS not only serves as a systemic process design tool, it also provides the process improvement tools with the process data and information to expedite process improvement implementation. More will be discussed in a subsequent chapter on how BPMS could help the process improvement tools.

The Value of Information Technology (IT)

We have talked extensively about IT as an enabling tool. BPR founders put strong faith in the value IT can create. Similarly, BPM also places emphasis on IT as an essential enabling tool. Is this merely a leap of faith or assumption on our part? From the academic studies surveyed, the benefits of BPR, TQM, and Six Sigma have been identified. Though BPR has suffered a high incidence of failures, successfull implementations can deliver substantial cost reductions. With the lessons learned from the initial BPR implementations, organizations that embark on large-scale business transformation projects will most likely have higher probability of success. Readers who are IT practitioners have undoubtedly heard complaints from business users and line managers about the value of IT. Business managers would remark why are we spending so much money on IT if our goal is to cut costs. Or, business users might say this new IT application is worthless, we are less efficient at doing our jobs. The fact is throughout most organizations IT is still seen as a necessary evil that does little to confer a competitive advantage. Questioning the value of IT does not stop with business users and line managers. Even academics were raising questions about the value of IT in the 1980s.

In 1987, noted economist and Nobel laureate Robert Solow remarked in the New York Times: "You can see the Computer Age everywhere but in the productivity statistics."[19] This quip by the famous economist was made in a book review he was writing and was not based on any studies he had done, but it does reflect the unfavorable data linking IT to productivity at that time. According to Bureau of Labor Statistics, the United States economy experienced average annual productivity growth of 2.9 percent from 1959 to 1973. Average annual productivity decreased to 1.1 percent from 1973 to 1995. This period of decline coincided with the rapid growth of the computer usage. This led economists to lament that the heavy investment in technology, accounting for more than 50 percent of all new capital investments by large United States firms,[20] had not produced increases in productivity. A study published in 1989 by Morgan Stanley economist, Steven Roach, looked at the productivity of the information workers. In his study Roach found that, output per production worker grew 16.9 percent between mid-1970s and 1986, while that of information workers grew only 6.6 percent.[21] He also found that the IT investment in the service industry grew much more than in the manufacturing industry from the early 1960s to 1987. By 1987, the service sector owned more than 85 percent of the installed base of IT. Drawing from this data Roach reached the conclusion that the productivity shortfall in the 1980s was concentrated in employers of white-collar workers and in sectors that have the greatest investment in IT. This type of rhetoric quickly became popular, and the value of IT was widely questioned in the early 1990s.

What Solow started with a casual statement, became a tide of rising interest in the academic world to understand this apparent paradox. Computers have automated a large number of manual tasks in the business world since they arrived on the corporate scene in the 1960s. Naturally, economists expected extensive investment in IT to be reflected in the productivity data. However, the productivity data from the 1980s did not seem to support that expectation. Consequently resolving the productivity paradox became a hot topic for research. A review of research in this area published in 2003, identified more than 50 articles from highly regarded academic journals published in 1990s that explored the relationship between productivity and computers.[22] This gives an indication of the number of studies that were undertaken during that time period. Erik Brynjolfsson of MIT's Sloan School, and Lorin M. Hitt of the Wharton School at the University of Pennsylvania did seminal works in this field. In a 1996 study that analyzed the IT investment performance at 367 large United States firms, Brynjolfsson and Hitt found gross returns on IT investments averaged 81 percent and net returns averaged 48 to 67 percent, depending on the depreciation rate used in the net return calculation.[23] Another study of United States firms discovered that one IT employee can substitute for six non-IT employees without loss of output.[24] Another Brynjolfsson and Hitt econometrics study based on 1987 to 1994 data from 527 large United States firms published in 2003, found that computer investment contributes roughly the same value in output as the cost over a one year horizon. However, the output growth contribution of computer investment is five times as much as the capital cost over longer time horizon (three to seven years).[25] Finally, the most comprehensive result is from the abovementioned review of more than 50 articles on IT and productivity. Finding that most of the articles reviewed show positive correlation, the authors concluded that IT does have a significant impact on productivity and computers do show up in productivity statistics. With a decade of research in this area, mainstream academics accept the idea that IT has a large impact on productivity, and they regard the productivity paradox resolved.

What caused the discrepancy between the results of studies in 1980s to the 1990s? Some of the causes put forth are faulty data from the United States Bureau of Labor Statistics (BLS), problems with dataset measurements, and the lag of computer investment's appearing in productivity data. Researchers found that BLS productivity data is not available for 58 percent of the service industry and the data is suspect in other industries.[26] The measurement criticism focuses on the failure to account for new technology outputs. One example is the value created by automated teller machines (ATM). One measure of productivity in the banking sector is the number of checks cleared. The introduction of the ATMs decreases the number of checks used, thus lowering output and productivity.[27] Finally, there is the lag time between the investment in IT and its productivity impact. Benefits of IT can take several years before they appear.[28] The effect of the lag is also supported by 2003 econometrics study by Brynjolfsson and Hitt.

Convergence of Process-Focused Management Practices

In discussing BPM principles and practices, we touched on the relationship of BPM to previous process-focused management practices. The proposal agreed to by both TQM and BPR experts is for these previous practices to exist under a BPM management approach. What exactly does this mean? The way we can view this is through Figure 2.2.

The goal of a process-focused organization is to become a process enterprise. As discussed in Chapter 1, the process enterprise is an organization that recognizes the centrality of processes to its business performance. That recognition leads the process enterprise to focus on the management of its processes and it treats its processes as assets that need to be invested in. In the process enterprise, employees are part of processes. The goal of the process enterprise is to create customer value by relentless focus on processes. To become a process enterprise, the BPM

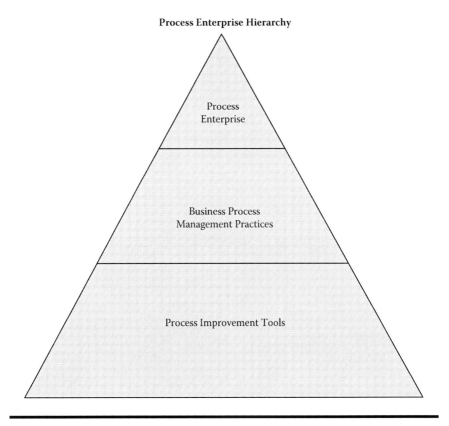

Figure 2.2   Process enterprise hierarchy.

principles and practices should be adhered to. These principles and practices are a collection from the various process-focused management practices, such as BPR and TQM. Therefore, it is the convergence of these process-focused management practices. When BPM practices are carried out, the process enterprise can function. In that sense, BPM is the foundation for the process enterprise. As the foundation, BPM provides information and process management business infrastructure for improvements to be carried out. The implementation of continuous process improvement is through process improvement tools. These tools are BPR, TQM, Six Sigma, and BPMS. BPR and Six Sigma DFSS are process improvement tools that can be utilized to improve business processes that are not meeting customer specifications (in other words, process output requirements). Six Sigma DMAIC and TQM methodologies are process improvement tools to incrementally improve business processes. These incremental tools are less risky and can generate consistent improvements over the long run. BPMS is the technological tool used in conjunction with all of the other process improvement tools. BPMS provides valuable design functions that will help in either incremental or more dramatic process improvement projects. It is also the technological foundation for BPM. Once BPMS has been implemented, it provides process data and analytics that help in the day-to-day management of business processes. The process data that BPMS contains is also valuable during process improvement projects. In summary, BPM provides the foundation and practices that enable an organization to reach the state of process enterprise. As the synthesis of other process-improvement approaches, BPM unifies these previous approaches under one framework. As the framework, BPM provides process information, organizational structure, and corporate culture to help the various tools succeed in process improvement.

Process Management Lifecycle

How should an organization implement BPM? Several scholars have explored this issue and have come up with their own approaches for implementing process management.[29,30] Their recommendations are generalized in Figure 2.3.

Elzinga et al recommend that the first step is to set organizational goals. This helps to align BPM to the organizational goals. The next step is to inventory all the business processes within the organization. The task of inventorying processes could uncover the need for processes that do not yet exist and have a large value proposition. While inventorying business processes, the current processes should be documented. After processes are inventoried, these processes should be ranked using a combination of criteria. These criteria could include relevance to organizational goals, process performance relative to available benchmarks, and potential return if the processes were improved. Once the ranking is done,

Process Improvement Life Cycle

1. Set organizational goals
2. Inventory all organizational processes
3. Rank organizational processes according to contribution to organizational goals, available benchmarks, and financial improvement potential
4. Choose the process that will contribute the most value
5. Determine whether an incremental or more radical process improvement tool should be used
6. Implement process improvement project
7. Monitor and measure process
8. Repeat step 4

Figure 2.3   Process improvement lifecycle.

the process that will contribute the most value according to the ranking criteria for improvement is chosen. The next step is to determine the appropriate process improvement tool to use for implementing the process improvement project. If the chosen process does not exist or needs a major change, DFSS and BPR are appropriate. A process that does not require major change is a good candidate for TQM (e.g., Plan–Do–Check and Act methodology) or DMAIC. During implementation, BPMS should be employed as the technology enabler. If the process were undergoing its first BPM improvement, BPMS would provide the real-time measurement capability that is critical for subsequent process monitoring, control, and analysis. For a process that has already undergone more than one BPM improvement, BPMS would provide the current process information and design tools for the process improvement project. Once the project is implemented, process should be standardized across the organization and procedures put in place to monitor and manage the process. The next step is to repeat the process improvement cycle by going back to the process inventory list to decide which process to improve next.

The generic and high-level approach illustrated above implies that only one process is improved at a time. This does not have to be the case, the process owners could decide when and how to improve the processes they manage. There are many methodologies for continuous improvement. The methodology illustrated here is by no means the best one. It serves as an example of how process improvement might be implemented. In Chapter 10, we will explore a BPM methodology that serves as a guide on implementing BPM as a business improvement initiative.

Notes

1. Anderson, J. C., Rungtusanatham, M. and Schroeder, R. G. 1994. A Theory of Quality Management Underlying the Deming Management Method. *Academy of Management Review*, 19: 472–509.
2. Hammer, M. 2002. Process Management and the Future of Six Sigma. *MIT Sloan Management Review*. Winter: 26–32.
3. Davenport, T. H. and Stoddard, D. B. 1994. Reengineering: Business Change of Mythic Proportions? *MIS Quarterly*. June: 121–127.
4. Elzinga, D. J., Horak, T., Lee, C., and Bruner, C. 1995. Business Process Management: Survey and Methodology. *IEEE Transactions of Engineering Management*. 42(2): 119–128.
5. Puah, P. and Tang, N. 2000. Business Process Management, A Consolidation of BPR and TQM. Proceedings of the 2000 IEEE International Conference on Management of Innovation and Technology — ICMIT-2000: Management in the 21th Century: 12–15 November 2000 Orchard Hotel, Singapore. IEEE: 110–114.

6. Huffman, J. L. 1997. The Four Re's of Total Improvement. *Quality Progress.* 30(1): 83–88.

7. Davenport, T. H., and Short J. S. 1990. The New Industrial Engineering: Information Technology and Business Process Redesign. *Sloan Management Review.* Summer: 11–27.

8. Davenport, T. H. and Beers, M. C. 1995. Managing Information about Processes. *Journal of Management Information Systems.* 12,1: 57–80.

9. Al-Mashari, M. and Zairi, M. 2000. Revisiting BPR: A Holistic Review of Practice and Development. *Business Process Management Journal.* 6,1: 10–42.

10. Davenport and Short, The New Industrial Engineering, 11–27.

11. Harrington, H. J. and Harrington, J. S. 1995. *Total Improvement Management.* McGraw-Hill, New York, NY. 449–457.

12. Ibid.

13. Hammer, M. 2001. *The Agenda.* Crown Business, New York, NY. 65–69.

14. Hammer, M. 2001. Q&A: Process Changed. *Journal of Business Strategy.* November/December: 11–15.

15. Pritchard, J. and Armistead, C. 1999. Business Process Management — Lessons From European Business. *Business Process Management Journal.* 5,1: 10–32.

16. Davenport and Stoddard, Reengineering, 121–127.

17. Hammer, *The Agenda*, 65–59.

18. Deming, W. E. 1982. *Out of Crisis: Quality, Productivity, and Competitive Position.* Cambridge University Press.

19. Solow, R. S. 1987. We'd Better Watch Out. *New York Times Book Review.* July 12, 1987.

20. Kriebel, C. H. 1989. Understanding the Strategic Investment in Information Technology. Chapter 7, *Information Technology and Management Strategy.* K. Laurdon and J. Turner (Eds.). Prentice Hall, Englewood Cliffs, NJ.

21. Roach, S. S. 1989. America's White-Collar Productivity Dilemma. *Manufacturing Engineering.* August: 104.

22. Dedrick, J., Gurbaxani, V. and Kraemer, K. L. 2003. Information Technology and Economic Performance: A Critical Review of the Empirical Evidence. *ACM Computing Surveys.* 35:1, 1–28.

23. Brynjolfsson, E. and Hitt L. M. 1996. Paradox lost? Firm-level evidence on the returns to information systems spending. *Management Science* 42:4, 541–558.

24. Lichtenberg, F. R. 1995. The Output Contributions of Computer Equipment and Personnel: A Firm Level Analysis. *Economics of Innovations and New Technology.* 3: 201–217.

25. Brynjolfsson, E. and Hitt, L. M. 2003. Computing Productivity: Firm-Level Evidence. *The Review of Economics and Statistics.* 85(4): 793–808.

26. Pinko, R. 1991. Is Office Productivity Stagnant? *MIS Quarterly.* 15(2): 191–204.

27. Brynjolfsson, E. and Hitt L. M. 1998. Beyond the Productivity Paradox. *Communications of the ACM.* 41(8): 49–55.

28. Brynjolfsson, E. 1993. The Productivity Paradox of Information Technology. *Communications of the ACM.* 36(12): 67–77.

29. Benner, M. J. and Tushman, M. 2002 Process Management and Techno-logical Innovation: A Longitudinal Study of the Photography and Paint Industries. *Administrative Science Quarterly.* 47: 676–706.

30. DeToro, I. and McCabe, 1997. How to Stay Flexible and Elude Fads. *Quality Progress.* 30,3: 55–60.

Chapter 3

Overview of Business Process Management System

Now that we have discussed Business Process Management (BPM) as a management approach, we shall look at BPM as an information technology (IT)–based enabling tool. There is confusion in the current literature on exactly what BPM is. According to Smith and Fingar's book *Business Process Management: The Third Wave*, BPM is the maturation and synthesis of process management practices and modern IT. This synthesis represents the falling in place of all the components that allow enterprises to achieve process management, which is the ability to control, monitor, and enhance business processes. This definition is a little vague, and it leaves the readers wondering whether this synthesis represents a management philosophy with its set of management practices or whether it is a technology. In some of the available literature, what has often been referred to as BPM is in fact BPM technology. Although technology has its practices and benefits, implementation of the technology does not automatically make an organization process-focused and put it on the path toward being a process enterprise. BPM principles and practices have to be adopted for that transformation to happen. In this book, we defined BPM as the holistic management approach that has its sets of principles and practices. These principles and practices span from organizational structure to employee compensation. Even though BPM technology is commonly referred to as

BPM, to avoid confusion, BPM technology will be referred to as Business Process Management System (BPMS) in this book.

Key Capabilities of Business Process Management System (BPMS)

BPMS is a new class of software that allows organizations to devise process-centric information technology solutions. Process-centric means BPMS solutions are able to integrate people, systems, and data. Organizations that utilize BPMS to accomplish IT–enabled business process change will gain the following capabilities:

1. Closer business involvement in designing IT–enabled business process solutions
2. Ability to integrate people and systems that participate in business processes
3. Ability to simulate business processes to design the most optimal processes for implementation
4. Ability to monitor, control, and improve business processes in real time
5. Ability to effect change on existing business processes in real time without an elaborate process conversion effort

Bridging the Business Information Technology (IT) Gap

One of the major improvements of BPMS over traditional IT–enabled business process improvement efforts is it brings IT closer to the business process owners. In traditional IT implementations, the functional analyst gathers the business requirements. The functional analyst reaches out to the business process owners and workers in the affected departments to learn what business and functional requirements the proposed IT–enabled solution needs to solve. In large business improvement projects, there is usually a team of business analysts that gather the business requirements. In this situation, the business analyst would pass the business requirements to the functional analyst, who would draft functional specifications to determine what functions each system in the proposed solution would perform. The functional specifications would also determine any new developments needed to bridge gaps between what the business requires and the functions provided by the systems in the proposed solution. Once the requirements are gathered and gaps determined, technical analysts would configure the systems according to functional specifications. If programming efforts are needed, the technical analyst would design technical specifications for the programmers to develop. Oftentimes the business requirements would go through three or four layers before they are implemented in the system. At every layer in the communication chain, the business requirements would have to be communicated, discussed, and potentially changed. By the time the requirements are implemented in the system, they usually do not satisfy the original requirements, or they are implemented in such a cumbersome manner as to make the solution hard for the business users to use. Essentially, there is a gap between what the business wants and how IT implements what the business wants.

BPMS is able to bridge the gap by allowing business process owners to be directly involved in designing the IT solution. The business process designer, offered by BPMS, is a Visio-like tool that allows the business process owners or business analysts to design the business processes in minute detail. The business process designers can automatically generate code that sometimes can be deployed without IT development help. In cases where development is needed, the BPMS already contains the process meanings and solution definitions. IT developers can use the same processes designed by business people and embed logic to them using the designer. This can be done using a scripting language that comes packaged with the process designer or development toolkit in a widely used programming language. The hand off from business people to IT people is more seamless than before. They are working from the same design using the same tool. This dramatically reduces the communication gap between IT and the business. Bridging the gap catapults BPMS into an essential component of any process management initiative.

Process-Centric Integration

The word process has been widely used in IT. However, there is no definition for process. Document-management vendors might view process as flows of documents to support a business transaction. Integration product vendors tend to view process as steps of integration between various applications. Workflow vendors view process as tasks that need to be performed by humans. To prevent the confusion the word process causes in IT, we will use the term process-centric integration, which means the integration of people, systems, and data. BPMS is the first software class that offers process-centric integration. This transcends the traditional work-flow capability that has been available for years. Although traditional workflow management systems can integrate human participants for a work-flow process, they lack robust application integration capabilities. Similar to workflow management system, BPMS offers workflow capability that can generate work lists for human participants in the business process to

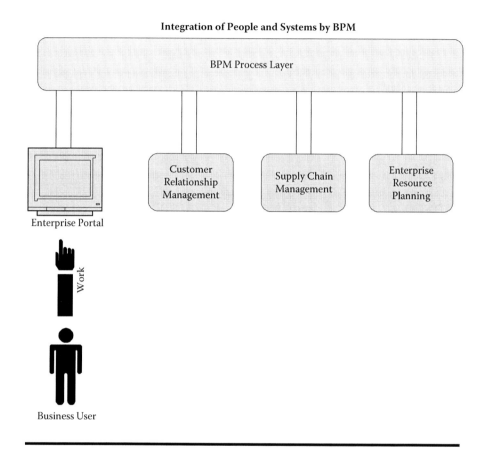

Figure 3.1   Integration of people and systems by BPMS.

perform their tasks (Figure 3.1). The work lists are presented to the human participants in a Web page through an internet browser. These work lists could be role-based and integrated with an internet enterprise portal for employees. For completing tasks in the work list, work is presented in simple, easily understandable Web forms for the users to complete. Systems involved in the business process are also integrated through rich application integration capabilities that BPMS offers. Process-centric integration allows BPMS to link every role and task specified in the business process designer.

In the business process designer, the analyst can specify roles, tasks performed by the various roles, and the sequence the process should follow. The roles could be for people or systems. A human task could be credit manager checks the customer credit for an incoming sales order that is on credit hold. An example of a system task is sending the sales order to the warehouse system after it is been released from credit hold.

Usually processes do not flow in simple sequential order. There are many exception scenarios and offshoot processes. The business process designer allows the analyst to set the conditions and the flows of these exceptions and sub-processes. In the process designer, the business analyst can design the process as dictated by the business environment without regard to the application functionality. It is not necessary for the business analyst to understand the inner workings of underlying applications. The business analyst does have to understand the logic and the flow of tasks for exceptions that need to be handled by applications and human participants. Once the business process solution has been implemented, work would be presented to the business users in a work list via the enterprise portal application. There the business users would click on a work item and a Web form would be presented for completion. Once the Web form has been completed, the process instance proceeds to the next activity, which could result in a transaction created in one of the business applications involved in the business process. The use of portal and internet technology greatly simplifies training and enhances user acceptance of the process solution. Business users only see Web pages that need to be completed. This shields the users from the underlying applications. Without having to teach users on how to operate the underlying applications, training costs could be greatly reduced. The Web presentation has a familiar look and feel that users would be more ready to accept than if other presentation formats are used.

Process Simulation

To help the business process owners and business analysts in the process design, BPMS provides the process simulation and modeling capability. Using the BPMS business process designer, business process owners or analysts can design the initial business processes and run the process designs in simulation mode. The simulation mode includes probability distributions of time for each activity in the simulated process. Obviously, preparation work has to be done to determine which simulation algorithm to use and what probabilistic distribution model fits each activity in the business process. Once the data have been collected, the process simulator identifies which steps are the process bottlenecks and any other weaknesses in the process design. Based on the results of the simulation, the initial process designs could be improved on iteratively. Simulation also reduces the chance of deploying a process design solution that performs dramatically differently than expected. This is a powerful capability. The process owners could use the data from the simulations to enhance the processes that are works-in-progress. This iterative approach to process design enables the best possible processes to be designed and deployed.

Process Management

BPMS serves as the supervisory system that oversees the business process once the process solution has been implemented. The supervisory aspect of BPMS provides the abilities to monitor, control, and improve business processes. Because BPMS oversees all the steps, whether manual or automated in the business process, it can provide valuable process information. BPMS software serves as the performance monitor for the processes. Process owners can obtain statistics such as average cycle time per transaction, the wait time before a process task is performed by human participants, and cost data. It is possible to assign cost figures to the time involved to complete each task in the process and the opportunity costs to the wait time while a process task is waiting in queue to be processed. These cost figures could be applied to the live process and real-time cost figures could be obtained. The monitoring capability could allow business managers to be notified of out-of-the-ordinary events. Examples of such events could be frequent large-sum banking transactions by a bank customer, in which case, the bank manager could be notified for investigation, or long processing times of a particular customer service representative.

Process data could be used to determine where process bottlenecks are. For instance, if a customer service representative takes 50 percent longer on average to process a customer inquiry, process owners will have the ability to know about this anomaly and about the performance statistics (i.e., how much time for logging, researching, and responding to a inquiry) of every task the customer service representative accomplished. Armed with this data, the process owner can determine the underlying cause of this anomaly. Another example is the time lapse between when products are shipped and when the invoices are sent to the customers. The process server will contain the statistics for such information down to the individual account executives. Advanced BPM servers come equipped with data mining capability. Through data mining, process variations can be discovered and the causes eradicated. In a way, this is not unlike Taylor's scientific management methods for business processes. The natural reaction would probably be to group BPM in the same way as Taylor and his rather functional and unhumanistic approaches to management. Inherently there is nothing wrong with using data to measure performance and diagnose problems. It is hard to imagine any kind of improvement initiative that does not utilize data. The criticism of Taylor is his theory treats workers as machines. Scientific management has been criticized as heartless, conservative, and discouraging to innovation.[1] However, these criticisms are of the management practices espoused by Taylor and not the effect of rigorous use of data to measure and enhance performance.

Real-Time Process Improvement

BPMS gives organizations the ability to implement real-time process improvement without the extensive process conversion effort. The original business processes already exist in the business process designer. This eliminates the need to gather current process information. When process bottlenecks have been determined, business process owners or analysts could incorporate improvements to the process using the business process designer. After the improved business process solution is implemented, BPMS allows any work that started on the original process to finish using the original process and any new work to be performed using the improved process. In essence, the system allows both the original and the improved processes to exist until all work from the original process is finished. Using BPMS process improvement could be made without disruption to process output. This is an important benefit to continuous process improvement.

Introduction of the Process Layer

How can BPMS deliver all of these benefits? One answer is the introduction of the business process layer in the traditional IT architecture. The business process layer is where BPMS resides. At the time business process reengineering was proposed, the technical solution for implementation consisted of the Enterprise Resource Planning (ERP) tools. These ERP systems served as the information backbone for organizations and laid the foundation for consolidated information to be produced. However, ERP tools are deficient in managing business processes, workflow, and collaboration among human participants. ERP tools have best practice business processes embedded in the software, and organizations are often forced to adopt these best practices. These deficiencies are not limited to ERP solutions. Any IT applications not developed from a process management perspective all suffer from these shortcomings. Business processes are typically embedded in these applications. There is no distinction between application functionality and business process requirements. In practice, application functionality can be incrementally improved. However, business processes, because they involve humans and other systems, are much harder to change once they have been embedded in the application. An example of a business process is the series of tasks that need to be performed for a sales order to be billed. Typically, this series of tasks would include completing a sales agreement with the customer, entering the sales order for the customer, pricing the sales order, performing a credit check, scheduling the order for delivery, informing the warehouse

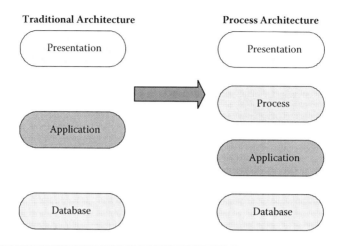

Figure 3.2   Three-Tier and Four-Tier Architectures.

to ship the products, shipping the products, and invoicing the customer. The sequence of tasks is programmed in the business application. It is not possible to perform these tasks in another sequence. What is needed is to separate the business processes from the underlying application software. This requires the introduction of the process layer to the enterprise information technology architecture.

The traditional IT architecture contains three layers: database, application, and presentation. In this structure, the database is physically where the data is stored. The application layer contains the business applications and process logic, and the presentation layer is what the users see. In the four-layer enterprise IT architecture, the process layer is situated between the presentation and the application layers. BPMS occupies the central role in the process layer. Figure 3.2 illustrates the layers of three-tier and four-tier IT architectures.

Deficiencies of Point-to-Point Interface

From a systems viewpoint, the process layer functions to integrate data and applications. In the three-layer IT architecture, integration with other applications is done point to point. When one application needs specific data from another application, an interface is created to link the two applications to transfer that specific data. As business requirements grow and applications are created and modified, the number of interfaces can grow to be unmanageable. There are several problems with the point-to-point approach to applications integration. First, the number of interfaces requires an army of programmers and a large budget to maintain them.

Software development is usually not a one-time expense. The cost of the initial development and deployment is obvious. After deployment, there is the ongoing cost for maintenance and enhancement. The more interfaces there are, the higher the cost of maintenance. Second, it is hard to impose common data standards to point-to-point interfaces. These interfaces usually link applications that have different data definitions. The lack of framework for data modeling and common definitions often leads to incompatible data transfer. An example is a financial planning application needing customer sales information for forecasting from the order management system. If, instead of net sales dollars, the order management system sends over sales dollars including freight, the result is inflation of sales dollars in the financial planning application in its forecasting function. Third, any change to the data model of an application that is linked by interfaces results in high costs to update the affected interfaces. For example, the definition of inventory on hand has been updated to exclude inventory that has been allocated for customer shipments in the inventory management system. If ten applications receive inventory–on hand data from the inventory management system, all ten interfaces would have to be analyzed for impacts and potentially be changed as a result of this change in the inventory management system.

Even though the advent of ERP has eliminated many systems, the need for application integration did not go away. The integration-free nirvana promised by ERP systems never materialized. What ERP accomplished was simplifying the complex Web of interfaces that characterized most enterprise IT architecture prior to ERP. Instead of hundreds of legacy applications to integrate, companies with ERP systems have to integrate one giant backend system and maybe dozens of satellite systems. These shortcomings of point-to-point interfaces call for a new paradigm for application integration.

Business Process Management System (BPMS) Application Integration Framework

What the process layer provides, through BPMS, is this new paradigm through an application integration framework. This framework comes complete with development tools, connectivity to commercially available systems, data mapping, and other tools. This application integration framework allows corporations to create enterprisewide data schemas that all applications will have to conform for data transfer. This is akin to Electronic Data Interchange (EDI) formats for the organization. Unlike EDI, the new technology of Extensible Markup Language (XML) enables these schemas to be less rigid and more extensible. Thus, for example, there is only one definition for open sales volume, and all applications requiring this data will receive the same information from the process layer. More importantly, the application integration framework represents the data hub where all applications transmit and receive information. The various applications are linked to the process layer by connectors and adopters, which are commercially available software to allow connectivity to business applications. The data repository in the process layer allows applications to retrieve the data needed for their functions without going directly to the originating applications. This eliminates the need for point-to-point interfaces and can drastically reduce the number of integration linkages to maintain. Figure 3.3 shows process-layer application integration versus point-to-point application integration. The application integration framework also provides common services like authentication, exception handling, and restart mechanisms. The result of the application integration framework in the process layer is lower development and maintenance costs and faster time for deployment.

Separation of Process from Business Applications

As alluded to previously, another important benefit of the process layer is the extraction of business process logic from the underlying applications. This is better explained with an example. In the high-tech industry, it is common for manufacturers to pay distributors rebate-like promotional allowances before sales orders have been placed. These payments are incentives to the distributors for specific products.

Salespeople can initiate this type of payment with management approval required for payment processing. When the term of the promotional agreement ends, the distributor is judged on how well it has performed compared to the promotional payment already made. If the distributor exceeds the volume the initial payment is based on, a subsequent payment is made for the difference. Similarly, if the distributor fails to match the volume of the initial payment, an invoice is sent to the distributor. By utilizing the process layer and BPMS, a solution can be devised (Figure 3.4). BPMS provides workflow, a process engine and database, and a design tool for process and logic creation.

The business analyst can define how this promotional process should work in the process designer. This includes the initial agreement with the customer, associated workflow for payment authorization, and subsequent settlement of the promotional agreement. Once the process has been designed, the IT analyst or programmer can create the process variables needed to support this process and embed the logic to create the payment, evaluate the distributor's performance, and settle the agreement in the underlying ERP system using application connectors and adopters. Using

Point-to-Point Interfaces

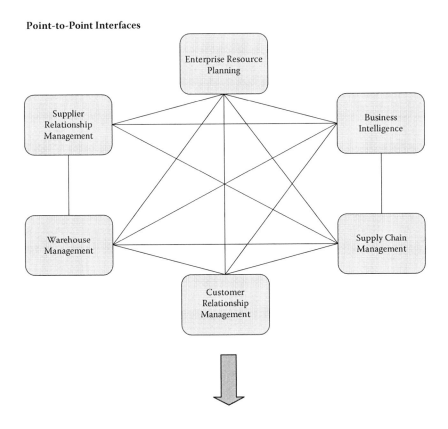

Process Layer Application Integration

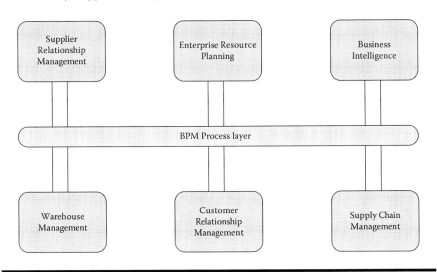

Figure 3.3   Point-to-Point versus Process-Layer Application Integration.

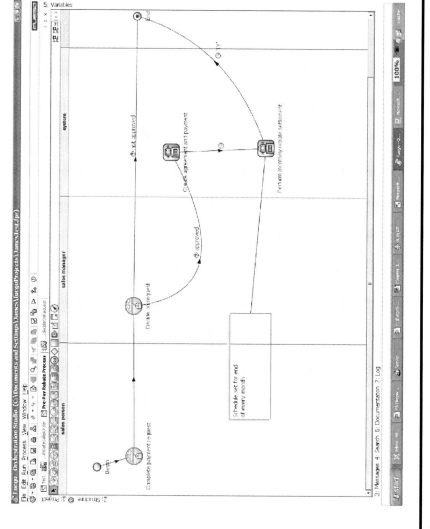

Figure 3.4 Pre-pay rebate process.

the BPMS development toolkit, information could be presented to users via Web pages. Once this solution has been deployed, the salesperson can go to a Web page to initiate a new marketing agreement. When this agreement is created, appropriate managers are informed by workflow that they need to authorize the payment. Based on the process design, the BPMS creates a payment transaction in the ERP when this agreement has been authorized. Through either automatic event (i.e., end of month) or human action, settlement is performed in the process layer. This creates a payment or an invoice in the ERP to send to the distributor. Because of the design tools and process management capabilities provided by BPMS, this solution (with the workflow, creating transactions automatically in the ERP, and user interface) requires significantly fewer resources to develop than creating a similar bolt onto the ERP. More importantly, it does not require alteration to the ERP, and it allows for measurements (i.e., time to process) on every step of the process.

In summary, BPM technology allows the business analyst to collaborate more closely with IT people in implementing projects. The various tools BPMS offers provide a new paradigm for how solutions can be implemented. Organizations are no longer tied to the business processes ingrained in their business applications. With automatic workflow generation and Web portal capabilities, workflow can be easily deployed across multiple applications, thus integrating people into the business processes. These technological innovations enable technology to better fulfill the ideals of process management. Processes can be managed in a process framework. This framework allows organizations to monitor, measure, and enhance their processes.

How Business Process Management System (BPMS) Can Benefit Business Process Reengineering (BPR) Initiatives

In Chapter 2, we have defined BPR as a large-scale redesign of core business processes. This redesign could be as dramatic as a total start-from-scratch reimplementation of business processes. Experience has shown that redesign of such dramatic scale rarely achieves success. However, when success is achieved, the results are often impressive. A more practical use of BPR is to redesign select key business processes. This revised BPR does not seek to remake the entire organization from scratch. Rather it seeks to redesign key business processes to obtain breakthrough jumps in process performance. The revised BPR approach could also be employed to implement new business processes that arise from entry into new markets or a dramatic change in business environments.

An example of dramatic change in business environment is the widespread use of the internet as a medium for conducting business. Companies are increasingly forced by the business environment to purchase, sell, and collaborate with business partners through the internet. This change usually results in new processes that have to be designed and deployed. As a tool in the process management toolkit, BPR is suited for the purposes mentioned above. BPMS offers the IT capability as well as new design and implementation approaches in fulfilling its role as an enabler. In that capacity, it serves to increase the efficiency and chance of successful BPR implementations.

To illustrate the strengths of BPM, we will first look at the shortcomings of a previous management practice and technology enabler tandem, BPR and ERP, and see how BPM and its new implementation paradigm can do better. For a period in the 1990s, ERP implementations were synonymous with BPR implementations. BPR's clarion call for massive change and structured, standardized business processes fit the ERP systems perfectly. ERP software contains one central database that ties all the data of the various functional departments. They also contain best practice business processes that have proven to work and promise seamless process integration if they are adopted. ERP came to be viewed as the implementation mechanism for BPR initiatives. Thus, the buzz generated by the rhetoric of the BPR gurus ushered in the golden age for ERP vendors. Many companies rushed to implement ERP as the BPR movement gained steam. Unfortunately, the BPR movement was not able to sustain success. The failures were not only due to the radical approach of the change program, which we discussed in the previous chapter, the state of IT and project implementation methodology also contributed to this outcome.

ERP systems are notorious for their rigidity and long implementation time. They come packaged with best practice business processes that corporations are nudged to adopt. Though it is possible to customize business processes, the risks to successful implementation are high. Once ERP systems have been implemented, the processes and business functions they carry are cast in stone. It is not a small feat to change a process to accommodate new business requirements. Though most of the ERP systems contain workflow functionality that can direct work to the appropriate employees, workflow usually requires custom programming, which is hard to change, and work cannot be directed outside of the ERP. Furthermore, integration technologies were not matured to the stage they have now. By most estimates, ERP systems cover at most 70 percent of the business requirements for a large organization. Custom and third party applications are required to satisfy the rest of the requirements. This presented integration challenges for ERP systems to integrate effectively with legacy and third party applications. Without seamless applications integration, it is difficult to achieve process management, which relies on the coordination of people and systems to be effective. The casting in stone of process logic in the ERP systems and their failures at integrating workflow with people and systems are the key systemic deficiencies of the ERP at achieving process management.

Despite these shortcomings, ERP systems did revolutionize corporate computing. Prior to the advent of ERP, most individual departments had their own IT systems that did not communicate with systems outside the departments. If there was any automatic communication at all, it was most likely the monthly reconciliation process at headquarters level. The most obvious problem with departmental computing was the lack of a clear picture of how the entire organization was performing. This reflected the Taylorist functional organizational philosophy that organizations adopted. Even with the reconciliation process, the data was suspect due to irreconcilable data differences that arose from how various departments defined their data. Thus, it was impossible to have an overview of information across departmental boundaries, let alone real-time information the managers could use to make decisions. ERP systems replaced many departmental computing systems in large corporations. After successful ERP implementations, managers were able to obtain accurate cross-functional information that was often close to real time. With the single database model, ERP brought to enterprise computing one integrated data standard and data model for the corporation. This allowed corporations to have the same meaning to their information enterprisewide. Reconciling different data from different information systems was no longer as challenging as it used to be. This increased the information accuracy for decision makers. The integrated nature of EPR also provided systemic linkages between functions. A sales order that has been shipped and invoiced would update the inventory levels, accounts receivable, revenue, and cost of goods entries. At a minimum, implementation of ERP helped a corporation establish the infrastructure for information synthesis and transactional processing, though it failed to serve as the platform for effective process management.

So how can BPMS help address these shortcomings? The creation of the business process layer permits a differentiation between application functions and business process functions. IT solutions no longer need to embed process flows into the ERP or other business applications. Because every organization is different, the line between application functions and business process functions will differ depending on each organization's definition. For example, application functions could be the calculation of customer prices, general ledger account assignments of various components that make up customer prices, or availability check of inventory to determine how much can be committed to a customer sales requirement.

Business process functions are on a higher level than application functions. They typically answer the sequence of tasks in a business process and who performs which tasks. Examples of business process function could be who performs order entry for which group of customers, what triggers a sales order to be generated, when is scheduling for customer shipments performed, and how are changes to customer sales performed. There are instances when the business process flows are embedded in the underlying business applications. Using SAP R/3 as an example, once the scheduling process of custom shipment has been designed to be contingent on successful credit checking results, it is not a simple task to alter this process for a select group of customers. In most instances, the underlying business applications do not contain the business process flows. These flows are kept outside any IT system and are enforced through training. In these cases, there are no monitoring and performance data on tracking the performance of these processes.

The BPMS process designer and the process layer allow organizations the option to separate business process functions from application functions. Critical processes that are not supported by the underlying applications or processes that are subject to change can be extricated from the business applications to reside in the process layer. At the minimum, this reduces rigidity by providing a dedicated IT layer to develop the business processes and eliminate business process logic from the business applications. More than that, the process designer allows the process owner to be intimately involved in the design of the business processes. The business process designer is a tool the business process owners can understand. Using this tool, the business processes can be designed to the most detailed level to reflect how the overall process solution should function. IT analysts can take these detailed process designs and decide how the application functions can fit into them. If the chosen business applications do not fit neatly into the desired process designs, the BPM process designer provides the development platform to customize functions needed to support the business process. Obviously, development and customization work could also be done in the application. However, the benefits of process monitoring, measurement, and cross-application workflow management will not be gained. Furthermore, this makes the underlying application more complex, which makes it more susceptible to future problems and results in higher cost for future changes.

The ability to customize business processes also could help in the change management process. Despite the shallow pretense of accommodation by project members in the past, business users have been forced to accept prepackaged business processes. This forced change undoubtedly raises rebellious feelings within the business user community. Before the solution has been put in place, the business users are already objecting to the usability of the solution. In fact, it is not unusual for business users to object to ERP products they have not seen simply because of the fear that their ways of doing business would be destroyed. Although utilizing sound change management practices would undoubtedly help the projects to succeed, the capabilities of BPMS would also help. As mentioned previously, the BPM tools and design methodology draws the business users and process owners closer to the solution design. This helps to empower the business users and process owners to the changes that are about to happen. The process empowerment shifts the accountability of the solutions to the business users and process owners. An even more important benefit to change management is the solution alternatives it offers to the business users, process owners, and IT specialists. With the arrival of the business process layer, organizations can create customized business process solutions that are outside the capability of the business applications or ERP. Thus, business users do not have to fear that their ways of doing business will be destroyed. The ability to customize processes will definitely help facilitate the change process.

How Business Process Management (BPM) Can Benefit Quality Programs

The focus of BPMS on process performance and the process analytics it provides make BPMS a close fit for quality programs. It is especially suited for the structured and analysis-heavy approach of Six Sigma. There are two well-known Six Sigma implementation methodologies, Define, Measure, Analyze, Implement, and Control (DMAIC) and Design for Six Sigma (DFSS). DMAIC is focused on improving existing processes, and DFSS caters to design of completely new processes or total redesign of existing processes. Table 3.1 illustrates the various steps of these two methodologies.

The main theme of Six Sigma focuses on eliminating process variability. Large process variability causes quality to decline. BPMS can be beneficial to Six Sigma projects to enhance existing business processes using DMAIC methodology. BPMS contains, in graphical form, the detailed business process flow of the business process to be improved. This helps project members to understand the current business process during the Define phase. Because BPMS contains rich statistics regarding process performance, this helps the Measure phase immensely. Without BPMS, the task of gathering business process performance statistics could be daunting. Oftentimes there is no detailed information on human process activities. Project team members might have to resort to unpleasant time studies to gather this information. For systemic activities, the quality of the process statistics could vary widely between applications. Using BPMS makes

Table 3.1 DMAIC and DFSS

Stage	Description
DMAIC	
Define	Customers identified and their requirements gathered. Measurements that are critical to customer satisfaction (Critical to Quality, CTQ) are identified. These will be the focus of the improvement project. Current process is studied to understand the cycle times and bottlenecks. Project charter created with business case and the goals and scope of the project.
Measure	Process output measures that are attributes of CTQs are determined and variables that affect these output measures identified. Data on current process are gathered. Establish current baseline performance for process output measures. Variances of output measures are graphed and process sigma calculated.
Analyze	Using statistical methods and graphical displays, possible causes of process output variations are identified. These possible causes are analyzed statistically to determine root cause of variation.
Improve	Solution alternatives are generated to fix the root cause. The most appropriate solution is identified using solution prioritization matrix. Solution validated using pilot testing. Cost and benefit analysis performed to validate the financial benefit of the solution. Implementation plan drafted and executed.
Control	Process is standardized and documented. Before and after analysis performed on the new process to validate expected results. Implement monitoring system to ensure process is performing as designed. Project is evaluated and lessons learned are shared with others.
DFSS or DFLSS	
Define	The project charter is drafted that includes goals, scope, business case and high-level project plan.
Measure	Customers are identified and their requirements gathered. These requirements are translated into definable measurements through use of Quality Function Deployment (QFD). Gather baseline from existing processes, competitor information, surveys, etc.

Table 3.1 (continued)   DMAIC and DFSS

Stage	Description
Explore	QFD functional analysis used to further prioritize functions most relevant to the customers. Generate multiple solutions to meet customer requirements. Most feasible solution is chosen.
Develop	Detail design is performed. Simulation and other design tools are used.
Implement	A pilot is implemented to verify design. If pilot is successful, the solution is implemented wide scale. Process controls and documentation are put in place.

consistent data on every process activity readily available. It is increasingly common to see analytical tools available with BPM technology. These analytical tools allow the process information to be mined and dissected. This capability would help the Analyze stage of the DMAIC implementation. These process analytical tools could also perform the statistical analyses (e.g., design of experiment) that are often done during the Analyze stage. The BPMS process simulation capability allows alternative solution designs to be tested. This function helps to identify the best solution alternative. The use of the business process simulator could also help validate the solution alternative. Thus, BPMS could greatly facilitate many steps performed in the Improve stage. BPMS business process designer is an ideal place to document the business processes. The business process designer keeps detailed documentation on each process activity. The documentation could be generated as Web pages or in other electronic formats. This function satisfies the process documentation step in the Control stage. Furthermore, BPMS could facilitate the task of implementing the control mechanism and monitoring of the business process. Process monitoring is inherently a BPMS function that automatically satisfies the DMAIC's process monitoring requirement. Process controls could be implemented by adding control steps in the business process design. These control steps could disallow actions that have been identified to cause variability or it could send automatic notifications to process owners if circumstances occur that could cause the process to become more variable. The functions BPMS provides clearly would facilitate DMAIC project's aim to improve business processes. In fact, with enhancements, BPMS would serve as a good project toolkit for DMAIC implementations.

For DMAIC projects aimed at processes that are not managed by BPMS, the use of BPMS could still be beneficial. As DMAIC is a process in itself, Smith and Fingar suggest the DMAIC process could be managed by BPM.[2]

The different stages and deliverables could be designed using the BPM process designer and implemented. For an organization that engages in a large number of Six Sigma projects, BPMS would show the status for each of them. By incorporating financial information, such as data from cost and benefit analysis and a business case, the organization can get real-time information on how much Six Sigma has cost and what financial benefits have been realized. BPMS also has rich analytical tools that will be useful to Six Sigma implementations. Six Sigma projects use simulation, such as Monte-Carlo simulation, to determine the best solution for implementation. BPMS already contains simulation and process modeling functionalities and its analytical capability could be utilized by Six Sigma project teams for data analysis. Another aspect where BPMS could help Six Sigma projects is in data gathering. With the application integration framework, BPMS has robust capability to extract data from applications and databases. During the Measure stage, a large quantity of data is required for analysis. Six Sigma projects could utilize BPMS's data extraction capability to gather the data. In essence, BPMS provides tools that manage Six Sigma projects and facilitate implementation of these projects. Standard Six Sigma toolkits available in the marketplace include functions such as Quality Function Deployment (QFD), Process Mapping, Failure Mode and Effects Analysis (FMEA), Statistical Process Control (SPC), Regression, Analysis of Variance (ANOVA), Design of Experiment (DOE), and Measurement System Evaluation (MSE). These functionalities could be added to BPMS, thus providing an integrated tool for Six Sigma projects.

In contrast to DMAIC, DFSS has multiple variants. There is no widely adopted methodology for DFSS. Methodologies have been developed to suit the needs of different businesses and industries. The one described above is the Design, Measure, Explore, Design, and Implement (DMEDI) methodology used in financial services and hospitals. Regardless of which variant is used, DFSS methodologies share the same tools. These tools include QFD, FMEA, DOE, simulation, etc. Because DFSS is focused on creating a new product, service, or business processes, it takes more time and usually requires more modeling and simulation than DMAIC projects. As with DMAIC, BPM could be helpful to DFSS projects. BPMS could be used to manage the process of DFSS projects. BPMS analytical tools could be used for Measure stage and BPMS simulation functionality could be helpful for the Explore stage of DFSS projects.

The usefulness of BPM does not stop with Six Sigma. The process data that BPMS contains is helpful to organizations in establishing baselines for continuous improvements. Once an improvement has been implemented, process performance is gathered in BPMS to establish the new baseline for improvement. The abundant process data stored in BPMS greatly facilitates the task of continuous improvement.

Notes

1. Peters, T. 1995. *In Search of Excellence — Lessons From America's Best-Run Companies.* HarperCollins Business. London. 42–52.
2. Smith, H. and Fingar, P. 2003. *Business Process Management: The Third Wave.* Meghan-Kiffer Press, Tampa, Florida. 147–150.

Chapter 4

Data Integration Technology

Ever since the birth of business applications, companies have been faced with challenges of integrating various applications to achieve consistent information. To overcome these challenges, technology vendors have put forth generations of integration technology. The integration technologies include simple database drivers, remote procedure calls, messaging queuing and workflow systems. With each new generation of technology, the task of integrating business applications becomes easier. When the process-focused management approaches emerged on the business arena, technology vendors started to incorporate the ability to integrate human participants into their integration technology product offerings. We will look at the various integration technologies. In this and subsequent chapters, we will look at data integration, messaging-based integration, Common Object Request Broker Architecture (CORBA), Microsoft component technologies, Java component technologies, and workflow technologies. After we have discussed the various integration technologies, we will investigate how these different classes of technologies can be used to build the different Business Process Management System (BPMS) products.

Data integration technologies allow an application to access data sources. The most prominent data source that comes to mind is of course the database. Other types of data sources are email, spreadsheets, word documents, etc. Data access technology allows an application to access any data source that conforms to the standard the technology is based on. To expose data to the outside world, data source applications (i.e.,

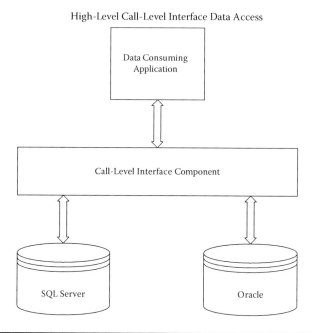

High-Level Call-Level Interface Data Access

Figure 4.1 Overview of database access using CLI.

databases) could incorporate a standard-based data access component for a remote application to perform functions on the database. The generic name for this type of standard is call level interface (CLI). The concept of CLI was originally created by the Structured Query Language (SQL) Access Group, an industry group created to define industry SQL standards. CLI shields the developer from the individual database. As long as the database is CLI–compliant, the developer can use the same code to access different SQL databases. Figure 4.1 is shows how the CLI component abstracts the data store from the data consulting application.

There are two main varieties of data integration technologies using CLI concept. The first variety is the one championed by Microsoft. It has its start with the Open Database Connectivity (ODBC) standard. From ODBC came several other Microsoft standards that facilitate data access. The other variety is the Java Database Connectivity (JDBC) standard from Javasoft.

Open Database Connectivity (ODBC)

ODBC is a CLI and has a set of standard function calls to a database. Microsoft provides the ODBC Driver Manager for its operating systems. There are other ODBC Driver Managers for other operating systems that are not created by Microsoft. In order for ODBC to work, an operating system-specific Driver Manager needs to be utilized. A Driver Manager dynamically determines which ODBC driver to use for a program to access a database that is ODBC–compliant. The ODBC driver takes the request from the calling program, translates it to a native format that the database can understand, and the database performs the request. As long as an ODBC driver exists for a database, an application can ask the database to perform a request that is supported natively in the database. Therefore, if a function supported by ODBC does not exist in the database, the ODBC driver for that database cannot support that function. Conversely, if a database has a function that is not supported in the ODBC standard, then the ODBC driver cannot support that function.

Using ODBC, an application can remotely access a database. Furthermore, developers do not care what database or platform is used to store application data. The same code for data access can work for any database that has an ODBC driver, as long as the right ODBC Driver Manager exists for that platform. This eases the task of data access. Initially ODBC has encountered database performance issues. However, it has evolved into a high-performance database access mechanism.[1] Figure 4.2 illustrates an

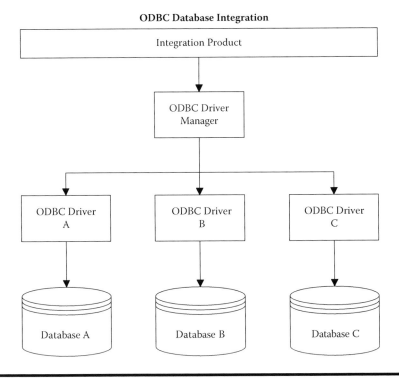

ODBC Database Integration

Figure 4.2   Overview of ODBC Architecture.

integration product that can access three databases (Database A, B, and C). The ODBC Driver Manager has access to three ODBC drivers, one for each database. During runtime, the ODBC Driver Manager will load the Driver Manager the integration product requests access to.

Object Linking & Embedding Database (OLE DB)

The downsides of ODBC are it is procedural based, requires SQL, and is relevant only for relational database. To address these drawbacks, Microsoft developed the Object Linking & Embedding Database (OLE DB) data access specifications. Like ODBC, OLE DB is also a standard and not a product. It is a standard on how the data consumer should interact with the data provider. A data provider could be a database and data consumer could be an integration product. OLE DB is a standard that follows Microsoft's Common Object Model (COM) component model and is object-oriented rather than procedural. In OLE DB, there is no ODBC Driver Manager equivalent. With OLE DB, the data consumer can access any data source that has an OLE DB data provider component. The OLE DB data component is akin to the ODBC data driver. An OLE DB component contains seven object types:

- Enumerator — provides information on data sources
- Data Source — provides connections to the data sources
- Session — provides context for transaction processing
- Transaction — commits or aborts changes to the data sources
- Command — executes a command (e.g., SQL) in the data source
- Rowset — provides data in tabular format
- Error — provides information about an error

According to the Microsoft Website, an OLE DB data provider must contain a data source, a rowset, and session objects.[2] These object types are similar to the function set in ODBC. If an application contains OLE DB objects, it can access any OLE DB data provider. This expands OLE DB to include not only relational database access but access to object databases, multidimensional data sources (Online Analytical Processing (OLAP)), emails, and spreadsheets. Microsoft also provides an OLE DB provider for ODBC, which allows the OLE DB data consumer to access ODBC databases. Because OLE DB is based on the COM component model, it is not available for non-Microsoft operating systems. The COM component model is utilized on Microsoft operating systems but not on the other major operating systems. The component model for Java is Enterprise Java Beans (EJB), and CORBA is the equivalent for Uniplexed

Information and Computing System (UNIX). This is a drawback of OLE DB when compared to ODBC. ODBC does have Driver Managers and drivers for non-Microsoft operating systems. There is an OLE DB driver for Microsoft's SQL Server database available for use on the UNIX operating system. This allows a UNIX application to access data stored in a SQL Server database.

Java Database Connectivity (JDBC)

JDBC is the ODBC–equivalent in the Java world. For the nontechnical readers, Java is a portable programming language. This means a Java application can run on any operating system that has a Java virtual machine. All the major operating systems support Java. In contrast to proprietary programming environments, such as Microsoft's Visual Basic and component environments, Java applications can be written once and run on multiple platforms. This obvious benefit is the application vendors do not have to create operating system-specific versions of their applications. This dramatically reduces their development costs.

Like ODBC, JDBC is a CLI and it has its own set of functions. It enables a Java program to access a database with a JDBC driver. The architecture of JDBC is similar to ODBC. There is the JDBC Driver Manager, which is supplied in the Java Development Toolkit. When using the JDBC Driver Manager, the developer has to register the driver with the Driver Manager in the Java program. There are four types of JDBC drivers:

1. Type 1 is the JDBC–ODBC bridge driver. This type of driver allows JDBC to access a database with an ODBC driver. Essentially this driver takes a data access request from a Java program, translates the request to an ODBC format, and submits the request to the database via the ODBC driver. Because of the extra layer of communication, data access using this JDBC–ODBC bridge driver has high overhead and can experience performance problems. Figure 4.3 illustrates the different components involved when a Type 1 JDBC driver is used.
2. Type 2 is what is known as native application programming interfaces (API) partly Java technology-enabled driver. This driver takes the JDBC command from the client application and converts the command to code the requested database can understand. Type 1 and Type 2 drivers both require native code from the requested database (e.g., Oracle, Informix, DB2) to exist on the client application. Figure 4.4 describes the participants in database access using Type 2 driver.

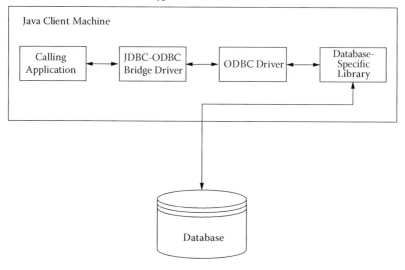

Figure 4.3   DBC Type 1 Architecture.

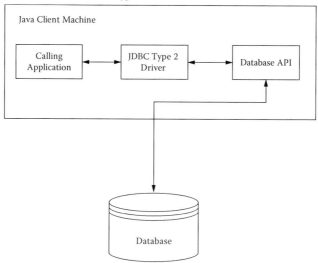

Figure 4.4   DBC Type 2 Architecture.

3. Type 3 is the net-protocol fully Java technology-enabled driver. This driver takes the JDBC command from the client application and converts the command to a standardized database-independent

JDBC Type 3 Driver Architecture

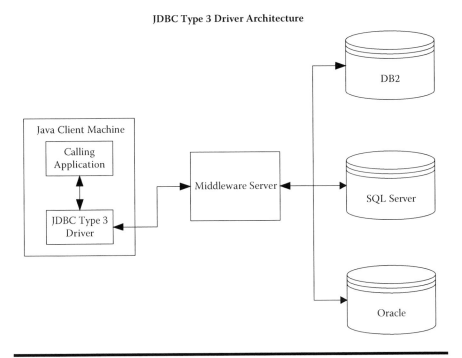

Figure 4.5   DBC Type 3 Architecture.

protocol. The database-independent protocol usually comes with a middleware server. The requested database takes the command in database-independent format from the middleware server, converts it to its own native format, and executes the command. Figure 4.5 shows a client application sending a database request to the database via the Type 3 driver and middleware server. Because this driver utilizes a database-independent protocol, and it requires no native code on the client application, it is the most flexible of the drivers. However, it requires a middleware server to communicate between client application and the database.

4.   Type 4 is the native-protocol fully Java technology-enabled driver. This driver takes a JDBC command from the client application and sends the command directly to the database. The difference between Type 4 and Type 2 drivers is a Type 4 driver does not have to convert the command to its native database code. A Type 4 driver sends the command in Java to the database, and the database has the mechanism to convert the Java code to its own native code. Figure 4.6 illustrates the participants of the database call using Type 4 driver. Unlike the other three drivers, this driver requires no native code on the client application and does not

JDBC Type 4 Driver Architecture

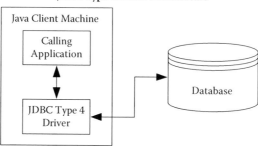

Figure 4.6   DBC Type 4 Architecture.

require a middleware server. It generally has good performance. The drawback is a database-specific JDBC driver has to exist for each database with which the calling application is interacting.

Each of the four JDBC drivers has its uses. The Type 1 driver is most applicable for databases that do not support JDBC but support ODBC drivers. Increasingly JDBC has become widely accepted, thus the relevance of a Type 1 driver should decrease in the future. A Type 1 driver is also useful for organizations that already have ODBC drivers installed on client machines. The Type 2 driver is not very common. It functions similarly to Type 4 drivers but requires native code on the calling application. Thus, the Type 4 driver is preferable to the Type 2 driver. The Type 3 driver uses the middleware server to perform conversion to database-specific protocol. This differs from a Type 4 driver. It performs the protocol conversion from the calling application using Java. Because the Type 3 driver uses an independent server, it has a higher level of security and it can support a higher workload than the Type 4 driver.

Notes

1. Linthicum, D. S. 2000. *Enterprise Application Integration.* Addison-Wesley, New York, 198.
2. Rauchs, S. 1997. Manage Data from Myriad Data Sources with the Universal Data Access Interfaces. Developer Relations Group, Microsoft Corporation, Internet: http://www.microsoft.com/msj/0997/universaldata.aspx

Chapter 5

Messaging-Based Integration Technology

The term application integration is used to denote technologies that allow a system or application to integrate to another system or application. These technologies incorporate mechanisms that a calling application can use to interact with a target application. There are many scenarios when a calling application wants to interact with a target application. One example is an application needs information from another application for its processing. In this case, the application needing the information would be the calling application that sends a request to the target application for information. Another example is the order fulfillment process involving an order management application and a warehouse management application. In this process, the order management application receives the order and the warehouse management application fulfills the order. Because the order is entered in the order management application, the warehouse management application only knows the need for fulfillment when the order management application creates a fulfillment request in the warehouse management application. In this scenario, the order management application is the calling application that sends the transaction to the warehouse management application. Application integration is important to Business Process Management Systems (BPMSs) because most business processes involve applications as well as people. Thus, BPMS incorporates application integration technologies to achieve process management. There are several types of application integration technology.

In this chapter, we will look at messaging–based application integration technology. In Chapter 6, we will look at the various component–based integration technologies.

What is messaging? Messaging is a mechanism that allows software components and applications to communicate without having the sending and receiving components or applications directly connected to each other. At a high-level, messaging allows a sending messaging client (or information producer) to send a message to a destination. A receiving messaging client (or information consumer) can receive the message at that destination. The sending and receiving clients do not have to know one another. They are linked by their shared knowledge of the message format and the destination to send and receive messages. In this manner, it provides a form of loosely coupled communications.

The message is the medium of communication. A message is a package of data that has a predefined format, and it contains the necessary context and information for all recipients to perform work independently. There are generally two sections to the message: header and body. The header typically describes the routing of the message and the origin of the message, and it contains descriptions of the body, such as the format. The body contains data for the receiver to process. The data in the body could be an explicit request to perform an action to be sent back to the sender, it could be a request for action that the sender does not expect a response, or it could be information that does not require the receiver to act. In addition to the message header and body, some messaging systems have their additional sections to the message format. For example, messages carried by Java Messaging Service (JMS) contain a properties section that allows application-specific information to be stored. The application-specific information allows the receiver to filter messages that have been sent to it.

For messaging to work, senders and receivers need to have messaging agents to facilitate the communication. The messaging agent is the messaging system, which is also commonly called the Message-Oriented Middleware (MOM). Here we are defining middleware as any program or software that facilitates communication among two or more software applications or systems. The function of a MOM is to facilitate communication, therefore integration, using messages. In this respect, it serves as the postal system for message clients, which are software components and systems that utilize the messaging system. A messaging client can send and receive a message from any other client of the messaging system. As in the case of the postal system, the receiving client does not have to be present (or active) to receive the messages. Another similarity to the postal system is senders and receivers do not have to know anything about each other, which is analogous to the mass mailings we receive from direct marketers. In this section, we will primarily refer to JMS to describe messaging. JMS contains a set of standard operations for passing messages in the Java environment. JMS has been widely adopted by various messaging vendors. The messaging operations contained in JMS represent the lowest common denominator for the various messaging systems.

There are two general models of messaging employed by MOM products: point-to-point and publish-and-subscribe. In point-to-point messaging, there is one information consumer per message, whereas in publish-and-subscribe, there are more than one information consumers per message. The differentiation between point-to-point and publish-and-subscribe messaging seems simple, but there are many functional differences arising from this high-level differentiation.

Point-to-Point Messaging Process

Point-to-point messaging is also known as message queuing. Message queuing allows a program to send communication to a queue accessible to the receiving program. The message queue serves as the middleware to facilitate communication. Unlike program-to-program communication, such as remote procedure calls, MOM does not require the receiving program to be active. Since the receiving program is not expected to be active, the sending program can proceed with processing without having to wait for a response from the receiving program. Thus asynchronous processing is the natural mode of communication for message queuing.

The message produced in point-to-point messaging is called the sender, the consumer is known as the receiver and the destination is called the queue. The sending client produces a message during its application processing addressed to a message queue. After the message has been completed, the sending client sends the message to the messaging middleware. The most common mode for the message producer to send the message is the asynchronous nonblocking send. In this mode, once the sending client has sent the message to the messaging middleware, it can continue with its processing without having to wait for a response from the receiving client. When the messaging system receives the message from the sending client, it places the message into a queue specified by the sender. The queue is a mailbox that is normally reserved for a single receiver. The receiving client can receive the messages in two modes: blocking and nonblocking. In blocking mode, the receiving client polls the queue for messages and suspends processing. It continues with processing until it has retrieved the message from the queue. In nonblocking mode, the receiving client uses a message listener to listen for

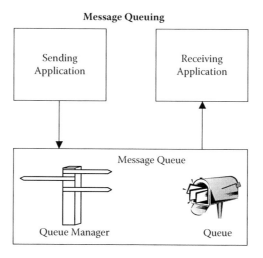

Figure 5.1 Operation of Message Queuing.

arrivals of new messages. The message listener prompts the receiver to retrieve a message once it has been placed into the queue by the messaging system. This allows the receiving client to continue application processing until a message is available for retrieval. It is possible for multiple receiving clients to be assigned the same queue, but the first receiving client to retrieve the message receives it. In this sense, message queuing is point-to-point communication to connect a sender to one receiver. Figure 5.1 describes a sending application posting the message to the messaging system. This message is placed in the queue of the receiving client by the messaging system.

After the receiving client has successfully received the message from the queue, it sends an acknowledgement to the messaging system. This is the signal to the messaging system that delivery is complete and the message can be deleted from the queue. The use of acknowledgement helps the messaging system ensure the message is only delivered once, and it helps to guarantee the delivery of the message. A message persists in the queue until a receiving client has acknowledged it or until the message expires. Messages can be set with expiration dates to prevent the storage system from being overwhelmed with unread messages. The receiving client can access the queue even when a message has not been sent to it. Thus, there is time independence of message processing between the sender and the receiver. Time independence means the sender and receiver do not have to be simultaneously active for communication to occur.

Publish-and-Subscribe Messaging Process

Publish-and-subscribe messaging is the second messaging model that has been widely adopted. In publish-and-subscribe messaging, there are an undetermined number of message recipients. The message producer is called the publisher. As in magazine subscriptions, the message consumers are known as subscribers. The destination of the message is called a topic. When a publisher sends a message, it is posted to a topic. Subscribers have to subscribe to that topic to receive a message. The publisher does not know the subscribers to the topic it is sending a message to. Similarly, the subscribers do not need to know the publisher of a topic. Thus, publish-and-subscribe messaging is more loosely coupled than point-to-point messaging, which uses a message queue that is known to be assigned to a receiving client. Publish-and-subscribe messaging systems keep track of which subscribers are interested in which topics so it can deliver the proper message. How is the management of a topic different from the management of a message queue? The difference is messages are retrieved in a first-in first-out (FIFO) fashion from the message queue. Messages to a topic are not queued. Any new message replaces an existing message in a topic. Thus, the messages in the publish-and-subscribe messaging model are generally pushed to the subscribers. This implies that only active subscribers (those that are online) will receive the messages. This is because the messages are not as durable as they are in message queues. JMS overcomes this deficiency by allowing durable subscriptions. Messages to a durable subscriber are stored for the subscribers to retrieve later. In this manner, durable subscribers use a messaging system similar to point-to-point receiving clients to receive messages.

Their loosely coupled nature and the ability to allow interaction among multiple participants make publish-and-subscribe messaging an ideal model for supporting business events. In the business context, an event is a change in status of a business transaction. Every event has an associated message in the business application. The trigger for creating the message is a business event that has been programmed into the application.

After the message has been created, the message producer (publisher) broadcasts the message to a topic. The message is processed by a broker component assigned for that topic in the messaging system. Other business applications interested in knowing about that business event subscribe to the topic in the messaging system. The broker delivers the message to the subscriber. In publish-and-subscribe messaging, the broker acts like a mini-messaging system. It has to receive messages from all publishers to a topic and ensure that only one copy of a message is delivered to every subscriber of the topic. A durable subscriber to the topic can specify how the subscriptions are stored. The subscriptions could be in one location or separate locations for separate topics. Publish-and-subscribe messages could persist on the messaging system. If the messages persist, a subscriber that subscribes after a message has been broadcasted could still receive the message. If a message did not persist in the messaging system, the subscriber would not be able to receive it.

As mentioned previously, messages could be pushed to the subscribers or polled by the subscribers. In the push mode, messages are sent to the subscribers once the messages have been broadcast. If a subscriber is offline and the messages are durable, the messages would be delivered to the subscriber once it is online. In the pull mode, the subscriber would access the messaging system at its leisure for messages addressed to it. Figure 5.2 illustrates two message producers, components A and B, publishing messages to a topic. The messages are delivered to subscribers, components C, D, and E, by the messaging system.

What are the uses of point-to-point and publish-and-subscribe messaging? In situations where a message producer sends a message to a

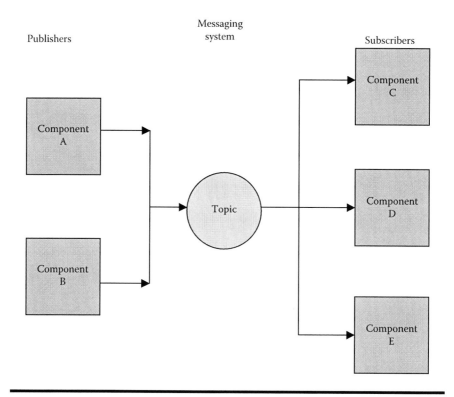

Figure 5.2   Overview of publish-and-subscribe messaging.

known recipient, point-to-point messaging is the obvious choice. In this scenario, the message will be routed to the queue of the message consumer and it will be there regardless of whether or not the consumer is active. Since there is only one recipient in point-to-point messaging, it is suitable in situations where the message should only be received once by one receiver. On the other hand, publish-and-subscribe messaging is useful for situations where many-to-many communication is required. Business examples of publish-and-subscribe include an auction system where anonymous auctioneers and bidders participate and disseminate by a pricing source.

The basic messaging process we just described utilizes asynchronous communication. There are several benefits to asynchronous messaging. First, asynchronous messaging clients can proceed with application processing independently of other applications. Loose-coupling of senders and receivers optimizes system processing by not having to block sending client processing while waiting for the receiving client to complete the request. Second, asynchronous messaging allows batch and parallel processing of messages. The sending client can send as many messages to receiving clients without having to wait for the receiving clients to process previously sent messages. On the receiving send, different receiving clients can process the messages at their own speed and timing. Third, there is less demand on the communication network because the messaging clients do not have to be connected to each other or the MOM while messages are processed. Connections are active only to put messages to the MOM and get messages from the MOM. Fourth, the network does not have to be available at all times because of timing independence of client processing. Messages can wait in the queue of the receiving client if the network is not available. MOM implements asynchronous message queues at its core. It can concurrently service many sending and receiving applications. To utilize MOM, the sending and receiving applications have to support application programming interfaces (API) of the MOM product to allow them to put and get messages.

Synchronous Messaging

Even though messaging is inherently asynchronous, most messaging systems have included synchronous messaging. They do so by combining two asynchronous messages and managing the combination so it appears synchronous to the sending client. Synchronous messaging requires a higher degree of interaction between the messaging clients and the messaging system. The messaging system serves as the glue that tightly couples the sending and receiving client in synchronous messaging. The sender must suspend processing and wait for a response from the receiver before it can proceed. When the receiving client finishes processing the message from the sending client, it sends its own message to the queue of the sending message with the response. The sending client listens to its queue for a response from the receiving client. Once the response message is in its queue, the sending client continues processing. The communication of one message is asynchronous. Thus, the sending of the initial request and the receiving of the response are two separate asynchronous messages. Synchronicity is only achieved when the sending and receiving messages are combined. Regardless of how the synchronicity is accomplished, the sending and receiving clients are tightly coupled. This means there is time dependence on message processing, and both the receiving and the sending messaging clients have to be online to process the messages.

Synchronous messaging is more difficult to implement using publish-and-subscribe messaging because of the more loosely coupled nature of publish-and-subscribe messaging. The mechanism for synchronous publish-and-subscribe messaging is similar to point-to-point in that the subscribers have to send responses to the publisher. When the publisher sends a message to a topic, it has to know whether it needs a response from one subscriber or all subscribers. If it needs a response from one subscriber, the anonymity of the subscribers is maintained. However, if responses from all subscribers are required, the publisher needs to know who the subscribers are. In the case of one response required, the subscriber sends a response to a reply topic, of which the publisher is a subscriber. When the response from the subscriber has been put to the reply topic, the publisher, which has been idle while listening to the reply topic, receives the response message and continues with its processing. Implementation of synchronous publish-and-subscribe messaging where responses from all subscribers are required is more difficult. In this case, the publisher blocks processing until it has received responses from all the subscribers in the reply topic. Using the publish-and-subscribe model for synchronous messaging is somewhat cumbersome. Messaging in general is loosely coupled. Publish-and-subscribe messaging model is even more loosely coupled. Synchronous communication entails the clients are tightly coupled. Implementing synchronous communication with the publish-and-subscribe model requires the developer to implement custom code to overcome the asynchronous foundation of messaging.

In synchronous messaging, every request from the sending client waits for the receiving client to process and responds to that request. It is possible to perform parallel messaging by creating multiple threads. Each thread is a connection to the messaging system and each thread performs

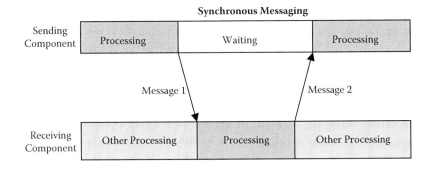

Figure 5.3   Synchronous messaging showing two asynchronous messages.

the synchronous messaging described above. To perform parallel messaging, the application has to handle simultaneous threads from the same application session. Every thread needs a connection to be active until the response has been received from the receiving client. As can be imagined, this increases the burden on the network and the session management in the sending client is more difficult because of the higher number of threads that need to be managed. In this sense, synchronous messaging has the opposite characteristics from asynchronous messaging. Synchronous messaging is tightly coupled, time dependent, places high network demand, and requires higher network availability. Figure 5.3 describes the operation of synchronous messaging. The blue boxes are processing by the sending and receiving components relating to the request-and-response messages. The sending component sends the message then blocks processing and waits for a response. While waiting for a message from the sending component, the receiving component is performing other processing not related to the request. After the receiving component receives the message, it processes the request and sends the response as an asynchronous message back to the sending component. The receiving component then proceeds with other work. Once the sending component receives the response from the receiving component, it continues with processing.

Despite the performance drawbacks, synchronous messaging has several benefits over asynchronous messaging. The tightly coupled nature of synchronous messaging means the sending client can better handle application errors in the receiving client. If an error occurs in the receiving client, the sending client can try to compensate for the error. This is especially important when the sending client requests a transaction to be performed in the receiving client. The better error handling ability of synchronous messaging means it is easier for programmers to develop synchronous messaging solutions. Since both the sending and receiving clients are online and connected, it is easier for programmers to debug errors that might occur during the development stage. Since most developers are also more familiar with programming using synchronous processing, this also facilities the development of synchronous messaging solutions over asynchronous messaging solutions

In addition to synchronous messaging, some MOM products also offer deferred synchronous messaging to allow for time-independent processing. In deferred synchronous messaging, the sending client sends the message to the messaging system and returns to its processing. Sometime in the future, the sending client polls its queue to check for a response from the receiving client. If the response has not returned, the sending client will continue periodically to check the queue for a response until the response has been received. The benefit of deferred synchronous messaging is it allows the sending client to continue with its processing without having to wait for a response from the receiving client. This is beneficial for messages that take the receiving client a long time to process.

Transactional Messaging

In addition to basic messaging processes, most messaging systems allow for transactional messaging. What is the meaning of transactional messaging? The classic definition of a transaction contains four properties: atomicity, consistency, isolation, and durability. These four properties are commonly known as the ACID properties.

- *Atomicity*: A transaction should be either all or not. If any part of the transaction fails, the entire transaction is undone.
- *Consistency*: Consistency requires that a transaction change a system from one consistent state to another consistent state. In other words, a transaction creates a new and valid state of data when it succeeds. When it fails, a transaction reverts the data to the state before the start of the transaction.
- *Isolation*: The data of a transaction should not be visible to another transaction until the original transaction has completed. This guarantees that the data in an intermediate state cannot be accidentally used by another transaction.
- *Durability*: A transaction should be durable in that the data of the transaction is available, even with system failure and restart, after the transaction is completed. This means the database will not write any partially completed transaction data to the database.

Typical messaging middleware supports transactions between the messaging client and the messaging system. In this transactional scope, the messaging client groups several messages in a transaction. The messages in the transactional group have to be sent to or received from the messaging system as a group. This means the message producer commits a transaction that contains several messages to the messaging system. If any of the messages failed in the send process from the message producer to the messaging system, the transaction does not commit, and none of the messages are delivered to the destination. Similarly, the message consumer can retrieve the messages in a transaction. In the transactional receiving process, all messages have to be received for the transaction to commit. If any of the messages failed the receiving process, the message consumer could receive none of the messages from the transaction. As long as the transaction is between the messaging client and the messaging system, it could contain sending and receiving processes. The messaging client could encapsulate sending a group of messages and receiving another group of messages from the messaging system in a transaction, provided the messages received are not a consequence of the messages sent. The reason is easy to understand. If the messages being sent have not committed, it is not possible for the message being received to have any dependence on the outgoing messages.

In a synchronous request using distributed objects, the request by the calling object and the response from the receiving object use one process. This ensures the calling object receives the response to the request in the same connection to the object-based middleware. In contrast, transactional messaging uses one process for sending the message and a separate process for receiving a response to the message. Because the processes are distinct, it is also not possible for most MOM products to encapsulate the sending of a message and the receiving of that same message into one transaction. The transactional context is lost once the message has been sent to the destination. This is a result of the asynchronous, loosely coupled nature of messaging.

An approach to implementing transactional scope across the sending and receiving messaging clients is for the programmer to include a compensating transaction in the application logic. The following example helps to illustrate the use of a compensating transaction. Let's say the sending client performs a database operation and sends a message to the receiving application once the database operation has successfully committed. The receiving application retrieves the message and performs its own database operation. Everything works great when the database operation of the receiving client is successful. However if the transaction in the receiving client fails, a message has to be sent to the sending client to inform it of the failure. When the sending client receives the message, it has to perform a compensating transaction to reverse the original database transaction it has performed. A basic MOM product does not provide this mechanism and it has to be custom developed. Due to the asynchronous nature of message queuing, it is difficult for MOM to maintain ACID properties of transactions. Even with a compensation mechanism, MOM cannot guard against the scenario where data has been deleted in the sending application prior to the reversal transaction in the case of a failure in the receiving application. An example is a transaction that debits one account in the sending application and credits another account in the receiving application. If the transaction fails to complete the debit entry in the receiving application, the compensating mechanism triggers a reversal transaction in the sending application. However, the overall transaction fails the isolation test if the account has been deleted in the sending application before the reversal of the debit entry can take place[1].

Message-Oriented Middleware (MOM) Interoperability

When MOM products came on the market, they were developed without industry-supported standards. IBM's product offering, Message Queueing (MQ) Series, has its own proprietary standard, and this is also true of Microsoft Message Queue (MSMQ) from Microsoft. This presented a problem for users of MOM and software companies that want to incorporate messaging in their product offerings. Organizations that wanted to utilize messaging for application integration had to standardize on one MOM product and ensure that all applications within the enterprise supported the protocols of the chosen MOM product. Software vendors faced the dilemma of choosing a MOM protocol or of duplicating the effort supporting multiple MOM protocols. The proprietary nature of the earlier MOM offerings adversely affected the ability for cross-platform application integration. The standardization problem was resolved when Java technology came to be widely adopted. One of the technology standards that Java offers is Java Messaging Service (JMS). JMS is a set of interface standards that allow MOM products to offer their functions. With JMS software, vendors only have to support JMS for their products to utilize MOM products that support JMS. Since most MOMs supports JMS, this effectively breaks down the proprietary walls of the MOM products.

Notes

1. Britton, C. 2001. *IT Architectures and Middleware*. Addison-Wesley, New York, 36–38.

Chapter 6

Component-Based Integration Technology

In this chapter, we will look at the various component-based integration technologies that are relevant for Business Process Management Systems (BPMS). Component technologies are important because programs built using one component technology can integrate with other programs using the same component technology. As we mentioned at the beginning of Chapter 5, process management involves people, data, and applications. Messaging technologies represent one mechanism for application integration. The other mechanism for application integration is using component-based integration technologies. A comprehensive BPMS product would contain both messaging-based and component-based integration technologies. In this chapter, we will discuss object-based technologies. Component technologies evolved from object-oriented technologies. In fact, components are made of objects. To understand component-based integration technologies, we will first look at the technologies that gave birth to component technologies.

Object-based application integration has its origin in the Remote Procedure Call (RPC) when distributed computing became fashionable in the late 1980s. Distributed computing is the evolution of information systems from the centralized computing of the mainframe world. Computing technology started with a centralized computer processor, the mainframe computer, which performed all the logic processing and data keeping. Users would access the applications on the mainframe through a terminal that performed no application logic. The information the users entered into the terminals was processed serially, in a queue, by the mainframe computer. The client/server technology of the 1980s made it possible to distribute the application processing among multiple servers and desktop computers. This also presented the challenge of integrating applications that no longer shared the same hardware or database.

Remote Procedure Call (RPC)

RPC technology was developed to solve this challenge. RPC is based on the function call technique in traditional programming. With RPC, the client application passes the arguments for the function call to a local stub. Stubs are code within the local system that handles communication and passing data to and from the remote system. When a local stub receives the arguments, it establishes communication with the server and passes the arguments for the procedure call to the stub on the server. The client application blocks processing while it waits for the response to its remote procedure call. When the server stub receives the arguments, it calls the procedure. After the server executes the procedure call, it passes the results to the server stub, which sends the results to the client stub. The client stub passes the results to the calling application. The connection between the two systems is closed only after the server returns the results of the request or the connection reaches a preset time limit. The client proceeds with its processing after it has received the response. Figure 6.1 describes the basic operation of RPC. In this example, the calling application in system A calls the RPC client stub. The stub then communicates with the RPC server stub in system B. After the target application in system B finishes processing, the result is sent back to the calling application via the client and server stubs.

RPC utilizes synchronous communication, which is different from the asynchronous nature of messaging. Using RPC, an application can invoke functions on another system as if they are on the same system. This is a tremendous help for application development. In a client-server development environment, developers can build distributed applications that span multiple computers using RPC without having to worry about network interface details. Unlike message-oriented middleware (MOM), RPC is not a discrete middleware layer. It requires stub codes on the client and the server. As long as the RPC stubs are available on the client and the server, the communication can be established directly without a discrete middleware intermediary. RPC technology comes with its set of specifications. When applications on different platforms follow the same set of specifications, these applications can interact with one another. Thus, RPC standards are platform-independent.

Basic RPC Operation

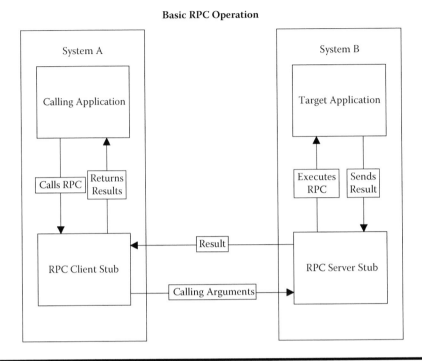

Figure 6.1   System A calling System B using RPC.

In addition to synchronous processing, RPC has developed several other modes of processing. One of the methods is asynchronous, or nonblocking, RPC. In some programming scenarios, it is not necessary to have a response from the server. In asynchronous RPC, the client sends the request to the server via the client-side stub. The server blocks while it waits for an acknowledgement from the server. The client-side stub initiates the communication to the server-side stub. When the connection has been made, the server-side stub sends an acceptance acknowledgement. Once the client receives the acknowledgement, it continues its processing without waiting for the server to reply. When the server finishes processing the call, it sends the response to the client-side stub via the server-side stub. We can consider the server response as another asynchronous call to the client. Once the client-side stub has stored the response, the client application that made the original RPC call is notified and it processes the response that has been stored on the client-side stub. The operation of asynchronous RPC is similar to request-response messaging. Just as messaging uses two messages to complete a request-response process, asynchronous RPC uses two calls to achieve request response. In contrast, synchronous RPC achieves request response with

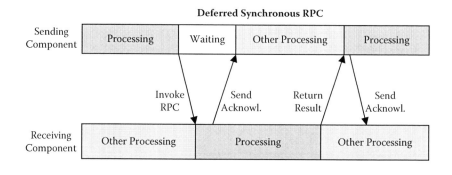

Figure 6.2   Deferred synchronous RPC with two one-way remote procedure calls.

one call. The difference between synchronous RPC and asynchronous RPC is in synchronous RPC, the connection between the client and server stays open until the server has sent the response and the client blocks processing until the response has been received from the server.

What we have described as asynchronous RPC is how most RPC technologies have implemented nonblocking RPC. Technically, it does not fit the rigorous definition of asynchronous processing. In asynchronous processing, the caller sends the request to the server and forgets about it. The client does not receive a result. A more appropriate term for the asynchronous RPC implemented by software vendors, which we have described above, would be deferred synchronous RPC. The call we described behaves like synchronous RPC except the receiving of the response is deferred. However, we will continue to use the term asynchronous RPC, or nonblocking RPC, when we refer to nonblocking request-response RPC. To avoid confusion, we will use one-way RPC to refer to RPC that performs remote procedure call without receiving a response. Figure 6.2 highlights the operations of deferred synchronous RPC, or, in our terminology, asynchronous RPC, using two one-way RPCs. The sending component invokes the remote procedure on the receiving component. Instead of blocking processing until the result is sent back from the receiving application, it continues with other processing after receiving an acknowledgment from the receiving component that the request has been accepted. After the receiving component finishes processing the request, it interrupts the sending component by sending a one-way RPC to return the result.

With the advent of object-oriented programming and component-based technology, several object-based integration technologies were developed based on RPC. In the following section, we will discuss the object-oriented programming and component-based technology. After we have a basic understanding of these technologies, we will look at the technologies available to integrate object- and component-based applications.

The Shift Toward Object-Oriented Programming

The advent of object-oriented programming represented the generational change in the information technology (IT) arena. In the object-oriented world, data and the code that supports that data are encapsulated in an object. In traditional procedural programming, the attributes (data) and the behavior (operations on data) are usually separated. Since there is no higher-level grouping (e.g., object) that binds the attributes and the behavior, a developer can never really know the entire result of a procedure call and therefore never knows exactly all the data that is affected by that procedure call. The detachment of the procedure from the data means that several unrelated procedures could change the same piece of data. This complicates the tasks of managing changes to data by procedures and testing to ensure that a new procedure does not adversely impact existing procedures. In contrast, the use of an object as a higher-level grouping of data and behavior implies that there is less risk of similar methods or procedures that perform same operations. It is easier to manage the data and access to the data because all operations on the same data are encapsulated in an object. The enhanced management of data and operations on data promotes higher code reuse. In the procedural programming world, developers have to understand the procedural code to know whether it is affecting the data the developer wants to affect. If the developer does not perform detailed due diligence, it is likely the developer might develop a procedure that is very similar to one that already exists. Whereas in the object-oriented world, the methods are contained in the object and they are easy for the developer to find and use. Furthermore, if an object does not satisfy the needs of the developer, he or she can create a new object from an existing object. The new object would inherit all of the attributes and methods of the existing object. The ability to inherit attributes and methods tremendously enhances code reuse. It makes maintenance easier because changes in the parent object propagate to the children.

In terms of design and modeling, object orientation is a more realistic representation of the real world than procedural programming. In real life, physical (e.g., car) and nonphysical (e.g., sales order) objects have attributes and behaviors. Attributes are changed by behavior based on some trigger (i.e., event). Objects can interact with each other such that the one object's attribute might be changed by its behavior to another object's behavior. An example would be the customer placing a sales order. In this example, the customer object performs an action that results in a sales order object. The sales order object has attributes (i.e., customer name, address, credit worthiness) that come from the customer object through the interaction. Object-oriented analysis and design allow dynamic and interactive modeling of objects that is hard to achieve with structured design methodology commonly associated with procedural programming.

Advent of Component-Based Technology

The next step in object-oriented technology is to encapsulate objects into components. Components take code reuse to a higher level than objects. The concept behind components is to create pluggable objects to ease software development efforts. In component-based programming, there is a library of components the developer can use. What is a component? In general terms, a component is usually a set of objects (though it could be procedural programs) that are self contained and perform functions that are not specific to any context. The nonspecificity property of a component means it can be used by any application, even a future application, which needs the functions it contains. It is meant to be used in a plug and play fashion, where the developer could use a component to perform desired functions without having to worry about how the component works. To the developer, the component is a black box. The developer only needs to know what a component does and not the implementation details.

How is a component different from an object? A component is a higher-level abstraction than an object. It is accessible to the outside only through well-defined interfaces. It is well encapsulated and cannot be used partially. In other words, when an application uses a component, it consumes the entire component. In contrast to objects, a component is typically more coarse grained. The granularity of a component depends on the number of tasks it performs. A coarse-grained component performs multiple tasks. A fine-grained component typically performs one task. An example of a coarse-grained component would be the purchasing component. The purchasing component could contain a purchase order, a purchase order item, and vendor objects. In this case, a call to a component that creates a purchase order would perform all the steps and updates to complete the purchase order without implementing and knowing the updates to the individual objects. Objects are typically finer grained. An object usually involves one data entity, for instance, the purchase order item entity, and it makes visible all the implementation details for the behavior of that entity. From a strict object-oriented analysis and detail perspective, we can generalize that objects are building blocks of components. However, components can be developed using procedural programming language. Conversely, objects do not have to be grouped into components. Object and component are two distinct concepts. One does not have to be dependent on the other.

Another difference between components and objects is the type of reuse they employ. As mentioned before, components are black boxes to the developer. The behavior and properties of a component are specified by the interface definition language (IDL). If the developer invokes an interface as described by the IDL, the specified behavior from the component will be obtained. This manner of reuse is black box because the software developer cannot see the implementation of the component, and the component cannot be modified to perform services outside of those described in the IDL. Interfaces of a component are like a contract. They promise the component, regardless of how often it has been modified, will perform according to the IDL. In contrast to components, objects use transparent, or white box reuse. The source code of the objects is available to the developer. The developer can modify the source code of an object to achieve the desired effects. This implies there is weak control over the services an object might perform. Depending on the way an object is used, the internals of an object might affect its services. Thus, the services an object offers might change when the object has been modified. The object offers no firm contract to its users as there is in a black box component.

Perhaps the biggest distinction between a component and an object is an object is not compatible with another object developed using different programming languages. A programmer developing in Visual Basic could not use an object created using C++. For a company like Microsoft, which supports multiple programming languages, the incompatibility of objects built using different programming language presents a problem in maintaining object libraries. These libraries contain objects for commonly used services and functions that help programmers in their application development. Furthermore, the incompatibility of objects developed using different programming languages presents a barrier to reuse for enterprises that use multiple programming languages. Development efforts have to be spent recreating an object developed in one programming language if that object is needed for an application developed using another programming language. Component standards were developed specifically to address the issue that pieces of code developed using different languages cannot be made to interoperate with one another. Software programs that adhere to a component model will be able to interact with other components developed for the same model. The major component models are, Common Object Model (COM) and its derivatives (such as COM+ and Microsoft XML Web Services platform (.NET), Enterprise Java Bean (EJB) and Common Object Request Broker Architecture (CORBA). We will discuss these different component models and the application integration capabilities that each of these component technologies provide.

Common Object Request Broker Architecture (CORBA)

When object-oriented technology started to take off in the late 1980s, it did not take long for software vendors to recognize the need for a standard allowing objects from different vendors to interoperate. In 1989, a group of eight companies formed the Object Management Group (OMG) to promote the use of object technology and create standards for object interoperability. OMG introduced CORBA 1.0 in 1991 as the first vendor-independent object standard. What CORBA 1.0 brought was the IDL and a set of application programming interfaces (API) that allow objects to request and receive services from other objects. CORBA is programming language independent and platform neutral. As long as vendors develop programs following CORBA standards, their programs can interoperate with other CORBA–compliant programs. The platform neutral feature of CORBA means that CORBA–compliant programs can be executed by any platform with a CORBA middleware. The CORBA standards have undergone several revisions. The current version is CORBA 3. Through the revisions, CORBA has evolved to include a component model, support for transactions, a bridge to the component models (EJB and COM), and support for messaging service (such aMessage Queueing (JMS)). Using CORBA standards, vendors have introduced middleware products to support CORBA components.

Elements of CORBA

The central building blocks of CORBA are the object request broker (ORB), IDL, dynamic invocation interface (DII), interface repository, and object adopter (OA). The ORB is the heart of the CORBA architecture. It serves as the middleware for object-based integration, similar to what RPC does for procedural programs. A client application can invoke a method through the ORB without worrying about the system platform, network connectivity, or object implementation details. A method in the object-oriented world is equivalent to a procedure in the procedural world. Methods are functions that an object has exposed to the outside world. In the component world, an object method could become a component interface. The client application sends a request to the ORB. The ORB delivers the request to the requested object, whether residing in a remote server or on the same server. Once the request has been processed, the ORB returns the results to the calling application. The ORB hides all of these concerns from the client application. To the client application, the method it is invoking appears to be implemented in the same platform and using the same programming language, even if the method might belong to a program executed on a different platform and constructed in a procedural language. The ORB abstracts all of these details to put the client and the invoked object on the same playing field. Every implementation of a CORBA ORB supports an interface repository. The client simply has to invoke an object using the interface definition stored in the interface repository.

A client application could invoke a remote object through the ORB using a static or a dynamic call. A static CORBA call uses the IDL stub program. An IDL stub exists for every interface of a target object called. The client application maps the call parameters to the IDL stub. The ORB takes the input from the IDL stub given by the client application and maps these parameters to the IDL skeleton for the target object. Whereas a calling client uses the IDL stub program, a target object could receive the call from the IDL skeleton program. The reason a call using IDL stub is static is the program has to know which IDL stub to use during design time. It is not possible for the calling application to dynamically decide at runtime which IDL stub to use for invoking a target object. A dynamic CORBA call, on the other hand, allows the client to decide at runtime, which target object interface to invoke. This is possible using DII. DII is the interface program the client application would call regardless of what target object it is invoking. In a dynamic CORBA call, the client dynamically builds and issues a request to a target object using the DII. Once the DII receives the request, it uses the interface repository to validate whether the request parameters from the client application fit what the target object is expecting. The interface repository (IR) is a CORBA object that contains all the target object interfaces the ORB supports. The client application can access the IR to find the target object interface definition that is not known during design time to dynamically construct a request. Obviously, if the target object interface is known, the client application could simply use the IDL stub program associated with that target object interface during design time. Figure 6.3 illustrates the interactions between the calling application, target object and the different elements of the CORBA architecture.

Once the ORB receives the request, it could send the request statically, as discussed above using the IDL skeleton, or dynamically, using dynamic skeleton interface (DSI). The DSI allows the ORB to deliver a request to a target object without design-time knowledge of the target object. Using DSI might be for the ORB to deliver the request to a non-CORBA object, such as a COM object. Since the COM object is not CORBA–compliant, there is no IDL skeleton for the COM object. The ORB passes the request

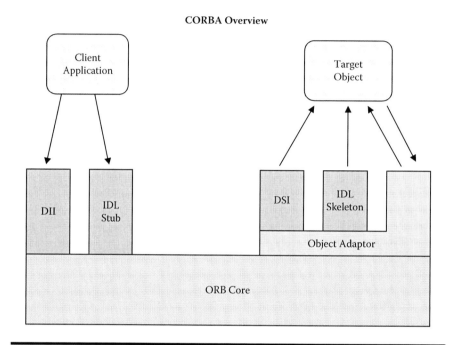

Figure 6.3 Overview of CORBA integration through stub, skeleton, and object adapter.

using the DSI to a servant object, which uses the information from the DSI to invoke the target COM object. The servant object serves as the bridge to the COM object. DSI is useful when linking two ORBs or for an ORB to pass to an object without IDL skeleton. In the case of two ORBs without using DSI, the first ORB receiving the request from its client application would have to know the IDL skeleton of the target object if the call is to be done statically. Since the target object receives request from the second ORB, which might not use the same IDL as the first ORB, it is not possible for the first ORB to have prior knowledge of the target object. When a client application makes a request, it does not have to know whether the ORB passes the request to the target object using IDL skeleton or DSI.

So far, we talked about the ORB, IDL stubs and skeletons, DII, DSI, and interface repository. The last major component of the CORBA architecture is the object adapter (OA). With CORBA 3.0, the current OA specification is called a portable object adapter (POA). A POA maps the request from the ORB to the target object. It is also how the target object accesses services provided by the ORB. That is why there are inbound and outbound arrows from the target object to the object adapter in Figure 6.3.

When the request is passed from the ORB, the POA accepts the request on behalf of the target object. It then maps the request to the appropriate IDL skeleton or DSI so the request is sent to the target object. It is possible for an application that accepts CORBA requests to have multiple POAs. Each POA could activate or deactivate a particular set of CORBA objects provided in the application. An important function provided by the POA is it is interoperable between ORBs of different vendors.

To summarize CORBA integration, a client application sends a request statically (IDL stub) or dynamically (DII). The request is received by the ORB, which forwards the request to the POA of the target object. The POA sends the request to the target object statically (IDL skeleton) or dynamically (DSI). After the request has been processed, the target object sends the response to the POA, which returns it to the calling application via the ORB.

CORBA Invocation Modes

CORBA ORB supports three different processing modes: synchronous invocation, deferred synchronous invocation, and one-way invocation:

- Synchronous invocation: The client sends a request to the ORB and waits for the response to be returned from the ORB.
- Deferred synchronous invocation: The client sends a request to the ORB and continues processing without waiting for a response. Later, the client polls the ORB to retrieve the result.
- One-way invocation: The client sends a request to the ORB without expecting a response. This is a send-and-forget processing mode, and the ORB provides a best effort guarantee that the request will be delivered. It is up to the ORB vendor to decide how best effort is implemented. An example of best effort implementation might mean the ORB will attempt to deliver the request without returning a delivery acknowledgement to the client.

The original CORBA standards are heavily focused on synchronous invocation. The two-way synchronous invocation requires the client and the server be tightly coupled to the ORB, and it requires that a client thread be used for each request-and-response lifecycle. Thus, it is deemed not scalable for large-scale implementation. Synchronous invocation uses an IDL stub to link to the remote object via the ORB. IDL stubs are similar to RPC stubs, and, like RPC invocation, synchronous CORBA invocation through IDL stubs requires the client be blocked from other processing throughout the entire request-and-response lifecycle. CORBA one-way invocation is scalable, but it does not always guarantee the request is delivered. The ambiguity surrounding the definition of best effort delivery also hinders portability of CORBA one-way implementation across different CORBA ORBs. Deferred synchronous invocation is the closest process mode for highly scalable implementation, but it is difficult to implement because it is heavily dependent on DII. In contrast to static IDL stub invocation, client applications can make nonblocking calls using DII, which are more desirable for achieving scalability. The issues with deferred synchronous invocations and DII are they are much harder to implement (require more code) than static invocation, and they use more memory.

To counter criticisms that CORBA communication is too tightly coupled, the current version, CORBA 3, includes specifications for asynchronous messaging, which is also called asynchronous method invocation (AMI). The asynchronous messaging comes in two processing modes: callback and polling. Both AMI modes allow the use of static IDL stubs. In CORBA callback asynchronous method invocation, the client sends a request to the ORB and continues processing. Once the ORB receives the response, it sends the response to the client via the callback interface. The callback is associated with the original request in the client and the callback is executed in the client application. In a sense, the response is sent to the client application as a request from the ORB. This forces the client application to be a target CORBA object as well as a CORBA client. Asynchronous polling operates in a similar fashion as deferred synchronous invocation. Instead of having the ORB notifying the client application through the callback interface, the client application polls the ORB to obtain the response from the target object. If the response has not arrived, the client application can either wait for the response to arrive, in which case it has to block processing, or continue with its processing and poll the ORB for responses later. In comparison to deferred synchronous invocation, AMI polling is easier to implement because it utilizes IDL stubs. AMI callback is more efficient than AMI polling because only one callback request is needed for the client application to receive the response. In contrast, AMI polling could result in multiple polling requests from the client or blocking of the client application processing while it waits for the response to arrive at the ORB.

In the earlier release of CORBA standards, the network communication mechanism is not specified. Thus, each ORB vendor could implement their choice of network communication protocol. This creates the problem of communication incompatibility between ORBs. One ORB might utilize Transmission Control Protocol Internet Protocol (TCP/IP), while another ORB might utilize Novell SPX. These two ORBs could not communicate with one another because of the different choices of network protocols. To resolve this incompatibility, OMG, the governing body of CORBA standards, has included Internet Inter–ORB Protocol (IIOP). The IIOP standard allows ORBs to make requests on each other over TCP/IP. Any ORB that adheres to CORBA 2.0 or later version will have incorporated IIOP as its network protocol. Since IIOP is at the communication level, application developers do not have to develop code using IIOP. It ensures a client application could make a request on an object linked to a different ORB than the ORB it is communicating with.

CORBA Services

As a standard, CORBA has evolved into a much more robust middleware than its predecessor, RPC. There are several ORB products available in the marketplace, and an ORB product usually resides on a server to which it is dedicated. As an integration server, ORB products offer many services that support integration of CORBA objects and clients. Using these services and CORBA objects, developers can assemble distributed applications in much the same way Java programmers can develop Enterprise Java Beans (EJB) that can execute on Java 2 Enterprise Edition (J2EE) servers. Since this is not a book on CORBA, we will not discuss all of the services CORBA offers. Some of the CORBA services that are most relevant for application integration are event, transaction, and query services.

Similar to events in a messaging context, CORBA event service allows objects to communicate asynchronously. It is the CORBA equivalent to MOM. It provides an event channel that allows consumer and supplier objects to exchange messages. The supplier sends the message to the CORBA event channel. The event channel forwards all the messages from any supplier to all the consumers registered with the event channel. The delivery of the event could be pushed to the consumer or pulled by the consumer. CORBA notification service allows consumers to filter the messages. The combination of a CORBA event and notification services is akin to the publish-and-subscribe messaging model.

CORBA transaction service allows the ORB to manage multiple requests from one or more client applications to one or more target objects as a transaction. The CORBA ORB functions as a facilitator when a client application utilizes the transaction service. When the client wants to implement a transaction, it first communicates with the ORB transaction service to obtain a transaction context. After the transaction context has been established, the client application makes multiple requests on target objects through the ORB. When the client is ready to commit, it sends the commit request to the ORB. If any of the requests fail, the ORB will roll back the updates performed by all the requests. This is possible if all the target objects support a two-phase commit. In a two-phase commit, the ORB is notified whenever a request has been successfully processed by a target object. Once all of the requests in the transaction have been successfully processed, the ORB instructs all the objects to commit the results. The target object withholds from committing the results of the request until the ORB has issued the commit command.

The last CORBA service we will discuss is the query service. This is similar to Java Database Connectivity (JDBC), but it is language independent. Query service allows a CORBA client application to access any database. The client sends the request to the query service of the ORB. The query service sends the request through a query skeleton to a wrapper program provided by a database vendor or a third party. After the database processes the request, it returns the result back to the client application via the query service skeleton program and then the ORB.

CORBA Component Model

We discussed all the various elements of CORBA. Although the discussions have been at a high level, readers should have a general understanding of how CORBA functions. Unlike Microsoft component technology and EJB, which were designed to provide a component standard for application development, the main aim of CORBA was to provide interoperability between existing applications. From its middleware roots, CORBA has evolved from a basic intermediary role of linking sender and receiver into a comprehensive component server. To support component-based application development, OMG introduced CORBA Component Model (CCM) in April 2002. CCM provides standards to define, develop, package, deploy, and execute CORBA components. CCM introduces the component container-programming model to CORBA, which allows components to be assembled in a container with security, transaction, persistence, and event services. The features included in CCM enable developers to assemble CORBA components and deploy these components as an application. CCM standards guarantee a CCM assembly can be deployed to run on top of a CCM–compliant application server. A CCM application could also be an assembly containing both CORBA and EJB components. The interoperability with EJB is one of the key features of CCM standards. The CCM–EJB interoperability standard enables vendors to offer development tools and runtime services that can automatically bridge the EJB and CCM environments. The availability of these tools and services, which are made possible by CCM standards, eases the tasks for developers to develop applications using both CCM and EJB components. In essence, CCM is analogous to EJB as a component development model, except CCM supports multi-languages while EJB is Java-specific. With the CORBA services and CCM, CORBA component servers serve the same role as Java and Microsoft application servers.

Microsoft Component Technologies

Microsoft developed the COM in the mid-1990s. COM provides a set of specifications for creating a COM component. A COM component can be created in several languages, including non-object-oriented languages, which are supported by Microsoft. Once the COM component is created, it is stored in binary code so programs developed using different programming languages can use it. COM is a component standard that provides black box reuse. A developer can access a COM component through interfaces provided by the component. Similar to CORBA, these interfaces are described using COM Interface Description Language (COM IDL). An interface is immutable in the sense that it is a contract for the service it provides. When a client application invokes an interface, it is guaranteed that the interface will always work the way it is defined in the COM IDL. A new interface has to be created if there is to be changes to an existing interface. As in CORBA interface, the immutability property is one of the core principles of component standards. In COM, there is a Microsoft Interface Definition Language (MIDL) compiler that generates a stub, and proxy objects from COM IDL for interaction with other components. A proxy object is a program of a target component that is local to the client application. If the client wants to invoke a method of a target component, the client sends the call to the proxy of the target component. The proxy relays the request to the stub object of the target component. The job of the stub is to receive the remote call on behalf of the target component and send the request to the target component for processing. When the request has been completed, the response is returned by the target component to the stub object, which relays the response to the client application via the proxy object. In comparison CORBA, integration using COM does not require a broker. Similar to RPC, the client application communicates directly with the target component through proxy and stub.

When a COM component is created, it is registered with the COM Object Library. COM Object Library is the facilitator of the communication between the client application and a target component. The COM Object Library is itself a COM component that contains the universally unique identification (UUID) references to all the registered components and their interfaces. The client application communicates with the COM Object Library to obtain the reference (UUID) to a remote object. The COM Object Library communicates with the local service control manager (SCM) to determine whether the component is active and where it is. If the target component is active, the reference is passed to the client application via the COM Object Library. This allows the call to be made from the client to the target component. If the remote component is not active, the local

SCM communicates with the SCM on the remote server to create an instance of the target component that is requested and it returns the reference to the client application for direct communication. The functions of the COM Object Library and SCM are critical. In fact, the COM Object Library provides the mechanism for COM to work. SCM is shielded from the developer. A developer would not have to invoke SCM directly. Access to the SCM is typically through interfaces provided by the COM Object Library. In terms of analogy to CORBA, SCM functions in a similar fashion to CORBA ORB. A local SCM communicates with a remote SCM similar to the way a local ORB communicates with a remote ORB through IIOP.

To enable transparent communication of components across the network, Microsoft created Distributed COM (DCOM). DCOM does not alter how COM operates. It simply provides a mechanism for the client application to communicate with a remote target component using the network. When the client application and the target component reside on the same machine, there is no need to use DCOM. The request can be sent by COM through inter-process communication. The main benefit DCOM provides to the developer is location independence. When making the call, the developer does not have to worry about whether the request from the client application is local or remote. DCOM automatically handles the communication. To accomplish remote communication, DCOM uses Object Remote Procedural Call (ORPC). This protocol is similar to IIOP which CORBA uses to communicate between ORBs. The combination of COM/DCOM is a competing component model to CORBA. Microsoft has implemented COM on its Windows platform and Apple's Macintosh platform. COM has also been implemented on specific versions of UNIX platforms.

Figure 6.4 describes the operation of DCOM. The client component communicates with the COM Library to find a reference to the remote component. The COM Object Library, in turn, checks with the local service control manager. If the target component has not been instantiated in the remote server, the local SCM communicates with the remote SCM to create an instance of the target component. Once the client component has the reference to the target component, it invokes the interface by calling the interface proxy residing on its local machine. The interface proxy communicates with the interface stub through ORPC, the DCOM communication protocol. As in COM, the interface stub is the program that directly calls the target component interface. Once the request has been processed, the target component returns the result to the interface stub. The result is received by the client component from the interface stub via the interface proxy.

Just as CORBA has implemented transaction service, Microsoft offers Microsoft Transaction Server (MTS) to provide transactional support for

DCOM Overview

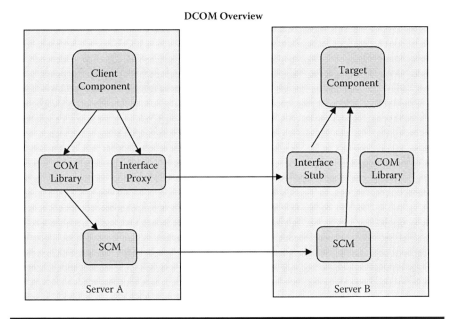

Figure 6.4 Client component invoking a remote component interface using DCOM.

COM components. The main function of MTS is to allow components to execute transactions. A client application would invoke a call to MTS to get transaction context. Then it would make calls to other COM objects. During the calls to the other COM objects, MTS keeps track of whether the calls are successful or not. If any of the calls failed, MTS can rollback all of the updates made by all the target objects involved in the transaction.

Since COM/DCOM is based on RPC, it naturally supports synchronous invocation. When a client application calls a target component, it blocks processing until the response has been received from the target component. The connection between the client and the target component also remains open until the request-and-response process has finished. The ability for COM asynchronous method invocation was introduced with Windows 2000 operating system. With asynchronous method call, the client application does not have to block processing while waiting to receive response from the target component. Result retrieval for the calling application uses the pull model. The client application calls a separate interface (the finish method) of the target component to retrieve the result. If the target component has not completed processing when the client application calls the finish interface, the client application blocks processing and waits until the results can be received.

Microsoft COM+

The next generation of COM technology is COM+, which could be thought of as the integration of MTS and COM. COM+ does not represent a revolutionary leap over COM. It fuses together different technologies (such as COM, MTS, Microsoft Message Queue (MSMQ) into one integrated platform. Although these various technologies could work together, integrating them into a platform simplifies development for programmers and offers integrated runtime services and administration. COM+ offers thread management, thread, and object pooling, security service, deployment, and administration services that are not available in COM. In terms of enhancements that are relevant for application integration, COM+ offers queued component, transaction, and event services. Transaction service is a core COM+ service that performs the same function as MTS. Because it is core to COM+, developers do not have to worry about managing the transactional context, as would be required using MTS, when there is a series of calls. COM+ automatically knows that component calls made by a component within a transaction context all belong to the same transaction. While the ease of use is important to developers, COM+ transaction service essentially offers the same capability as MTS.

COM+ Queued Component Service

COM+ queued component (QC) is based on the MSMQ technology and is offered as a core COM+ service. As we have discussed, traditional COM uses synchronous RPC to invoke a remote component. Since Windows 2000, Microsoft has introduced asynchronous COM for performing asynchronous COM calls. However, asynchronous COM calls cannot be made from every COM component. For instance, interfaces that inherit from the IDispatch interface standard cannot work with asynchronous COM. IDispatch is the standard COM interface for a component to be invoked by other components dynamically. IDispatch interface looks the same for every component. A calling client could invoke the same IDispatch interface when accessing a wide variety of components that support IDispatch. Visual Basic, in its earlier versions, requires all components to be invoked through IDispatch. Another disadvantage of the asynchronous COM call is it does not work with components that are part of a COM+ application. This limits the use of asynchronous COM in a COM+ environment because asynchronous COM interface calls cannot utilize COM+ services such as transaction, security, etc.

Almost as a replacement for asynchronous COM technology, Microsoft introduced QC service as the model for asynchronous method invocation for COM+. Prior to COM+ QC service, developers could utilize MSMQ, in addition to asynchronous COM, to invoke a remote component interface asynchronously. However, the developer has to implement a different code to invoke the remote component interface with MSMQ as the code to invoke the remote component using COM call. This presents a new programming technique the developer has to master. COM+ QC service is based on MSMQ. One of the important features of QC service is it hides the complexity of MSMQ from the developers. A developer does not have to implement the extra code to enable a component to be called asynchronously. Similarly, no special step (such as MSMQ code) is required for a client application to invoke a COM+ component asynchronously using QC. The only requirement is for the target COM+ component to be instantiated as a queued component. The proper instantiation of the target component indicates to COM+ that MSMQ should be used as the communication transport.

When a client application calls a target component interface synchronously using QC service, the client application actually calls a recorder interface created automatically by COM+ to handle asynchronous calls. The recorder interface looks like the real target component interface to the calling application, and it resides on the same server as the calling application. Once the request has been sent to the recorder, the connection is released from the calling application. The recorder interface is a proxy for the target component interface. It converts the request to a MSMQ message and delivers the message to a MSMQ queue reserved for the recorder interface. Once the message has been placed into the recorder queue, MSMQ picks up the message and delivers it to the application queue for the target component. When the message reaches the queue for the target component, a listener object that COM+ maintains detects the presence of the new message. Every COM+ application has one listener object. After the application listener object detects the message, it creates a player object for the target component and the listener object instructs the target component player object to retrieve the message from the application queue. The player retrieves the message from the application queue and it makes the call to the target component interface. Figure 6.5 shows the elements involved in making the interface call using queued component. In equivalent terms to conventional synchronous COM RPC, the player has the same role as the target component stub. As the remote component receives the call, the remote component does not know whether the request is made asynchronously through the player object or synchronously through RPC.

Since COM+ QC service is asynchronous, the client application does not expect to receive a response. Using QC service does not guarantee the request will be processed by the target component. In scenarios where response from the target component is required, a synchronous call is

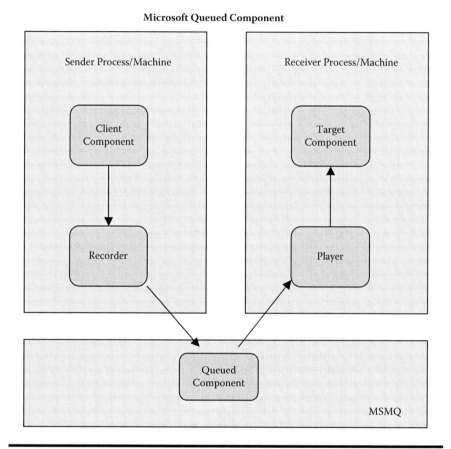

Figure 6.5 Operation of asynchronous call using COM+ Queued Component.

probably the way to go. COM+ QC does offer a notification function. It is possible for the recorder object to forward a callback request with the message for player object of the target component. The callback request indicates to the target component to send an acknowledgement to a callback object that the client application has created to process the acknowledgement. This is essentially a series of two one-way asynchronous calls. The difference is the client application specifies which component interface the target component should invoke for the acknowledgement.

COM+ Event Service

In addition to QC service, COM+ also offers event service to perform publish-and-subscribe messaging. QC is a service for point-to-point asynchronous communication. Using COM+ event service, publisher components can send events subscriber components can receive. An event is a message a publisher sends to inform others of some change in data. The concept is similar to publish or subscribe MOM. A component that wants to send an event is called a publisher, and it can register with COM+ the event it wants to send. An example of an event is a change in stock prices. The publisher might be an application that keeps track of stock prices. Once the event has been registered, components interested in the event can register with COM+ as subscribers of that event. COM+ event service keeps track of publishers of events and all subscribers to each event. Using the stock price example, a subscriber might be a customer account summary component that uses the stock price to determine customer account value. When the publisher sends an event, the COM+ event service has the responsibility of delivering the event to the subscribers. The COM+ event service determines all the registered subscribers to whom the event will be sent and it connects to the subscriber to deliver the event. Available connection options for COM+ event service to call sub-scribers include synchronous call and QC service. One interesting point to note is the default connection option from the publisher to the COM+ event service is synchronous. Thus, the connection between the publisher and the COM+ event service is not broken until after the COM+ event service has connected with each subscriber. The performance implication is it might take a long time for a publisher to send an event that has been subscribed to by a large number of subscribers.

With the various component services, COM+ has become a robust platform for component development. It has extended beyond the RPC mechanism for component integration by including QC service and event service. With COM+, it is possible to develop large-scale distributed applications that require asynchronous connectivity.

Microsoft .NET

The next evolution in Microsoft component technology is .NET. .NET is considered a major leap over the COM+ component model. With .NET, Microsoft introduced several features that are important to component development. These features include common language runtime (CLR), a new way of component deployment through assemblies, Web services to expose component services through Extensible Markup Language (XML), and Simple Object Access Protocol (SOAP). Most of the features introduced in .NET are important to component development. Since this is not a book on component development, we will focus on the features that are important to application integration and CLR, which is the foundation of .NET component development. The features we will discuss include .NET remote method calls and Web services. See Figure 6.6.

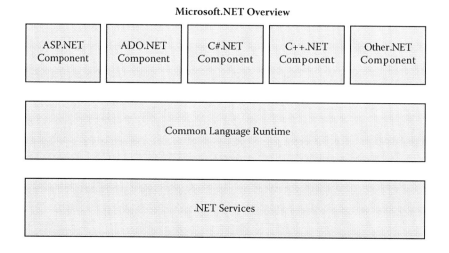

Figure 6.6 High-level overview of Microsoft .NET architecture.

CLR is the key point of the .NET technology offering. CLR replaces COM as Microsoft's component environment. Though COM allows components to interact with one another, the COM standard does not represent the lowest common denominator of all the COM–compliant languages. Therefore, COM components developed using one language might not be 100 percent interoperable with COM components developed using another language. One of the common interoperability issues is data type compatibility. A component developed using one language might contain data types not supported by components developed using another language. Because of compatibility issues, it is not feasible to assemble a COM application from components developed using different languages. CLR resolves the language dependence issue by introducing a revolutionizing intermediate layers. CLR converts code developed using a CLR–supported language into an intermediate language format. The Microsoft Intermediate Language (MSIL) code is the byte code that is executed. Because of MSIL, components are compatible regardless of which CLR–supported languages are used to develop them. CLR is similar to CORBA's CCM in that both aim to provide true language neutral component support. The language neutral feature allows an application to be assembled from components developed using multiple programming languages. CLR is also similar to Java Virtual Machine (JVM) in concept. It is technically possible to run a .NET component on any platform that supports CLR, just as Java programs can be run on any platform that has a JVM installed. However, the possibility that CLR will gain momentum on a non-Microsoft platform is probably low. Such a development would probably not be desirable for Microsoft because of the potential negative impact to its platform sales. As for third-party open-source initiatives, there are the Mono project, sponsored by Novell, and the DotGNU project from the Free Software Foundation that aim to bring .NET environment to LINUX platforms. Unlike COM, which is replaced by .NET, COM+ component services are used by .NET. In the .NET world, the COM+ component services are retained and they are relabeled as .NET component services.

.NET Remoting

The unit of deployment for .NET is an assembly. It is the .NET equivalent of a COM component. A set of assemblies could form a .NET application. An assembly is a set of files including the MSIL code, a manifest that contains information about the assembly and its metadata, and resources (immutable data such as Joint Photographic Experts Group (JPG) file) for the assembly to function. CLR uses a just-in-time compiler (JIT) to compile the MSIL code in the assembly to native code. The native code is specific to the Central Processing Unit (CPU) for the computer that runs the CLR. When a component calls another component's interface and the target component is not active, the CLR loads the target component, translates the MSIL code to native code, and executes the interface. Similar to DCOM for remote COM interface call, .NET components utilize .NET Remoting to accomplish component integration across the network. In terms of technical foundation, .NET Remoting and DCOM are both based on RPC. They both use proxies and stubs, described earlier. DCOM is based on proprietary binary network communication that is not supported by non-DCOM platforms. This limits DCOM use to only Windows-based applications. Because of the proprietary nature of DCOM, it is cumbersome to allow DCOM calls to get past firewalls. On the other hand, .NET Remoting utilizes HyperText Transfer Protocol (HTTP), SOAP, and Transmission Control Protocol (TCP) for network communication protocols. This feature makes .NET Remoting more adaptable to environments that need to support multiple platforms.

Remotable components in .NET are exposed to the outside world through a listener in the .NET Remoting system. When an application has been created, there needs to be a listener process that is registered with the .NET Remoting system. A client component sends a request that is received by the listener for the target remote component. The listener submits the request to the remote component and sends back the request to the client component via a channel. In .NET Remoting, a channel transports the data from the sender to the receiver. There are two standard channels, TCP and HTTP. It is also possible to create custom channels for the message transport. TCP generally has faster performance than an HTTP channel. Before the request and response are transported, they have to be formatted to a protocol to transport across the wire. There are two standard formatters that come with .NET Remoting, binary and SOAP. The binary formatter packages the request or response into binary format to carry across the TCP or HTTP channels. The SOAP formatter packages the message into an XML format according to its protocol. It is a cross-platform protocol allowing Web services to be invoked. SOAP is a standard that has garnered increasing acceptance within the technology industry and it has been accepted as a standard by the World Wide Web Consortium (W3C). The default processing mode for .NET Remoting is synchronous. It is also possible to communicate asynchronously. In a .NET Remoting asynchronous call, the client sends the request to the target component with a callback delegate. The callback delegate is an object of the client application that is sent as a reference to the remote target component. After the target component finishes processing, its state information is sent to the callback object. The callback object sends a notification to the client component indicating the target component has finished processing the request.

In summary, .NET Remoting provides an easy way for developers to invoke remote components. It uses the .NET Remoting system for brokering the communication. Remotable components and channels are registered with the .NET Remoting system. A client component submits a request to a listener for the target component. The request and response are communicated via a channel that has been assigned to the remote component.

.NET Web Service

The most marketed feature of .NET is its ability to create and invoke Web service. In evolutionary terms, Web service can be viewed as a component interface that has been exposed to the internet. Instead of utilizing RPC or messaging, Web service is invoked through SOAP and it uses HTTP as the transport for carrying the request. The request and response which are embedded as XML documents follow the SOAP standards. As discussed previously, SOAP is the industry standard protocol for invoking a component interface across the internet using Web service. The SOAP standard defines the XML format that the request-and-response message should contain and it uses HTTP as the transport for communication across the internet.

So how does Web service work? Like the IDL that exists for COM interfaces, Web services are described by Web Service Description Language (WSDL). The WSDL serves as a metadata for the Web service. It contains the format of the request message the client sends to invoke the Web service, and it also contains the format of the response message the Web service returns to the client. A WSDL file serves more than a descriptive purpose, it is meant to generate proxy code by any platform that supports Web service. For example, a J2EE application server should be able to automatically generate proxy code in Java, based on the WSDL for a Web service created using Visual Basic.NET. Once the proxy code has been generated, other Java programs can call the proxy as if it is a Java interface. The Java proxy code generated by the WSDL knows how to connect to the Web service when the proxy code has been called, and it packages the request and response into SOAP messages.

The .NET development platform makes it easy for developers to publish their component interface as Web services. For existing COM components, the .NET development platform provides the SOAP toolkit to expose the COM components as Web services. If a component is developed as a .NET assembly, Visual Studio.NET (Microsoft's .NET development tool) can create a Web service file that references the assembly. Once the Web service file has been created, Microsoft provides a WSDL utility, WSDL.exe, to automatically generate proxies for the Web service in a .NET-supported language. Of course, a Web service does not reference a component. It could simply be a .NET class that has been declared as a Web service. Using Visual Studio.Net, a .NET class can be updated to a Web service with a couple of lines of additional code.

After the Web service has been created, .NET can automatically create a WSDL for the Web service. The WSDL can be registered with a Web service registry such as Universal Description, Discover, and Integration (UDDI). Applications interested in Web services can search the UDDI directory to discover Web services that are appropriate for its needs. In this way, UDDI functions as the white pages and the yellow pages of Web services. Once the Web service has been discovered by a client application, the WSDL of the Web service can be converted to proxy code that is usable by the client application. When a client application invokes a Web service, the Web service proxy generated for the client application formats the request into a SOAP message, then the proxy sends the SOAP message to the Web service by HTTP. The request is received by a listener for the Web service residing on the recipient server. The Web service listener dispatches the request to the appropriate component interface. If the Web service call produces a result message, the listener is responsible for packaging the result message into SOAP format and transporting the result back to the client application.

Our high-level discussion of Microsoft component technologies has taken us from COM to .NET. The goal of component technology has always been to enable seamless integration of components. COM was Microsoft's first comprehensive component model. It made the first major step to enabling component-based development. Though type compatibility hinders interoperability of components built using different programming languages, COM allows components to interact remotely. COM+ added component services that made component-based development easier. .NET brings true language neutrality, as long as the programming languages support CLR. The language neutral feature takes the choice of programming language out of the equation for component interoperability. Finally, .NET greatly facilitates the development of Web services. As much as COM was touted as an open standard, the truth is that COM never gained popularity outside of the Windows platform. The advent of Web service might be the integration standard that finally brings the components of the various component standards together.

Java Component Technologies

In 1995, Sun Microsystems introduced the Java development technology. The impetus behind Java was to create a development technology that could be run on any platform. Platform neutrality has always been the challenge software vendors faced. Prior to Java, software vendors had to develop several versions of their products for the different platforms their customers were using. The duplicated development efforts were a huge cost to the vendors. Java's motto is, ìWrite Once, Run Anywhereî. Instead of writing several versions of their programs, applications written in Java can be run on any platform that supports a JVM.

In contrast, Microsoft COM technology does not offer platform neutrality in the sense that there is a common programming language for developing components that can work on many platforms. COM offers a component model but not a development language. Furthermore, the COM component model has not been widely accepted outside Microsoft platforms. Though the CORBA component model has wider platform acceptance than Microsoft COM, it also does not offer a development language as provided by Java and J2EE. In fact, the new CCM specification has tight EJB interoperability. This means J2EE components will work in a CORBA component model environment. It remains to be seen whether CCM will garner wide acceptance. If it does, it will also mean that J2EE component technology has extended its footprint because of the tight CCM–EJB interoperability. Though all the component technologies hope to accomplish platform- and language-independent component interoperability, Java has the distinction of offering a programming language that allows components created using this language to be used in any platform that supports JVM. This unique offering has made Java into one of the most widely used programming languages. Microsoft .NET component model offers the CLR layer functions similarly to the JVM. Microsoft is offering what J2EE has offered to the development community with the introduction of CLR. The main difference between J2EE and .NET is .NET allows the developers to choose from any CLR–compliant programming language. However, it remains to be seen whether CLR will be as widely accepted by non-Microsoft platforms as J2EE is.

So what comprises the J2EE component technology? The main elements of J2EE technology are components, container services, and Web services. J2EE offers two different component models, servlet or Java Server Page (JSP) for the Web component, and EJB for the server component. After we discuss these two component models, we will investigate the various container and Web services that are relevant for application integration.

Servlet and EJB

It is a little confusing when one talks about a J2EE component. There is not one standard J2EE component model. The J2EE platform is made up of several different component models. As new technologies are introduced, the number of Java component models seems to increase. In this discussion of Java component technology, we will focus on JSP, Servlet, and EJB. The servlet and JSP are primary J2EE component technology for Web development, while EJB is the component model for application logic. JSP and servlet usually work together. JSP is a text-based document that contains static content (i.e., images, text, etc.) and dynamic data. The JSP static data could be expressed in HyperText Markup Language (HTML) or XML code, while the dynamic data is controlled by Java code. JSP is an extension of servlet. When the JSP is being run, the JSP code is translated into a Java servlet. Both the servlet and EJB operate in a separate container. The servlet operates in a Web container and the EJB operates in an EJB container. A container is a runtime environment that hosts and manages a component. The container provides services that allow the component to operate. These services include transaction, messaging, remote access, security, and other services. We will discuss some of these services a little later in this chapter. The component is shielded from the outside by the container. Any interaction between the component and the outside is by means of container services. This makes programming easier for the developer, because the developer can focus only on encapsulating business logic when building the component. The container will automatically use a container service during runtime depending on policies specified by the developer during design time. A policy might be to use messaging for remote communication rather than RPC. Although Microsoft .NET does not specifically use the term container, the .NET services and the .NET runtime environment effectively functions as a component container for the .NET components. Whereas .NET uses the same container model for all .NET components, J2EE utilizes separate container models for Web and EJB components.

What are the differences between the servlet and EJB components? The main difference is probably the servlet specializes in communicating with Web browser. Thus, it takes requests using HTTP. An EJB communicates with other Java components using the Remote Method Invocation over Internet Inter–ORB Protocol (RMI–IIOP). According to J2EE 1.4 specification, the J2EE applications are required to access EJB through RMI–IIOP. Servlet can respond to HTTP commands, such as HTTP–POST and HTTP–GET. Following the J2EE specification, EJB should not interact directly with the Web browser. The one Web interaction allowed for EJB under J2EE specification is SOAP/HTTP protocol for Web services. Because of the differences in the container, servlet resides on the Web server that has the servlet container, while EJB resides on the application server that has the EJB container. Other than that, both the Web and EJB containers provide similar services. Because of the similarities of these two component models, some software vendors developed their products purely using servlet technology. The advantage of this approach is their products can be run on any Web server that supports a servlet container. This minimizes the system footprint necessary to run their products. Web servers are originally designed to serve static content that do not require high performance and distributed computing features. However, most Web servers that support servlet containers are now offering high performance features such as failover, clustering, and load balancing. Increasingly the main difference in the Web server that supports servlet container and the application server is the support for integration with other systems and platforms. Since most J2EE application servers support both servlet and EJB containers, servlet applications can be run on application servers when the rich integration capability is desired.

We talked about the increasing blurring of the line between the Web components and EJB. In traditional Java programming paradigm, the Web components and EJB play distinct and complementary roles. How should the Web components interact with EJB components? JSP, servlet, and EJB are created to work in conjunction with the Model-View-Controller (MVC) programming model. The MVC design paradigm separates an interactive application into three modules: model, view, and controller. The model module is the application logic and data. It is the heart of the application processing and corresponds to the application and data layer in the traditional three-layer application architecture. The view component is the presentation to the user. Typically, in a Web program, this component would contain the Web pages that are displayed to the users. The controller component is the link between the model and the view. It dispatches the requests from the views to the model and it mediates the application flow. Using something we previously discussed as an analogous, the controller functions similar to the ORB. Both the ORB and the controller take requests from the client, dispatch the requests to the receiver, and return the results to the client. Because of the interactive nature of Web applications, the controller performs the additional task of selecting and synthesizing the view to display to the user following a request. In this manner, the controller can be viewed as a specialized view that can display dynamic views.

According to the MVC model, the controller is typically performed by the controller servlet. This servlet takes the request from the user and invokes the appropriate model component(s). Once the request has been processed, the controller servlet selects the appropriate HTML or JSP to display to the user. However, this does not mean the servlet only functions in the controller role under the MVC model. As mentioned previously, JSP is translated into the servlet when it is run. Thus, JSP and the servlet usually perform together. Therefore, the controller servlet does not render the view; it sends the request to one or more objects to render the view to the user. As for the model under the MVC paradigm, the EJB is an ideal candidate to serve that role. In a typical flow, a request could be generated by the user from the Web browser. The controller servlet takes the request and invokes the appropriate EJB component interface. When the result of the EJB component call has been received, the controller servlet assembles the view to display to the user. The view is then rendered by the JSP.

Java Component Container Services

To recap our discussion of component container, we have defined the container as the runtime environment that hosts and runs Java components. Components exist inside the container and there is no direct interaction with the component by another component. A container can simultaneously host multiple components. The container is equivalent to the .NET runtime and COM runtime environments. The illustration below describes a typical J2EE architecture in terms of containers.

In this typical J2EE architecture, the client (whether an application or a Web browser) interacts with the Web container through HTTP. None of the components interact directly with other components. Once the request has been received by the Web container, it invokes the appropriate servlet or JSP to process the request. If application processing is required, the servlet or JSP could utilize the RMI–IIOP API in the Web container to communicate with an EJB in the EJB container. Again, the communication is indirect. The Web container communicates with the EJB container, which invokes the appropriate EJB component interface to process the request. The Web client application could also interact directly with the EJB container through RMI–IIOP. In this case, the Web application's client container sends the request on behalf of Web client application. The container provides several different services through APIs to the components it hosts. Table 6.1 describes the services available to both Web and EJB container.

These services are intended to make development, deployment, and management of components easier. All of these services are available as system programming interfaces or application programming interfaces. If a container service is required by a component, this container service is accessed through the appropriate programming interface. The service provided to the component by the interface will be supported regardless of the Java platform provider. Figure 6.7 depicts the overview of J2EE architecture. In this illustration, the J2EE application server supports both the Web container and the EJB container. The common container services are shown. The figure also shows the typical interaction between the J2EE components and other enterprise applications and components. In the next sections, we will discuss some of the container services that are important to application integration. These services include RMI–IIOP, Java Transaction API (JTA), Java Naming and Directory Interface (JNDI), J2EE Connector Architecture, and support for Web services. Please refer to previous section for a discussion of JMS and JDBC, two other container services that are relevant for application integration

Remote Method Invocation over Internet Inter–ORB Protocol (RMI–IIOP)

RMI–IIOP is the standard communication protocol among Java components. Prior to the introduction of RMI–IIOP, Java RMI was the standard object invocation service. RMI is the Java component equivalent of the RPC. It allows one Java component to communicate with another Java component on a remote server. The client component calls Java RMI service to invoke an interface of a remote component. RMI takes the request to the remote component and returns the response from the target component back to the client component. Unlike COM or DCOM, there is no IDL because all Java components are built using Java, hence no mapping from one language to another is necessary. Similar to DCOM, which uses ORPC as its transport protocol, Java RMI uses the Java Remote Method Protocol that is proprietary to Java. The client component looks in the RMI registry of the JVM on which it is running to locate the reference

Table 6.1   Services for Web and EJB Containers

Service	Description
JTA (Java Transaction API)	JTA allows the component to define the transaction scope. It also serves as the transaction manager that coordinates the various resources that participate in the transaction.
JMS (Java Messaging Services)	JMS is a MOM that allows components to interact through messaging. Please refer to the previous section on messaging for more details.
JNDI (Java Naming and Directory Interface)	JNDI is standard Java API that allows a component to access different kinds of naming and directory services. Naming services that JNDI can access include LDAP (Lightweight Directory Access Protocol) and DNS (Domain Name Service).
Java Database Connectivity (JDBC)	JDBC is standard Java API to execute SQL statements on SQL–compliant data sources. Please refer to previous section of data integration technology.
RMI–IIOP (Remote Method Invocation over Internet Inter–ORB Protocol)	RMI is Java's RPC protocol for invoking an interface of a remote Java component. With RMI over Internet Inter–ORB Protocol, a Java component can use the same protocol to invoke another Java component or a CORBA component.
HTTP (HyperText Transfer Protocol)	J2EE supports HTTP and HTTPS (HTTP Secure) for client and Web component (JSP/Servlet).
Java IDL (Interface Description Language)	Java is used in conjunction with RMI–IIOP. It allows Java component to invoke CORBA component through IDL mapping for the CORBA component model.
JavaMail	This service allows Java component to send email.
JAF (JavaBean Activation Framework)	JAF is used by Java Mail API. It converts MIME objects in an email to Java objects so these MIME objects can be handled by Java components.
JAXP (Java API for XML Processing)	JAXP allows a Java component to parse and manipulate XML documents.
J2EE Connector Architecture	J2EE Connector Architecture is a system programming interface that allows connectors to legacy or non-Java applications to be plugged to a J2EE server. These connectors allow Java components to interact with non-Java applications that do not support CORBA.

Table 6.1 (continued)   Services for Web and EJB Containers

Service	Description
JAAS (Java Authentication and Authorization Service)	JAAS is security service that authenticates users and manages access control on the users.
Web Services	J2EE provides support for Web service caller and receiver. The support includes Web service call using SOAP/HTTP and access to Web service registries.
Management	J2EE provides runtime management support for the J2EE server.
Deployment	J2EE provides API that allows deployment tool to plug into the J2EE server.

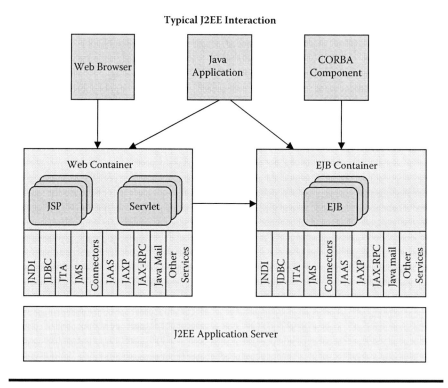

Figure 6.7   Overview of J2EE architecture with component services and typical interaction among different participants.

to the interface it wants to call on a remote component. After the interface reference has been obtained, the client calls the remote interface as if that remote interface is local. The RMI service hides the complexity of the remote call from the developer.

With the convergence of Java and CORBA component technologies, J2EE 1.4 offers the RMI–IIOP to allow a client Java component to invoke another RMI–compatible component using IIOP as the protocol. RMI–IIOP is an ORB that can communicate with other CORBA ORBs. Code that has been written using RMI–IIOP can run in a pure Java environment. In the pure Java environment, RMI will be used as the protocol. When the landscape includes both Java and CORBA components, RMI–IIOP is the Java ORB that can communicate with the ORB that supports remote CORBA components using IIOP. Once a Java component has been created to the RMI–IIOP interface, it can be accessed by CORBA components. RMI–IIOP has a compiler that can generate a IDL stub. Any CORBA client component can access the Java component because of the IDL stub provided by the RMI–IIOP. The IDL stub is the CORBA interface description language that describes an interface. The client CORBA component maps the interface call from its native language (whether it is C++, Java, etc.) to the IDL format. This allows components in different languages to communicate with one another. When the RMI–IIOP receives a call from a client CORBA component, it takes the request and maps the data from the client request from IDL format to Java format. It utilizes the Java IDL service to accomplish this.

In similar fashion, Java IDL is used when a Java program wants to invoke a remote COBRA interface. Java IDL is an ORB and a compiler that can map IDL to Java. Java IDL translates the request from the Java component client. Then Java IDL ORB sends the request to the CORBA ORB of the remote interface. When the request has been executed by the remote CORBA interface, the CORBA ORB sends the response back to the Java IDL ORB, which translates the result back to the client Java component. In summary, RMI–IIOP and Java IDL effectively integrate CORBA components and Java components. J2EE 1.4 requires that all EJB implement interfaces use the RMI–IIOP protocol.

Java Transaction API (JTA)

JTA is a set of J2EE container APIs that are available to the component developer to demarcate transaction boundaries. The developer can programmatically control the transaction boundary using the JTA API. Transactions could be simple transactions, such as updates to one database through a JDBC driver, or distribute transactions. The definition of distributed transaction is when more than one network resources are involved in the transaction. JTA provides a user transaction management API that is used by the developer to define the transaction boundary. Some of the methods available with the user transaction API are to define the beginning of a transaction boundary, to commit a transaction, or to rollback a transaction. The JTA transaction manager then manages the transaction. The transaction manager, through a standard XA resource interface, accesses all the resources involved in the transaction. X/OPEN XA, is an accepted industry standard interface specification for a resource manager to communicate with a transaction manager. In a transactional context, a resource manager provides access to shared resources. Examples of resource managers are database and JMS. Once the transaction has been started, the transaction manager coordinates the various resource managers. If any of the requests fail in the transaction boundary, the transaction manager can issue a rollback, which is executed by the various resource managers. Similarly, when the entire transaction is successfully executed, the transaction manager instructs the various resource managers to commit the transaction.

Java Naming and Directory Interface (JNDI)

JNDI is a set of APIs provided by J2EE for a Java program to access external naming and directory services. Since it is designed to be compatible with most naming and directory services, JNDI provides APIs that access common functions of these external naming and directory services. What are naming and directory services? A naming and directory service is like a phone book. It associates names with attributes. For instance, a file system has a naming service that allows a user to know in which directory the file is stored. Another example is the employee directory. One can access the employee directory to retrieve a record that contains the employee's email address, phone number, address, password, etc. In the technical context, the employee directory could be implemented in a product that supports Lightweight Directory Access Protocol (LDAP), such as iPlanet LDAP or Microsoft Active Directory. In high-level terms, we can think of the naming service as a service that can take a name as input and give the location of the service or the data provided by that name. Directory service is like a database. It stores attributes with a name, just like a database stores a unique record given a set of key fields. With naming and directory service, a program can access the information such as corporate organizational hierarchy, user records, and the location of objects and components. This sort of information is useful in workflow (where organizational structure might come in play), single sign on and not so glamorous functions such as providing a component the ability to locate an interface of a remote component. JNDI is essential for creating distributed applications. In a distributed network environment, resources are stored in various places in the network. JNDI allows the component to find these resources by accessing available naming and directory services. Without access to these services through JNDI, Java has no mechanism to find the resources it needs to complete its functions.

J2EE Connector Architecture

The most important component of the J2EE platform to application integration is perhaps the J2EE Connector Architecture. J2EE Connector Architecture offers a standard architecture to connect J2EE platform to Enterprise Information Systems (EIS). In this context, EIS is used to define software that enterprises use as their information infrastructure. Enterprise Resource Planning (ERP) software applications are examples of EIS. Other examples of EIS are mainframe transaction processing systems and database systems. Just as JDBC allows J2EE applications to connect to a variety of database systems, the J2EE Connector Architecture defines specifications that software vendors should use to connect their applications to the J2EE platform. While JDBC limits connectivity to only relational databases, J2EE Connector Architecture allows the J2EE platform to connect to any EIS or other information source. This is of tremendous help to both enterprises that have standardized on J2EE as their technology platform and enterprise application software vendors that support their products on J2EE platform. See Figure 6.8.

In the case of software vendors, the introduction of J2EE Connector Architecture eliminates the need to customize their products for every Java application server. Prior to J2EE Connector Architecture, there was no set of standardized interfaces and services that all application servers implement for EIS application vendors. EIS application vendors needed to create a custom resource adapter for every application server it supports. J2EE Connector Architecture introduces system contracts that all J2EE application servers should implement. Using these system contracts, the EIS application vendor can expect standardized services, thus eliminating the need to use interfaces that are specific to each application server. The standardization of systems services allows the EIS application vendor to provide one resource adapter that can be used on all the different J2EE application servers.

J2EE Connector Architecture also eases the task for the application developer by providing Common Client Interface (CCI). The reason JDBC works so well and is so widely used is all relational database systems comply with Structured Query Language (SQL) standards. Because of the

J2EE and Resource Adapter

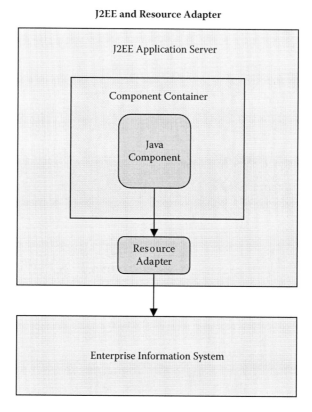

Figure 6.8   Integration to EIS through resource adapter.

standardization of SQL, it becomes possible to have a set of APIs that all relational database systems support. In the EIS world, there is no standard set of APIs available for EIS systems. With the CCI, the J2EE Connector Architecture provides a standard interface for J2EE applications to interact with EIS through resource adapters. Using the CCI, a J2EE application can invoke interfaces from the EIS through the resource adapter. Used in conjunction with middleware technology, J2EE Connector Architecture allows the possibility for a J2EE application to invoke one interface that could be used to access multiple EIS.

The participants of the J2EE Connector Architecture can be categorized into four components: application component, component container, resource adapter, and EIS. The application component is a J2EE component that wants to interact with an EIS. The component container is the runtime environment for the application component. It supplies the application component with various component services, which includes the interaction with the CCI of the resource adapter. The resource adapter is the gateway to the EIS provided by the EIS vendor. It exposes functions of the EIS to the J2EE world. The resource adapter is supported by the component container, which provides transaction, connection, and security management to the resource adapter. Finally, the EIS is the information system that performs the backend processing requested by the Java component.

To integrate all these components, the J2EE Connector Architecture provides two sets of contracts: system-level contract and CCI. The system-level contract is the specification that all resource adapters should support. By following these system-level contracts, the resource adapter is guaranteed to receive the service specified by the contract. The basic system-level contracts are connection management, transaction management, and security management. The connection management contract specifies a standard way a J2EE application component should be able to connect to the resource adapter. It also specifies how connections can be pooled. The connection pooling optimizes the throughput for requests with a limited number of connections. Transaction management extends the JTA service to the EIS and allows the EIS to participate in a multi-step transaction. The third basic system-level contract is the security management. This contract extends J2EE security service to the EIS and it enables single–sign-on capability across J2EE and the EIS.

CCI is the second set of contracts specified in the J2EE Connector Architecture. It standardizes the interaction from the application component to the resource adapter. The CCI is the interface exposed by the resource adapter component, in a way much like a J2EE component would expose its interfaces to other remote J2EE components. CCI is generic in that it is not specific to an EIS. It can use the metadata from the EIS to build specific remote function calls. With the CCI, the EIS's API could be exposed to the J2EE application component. For instance, if the EIS has an API to create a sales order, it can be made available as a J2EE component interface to other J2EE components through the common client interface of the resource adapter. The CCI is probably of more use to enterprise application integration vendors than application component developers are. To use a CCI, the application component developer has to prepare an input record format to send the CCI and the output record format to receive the results from the CCI. Enterprise application integration products are well suited to handle the input and output formats. EAI products also have the transformation capability and the repository to allow quick conversion from one format to another. The application component can interact with the EAI product without regard to which EIS it wants to interact with. The EAI product would perform the transformation and preparation for the connection to the EIS. Using EAI provides a level of abstraction that shields the application component developer from the details of the interaction with an EIS. An application component developer would provide the same input data for a specific business transaction such as a sales order create to the EAI tool, regardless of what EIS it is interacting with. It can expect the EAI tool to return the data in a standard fashion regardless of which EIS it is coming from.

J2EE Support for Web Services

As Web service has gained popularity as an integration technology, J2EE has included several services that support Web services. Like everything else, these services are denoted by acronyms, and they provide support for both clients calling Web services or endpoints that process the Web services. Some of these services are Java API for XML Processing (JAXP), Java API for XML–Based RPC (JAX–RPC), and Java API for XML Registries (JAXR).

Java API for XML Processing (JAXP)

Java API for XML Processing (JAXP) is a development tool that is part of the Java Web Service Developer Pack. It allows the application developer to process XML documents using a variety of different processing models. According to J2EE 1.4 specifications, JAXP includes one DOM parser, one Simple API for XML (SAX) parser, and one Extensible Style Sheet Language Transformation (XSLT) transformation engine. Document Object Model (DOM) and SAX are different models for processing XML. In the DOM, the XML document is converted to a Java object and stored in memory of the JVM by the DOM parser. When the DOM parser converts the XML into a document object, it stores the XML in a tree structure. The developer does not manipulate the XML file directly. Any interaction with the XML is through a set of DOM API that allows the developer to traverse the hierarchical structure of the XML document object and make any changes.

The other processing model is the SAX model. The SAX parser does not read the entire XML document as the DOM parser does. It reads the XML document and creates a sequence of events as it encounters XML tags in the document. It is up to the developer to capture the events the SAX parser is sending. In contrast to DOM, the SAX parser is much faster because it does read the entire XML document, and it does not store the document in memory as a tree structure. However, it requires much more development work, because the developer has to handle listening for the events the SAX parser triggers as it reads the document and capturing the data read by the SAX parser. The benefit of the SAX parser is the developer gets to decide what data to store for the XML document. This speeds performance because not all data from the XML file is stored.

The third JAXP component is the XSLT transformation engine. After the XML document has been read by the parser (whether SAX or DOM), the data exists for the developer to manipulate. XSLT is a language that describes how an XML document is to be transformed into another XML document. During design time, the developer would develop a XSLT that would define how one XML document is to be transformed to produce another XML document (it could also produce a HTML document). The XSLT contains rules for transforming the source document to produce a target document. In the runtime environment, the XSLT is applied to the XML by the XSLT transformation engine after the XML document has been read by the parser. The application of XSLT to the XML document object produces another XML. How do all these technologies fit into JAXP? JAXP provides separate layers that can take in the DOM parser, the SAX parser, and the XSLT transformation engine from a variety of software vendors as plug-in components. This shields the developer from the individual parsers and transformers. When different sets of parsers and transformers are used with JAXP, code developed using the original set of parsers and transformers will still work.

Java API for XML–Based RPC (JAX–RPC)

Now we have a way of reading and transforming a XML document using JAXP, how about invoking a remote interface using XML? That is the raison d'etre for JAX–RPC. This API allows the developer to send and receive method calls using an XML–based protocol. The widely used XML–based protocol is SOAP. SOAP is a standardized message format that defines the RPC request and response. All the information between the requester and the receiver are encoded in the SOAP XML message. When JAX–RPC is used, a component can make a request on a Web service by sending the request as a SOAP message and transporting the message using HTTP. To the application developer, JAX–RPC hides the complexity of invoking that remote interface. The call is made similar to a local call. JAX–RPC packages the SOAP message and communicates with the Web service using HTTP as the transport protocol. The benefit of JAX–RPC and the Web service is their platform and language independence. As long as the Web service can take a SOAP request, it does not matter which platform or component model the Web service is built on.

Java API for XML Registries (JAXR)

With JAX–RPC, we have a way to invoke a Web service. What about finding the Web service to use? JAXR is the answer to that question. JAXR is a standard API that allows the developer to access different registries. Examples of registries are Electronic Business Extensible Markup Language (ebXML) Registry & Repository and (UDDI). JAXR API shields the developer from having to code for the specific registry that is to be accessed. The API provides standard querying service that allows a client component to search the registry to find the appropriate Web service. Once the Web service has been located, the client component can use JAX–RPC to send the request via SOAP over HTTP. When the Web service has returned the result, the client component can read the resulting XML using its JAXP parser.

Summary

In this chapter, we discussed the three main component standards (Microsoft, Java, and CORBA). We also discussed the evolution of RPC technology to the component-based technologies. Java and Microsoft are the most widely used component development technologies. CORBA started as a component-interoperability standard. It has only recently developed into a full-fledged component development standard. In a large organization, it is not unusual to find multiple component technologies used in the organization's enterprise application landscape. Thus, the potential exists for a business process to encompass applications that are built using different component technologies. For business process management to be deployed, the BPMS product has to integrate to products built using different component technologies. In Chapter 5, we discussed messaging as a mechanism for BPMS to accomplish application integration. In this chapter, we discussed component-integration mechanisms offered by the major component standards. While it is unlikely for a BPMS to cover all mechanisms for application integration, the ideal BPMS product should include as many mechanisms as possible.

Chapter 7

Workflow Technology

In the previous chapters, we discussed data- and application-focused technologies that are the building blocks of Business Process Management Systems (BPMSs). These technologies are integration components that can be coordinated to form a business process management solution. The platform to design and deploy the business process management solution is the BPMS. Database-integration components offer BPMS the ability to interact directly with data sources. As unglamorous as data integration might seem, analysis of a process is impossible without data. The flow of data is central to the execution of any business process. Application-integration components provide BPMS with the ability to integrate and control applications that are part of a business process management solution. If data is the source for analysis, applications are the workhorses of a business process. Applications perform calculations needed for the business process to provide its output. These calculations include supply chain optimization, customer pricing, work order scheduling, etc. Applications also record transactions that happen as part of a business process. Transactions are often necessary for bookkeeping purposes. Other times, transactions serve as input for further calculations needed for the business process. Because applications are the workhorses of a business process, the ability to control and integrate applications is critical to business process management (BPM). Some applications interact with other systems using messaging. Other applications interact using interfaces exposed through a standard component model (Common Object Request Broker Architecture (CORBA), Microsoft XML Web Services platform (.NET), Java 2 Enterprise Edition (J2EE), etc.). The various application integration components we discussed in Chapter 5 and Chapter 6 provide BPMS with capabilities to control these applications when executing business process management solutions. Workflow is the other key technology component essential to BPMS. From workflow management system (WfMS), BPMS obtained a process design tool that allows business process management solutions to be modeled. In addition to design functions, workflow also gives BPMS the ability to integrate people into business process management solutions. In this chapter, we will discuss the WfMS in detail.

Like many terms in the technology industry, the term workflow has many different meanings. Used in the imaging context, workflow is the routing of business documents. When an image is imported into the imaging system, the image can be sent to the appropriate reviewer, based on predefined attributes, for review and approval. In the messaging context, workflow represents a series of actions that arise as a result of events. When an event happens, predefined rules trigger activities performed as a result of the event. The event-based use of workflow also extends to the database management system. Some database management systems use event–condition–action rules that trigger database actions when events that satisfied predefined conditions occur. Another use of workflow is related to electronic forms. This is similar to the imaging scenario. When a form such as a loan application is populated, the form is routed to the proper person for review and approval based on predefined attributes. The difference between imaging and electronic forms is images are not editable while forms can be edited. The line is blurring as imaging systems can now be used to populate electronic forms automatically based on the content of an image.

Some of the uses of workflow are related, but others developed independently. To help standardize and coordinate the various uses of workflow, an industry group, Workflow Management Coalition (WfMC), was created in 1993. The charter of WfMC was to develop interoperability standards and common terminology for use by the various workflow vendors. Even though workflow is used for different contexts, the various uses of workflow all share common themes. According to the WfMC, workflow is defined as:

> "The automation of a business process, in whole or part, during which documents, information or tasks are passed from one participant to another for action, according to a set of procedural rules."

This definition is so generic it can apply to the various workflow scenarios. Regardless of whether the participants are humans or systems, workflow is the passing of work from one participant to another. The passing of work is determined by predefined rules or conditions, and the receiving participant is expected to perform action once work has been received. The general phrase workflow management system was defined to cover the various products that have been developed to support workflow. The WfMC describes WfMS as follows:

> "A system that defines, creates, and manages the execution of workflows through the use of software, running on one or more workflow engines, which is able to interpret the process definition, interact with other workflow participants and, where required, invoke the use of IT tools and applications."[1]

The definitions of workflow and WfMS sound similar to the definitions of business process management (BPM) and BPMS defined in the previous chapters. In fact, the functions of WfMSs are identical to some components of BPMS. Just like BPMS, WfMS serves to integrate people and applications so that they can participate in a process. WfMS and BPMS both manage processes. We will compare WfMS and BPMS at the end of this chapter, after we have a chance to look at WfMS in some detail.

Different Types of Workflows

There are many proposals to classify workflow. The most widely accepted classification, one that has been endorsed by WfMC, divides workflow into four categories: production, administrative, ad hoc, and collaborative.[2]

Production Workflow

A production workflow is one that performs large number of repetitive tasks that have high business value.[3] The goal of a production workflow is to automate the process as much as possible. This type of workflow began as a feature of the document imaging system. The financial services sector uses document imaging for processing large amounts of transactions, such as loan processing and insurance claims. These transactions are structured and repetitive. Any automation of these processes usually yields significant financial savings. To speed up the routing and processing of these paper-based forms, workflow was added to the document imaging system to help reduce process cycle time. The concept of routing documents and images has expanded beyond the financial services sector. Now production workflow characterizes highly automated workflow processes.

Many WfMSs in the market were developed to handle production workflow scenarios. Production WfMSs can be further categorized into autonomous and embedded WfMSs. An autonomous WfMS is a stand alone system that does not need to function in conjunction with a business application. It can be used to manage workflow processes that involve an application and human participants. During runtime, an autonomous WfMS can invoke external business applications and pass data between different workflow participants. The integration of autonomous WfMS to other business applications usually requires application development. Integration is getting easier with interface standardization and connector technologies that are available for enterprise information systems.[4]

In contrast to an autonomous WfMS, an embedded WfMS requires the host system to function. In other words, an embedded WfMS is a workflow system that is specific to a business application and it is used to perform workflow within the scope of the host business applications. An example is the business workflow of SAP Enterprise Resource Planning (ERP) offering. Business workflow exists as a module of SAP ERP and it uses the SAP ERP's infrastructure to perform its functions. Use of embedded workflow does not require an application integration effort because it is already part of a business application. It also offers the same user interface and it operates in the same platform as the business application. These characteristics make embedded workflow easier to implement and maintain than an autonomous WfMS. On the flip side, an embedded WfMS cannot be used to manage complex processes that span multiple applications. Its use is limited to the events and triggers provided by the host business application.

Administrative Workflow

Administrative workflow arose from office automation. It is used to perform workflow processes with defined procedures although each instance of the workflow can have different work performed on it. In contrast to production workflow, administrative workflow is not as structured. The process for an expense report approval can be considered as an example of administrative workflow. The employee would fill out the expense report. The expense report is reviewed by an accounts payable clerk for whether any items fall outside of guidelines. Once the expense report has been reviewed, it is approved and can be paid. In this example, the flow of work is well defined but the content of the work is different (e.g., the content varies from one expense report to another expense report). Office automation products (such as Lotus Notes) first included administrative workflow functions to manage these types of processes through emails and messages. Using an administrative workflow product, the employee would attach the expense report to a workflow template. The workflow template contains the name of the person to receive the expense report and instructions on what the receiver has to do to the expense report. When the workflow is sent, the workflow system routes the expense report to the appropriate person as an email. Simple rules could be predefined in the routing (such as sender–receiver relationships), but it is not designed to handle complex logic. The same expense report approval process can also be implemented using a production workflow system. In the production workflow scenario, the employee would complete an electronic form. When the expense report has been completed, the system automatically routes it to the accounts payable clerk for review and approval. The differences in an administrative and a production workflow system are administrative workflow is simple to implement, unsophisticated, and uses email technology. The production workflow is sophisticated, can handle complex logic, and it requires a high degree of process design.

Ad Hoc Workflow

The third type of workflow is ad hoc workflow. As the name suggests, an ad hoc workflow is one implemented by a user to perform a string of actions that arise for a business scenario. This type of workflow is very individualized; every user can design specific workflow for a business process. There is no standardized routing and structure. The workflow model is not predefined for the business process that it is serving. Every workflow instance is different. Ad hoc workflow is for processes that are individualized and not repetitive. In an implementation of ad hoc workflow, the sender decides the recipient who will receive the activities of the ad hoc workflow. The recipient can forward the workflow instance to other recipients. The workflow ends when there is no recipient to forward to. What differentiates ad hoc workflow from email? The difference is email is only a message, ad hoc workflow can have actions and rules that can be included in the workflow. During design time, a user can specify actions the workflow should have based on rules. There are several formats for workflow business rules. One of them is the event–condition–action–alternative action (ECAA). In ECAA, the event is the trigger that starts the business rule. After the rule has been triggered, the condition is evaluated. If the condition holds true, the action is taken. The alternative action is performed if the condition is false. An example of an ad hoc workflow with rule is checking customer credit. The event could be the receipt of a sales order by the account executive. The condition is customer has good credit. If the condition is true, the action is pass the order to order fulfillment for scheduling. If the condition is false, the alternative condition is to send notification to the customer regarding a credit problem. This credit checking rule would be one ad hoc workflow process. The recipient of the workflow could define his own subsequent ad hoc workflow.

Collaborative Workflow

The fourth type of workflow is collaborative workflow. This type of work-flow involves a team of people working together. An example would be a product development project. Everyone has a defined role, but the work-flow process model is not rigid. There are frequent changes to the workflow process. An Information Technology (IT) project plan could be considered an example of collaborative workflow process. Every project plan is tailored specifically to the project at hand. Revisions are usually made to the project plan. The participants in a collaborative workflow need to be able to share documents and to pass documents for review and comment. Another example of collaborative workflow is engineering change management. In this type of scenario, people from several func-tional departments are involved in reviewing and commenting on changes to a design. A collaborative workflow would allow the participants to share design documents, comment on changes, and approve the changes. The products that have been developed to cater to this workflow are generically called groupware. Unlike the production workflow system, collaborative workflow systems are not transaction oriented. They usually do not create business transactions in backend systems.

The above categorization of workflows is not meant to be exclusive. There are workflow processes that could fall under multiple categories. Production workflow is the most rigorous of all the workflow types. It requires detailed routing and structure to be included in the workflow. Administrative workflow is less structured and is usually based on a form, such as an expense report. Administrative workflow products represent the lower end of the workflow product market. They are cheaper to purchase and are more flexible than a production workflow system. On the other hand, they have a lower degree of automation and they do not have the integration and modeling functionalities of production workflow systems. In terms of product categorization, there is a blurring of the lines among the various workflow types. Many production workflow vendors also include capabilities to handle the other three types of workflow.

Workflow Reference Model

In our discussion of the various workflow types, we said these workflow types arose from different origins. For example, production workflow arose from document imaging systems and administrative workflow arose from office automation products (such as Lotus Notes). Because of the varied origins of the workflow products, there was no standardization for these products to interoperate. Workflow vendors are not using a standardized terminology. In 1993, the WfMC recognized there was a need for standardization for the various workflow products that were on the market. They created the workflow reference model to address the standardization. The workflow reference model provides three guidelines. The first guideline is a common terminology for the workflow product category. Without a standardized terminology, it is very difficult for customers to understand the workflow product segment. Not only is it confusing for the customers, it is also detrimental to the establishment for a workflow ecosystem of developers and consultants. The second guideline of the workflow reference model is the functional components necessary in a WfMS. This serves as a guide for workflow product vendors to design their workflow products. By following this reference system module, the chances of product interoperability increase. The third guideline is the set of interfaces that connect the various functional components. The initial interface definitions are described in functional terms. Thus, they do not provide the technical specifications to allow for interoperability. The functional interface definitions provide the foundation for workflow system interoperability. Technical interface binding definitions were developed later that would allow different workflow systems to interoperate once they have implemented these interface bindings.[5]

The workflow reference model divides the workflow system into five components: process definition tool, workflow engine, workflow client application, invoked application, and administration and monitoring tool. These five components interact with one another through the set of five interfaces. Figure 7.1 depicts the workflow components and the five interfaces.

Workflow Process Definition Component

The process definition tool is the design tool that allows the workflow designer to design and model the workflow process. It is normally part of the WfMS. However, the process definition could be defined in a separate business modeling product. If a separate product is used for process definition and modeling, interface 1 of the workflow reference model is the conduit for transferring the business process definition to the workflow engine. A typical process definition tool provides a graphical interface for the process designer to graphically design the business process. The process designer would specify the steps, participants, and the transitions between the different steps of the workflow process in the process definition tool. The result of the design activity is a workflow process model. The WfMC defines the workflow process model as:

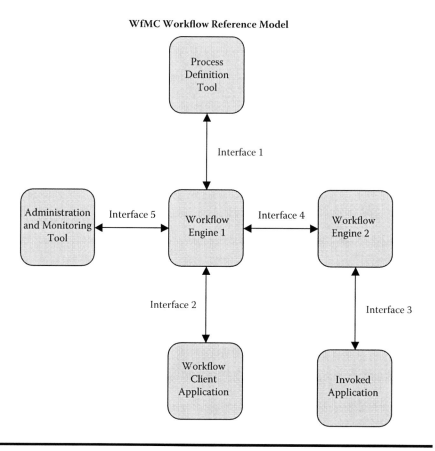

WfMC Workflow Reference Model

Figure 7.1 Components and interfaces of the Workflow Reference Model.

"The representation of business process in a form which supports automated manipulation, such as modeling, or enactment by a workflow management system. The process definition consists of a network of activities and their relationships, criteria to indicate the start and termination of the process, and information about the individual activities, such as participants, associated IT applications and data, etc."[6]

Once the workflow process model has been designed, the process definition tool creates an output of the model using a process definition language. The generic format included in the workflow reference model is the Workflow Process Definition Language (WPDL). The goal of the WPDL standard is for interoperability of process models created using different process definition tool. As long as a workflow engine supports WPDL, that workflow engine can enact any workflow process model created using WPDL. In 2002, an Extensible Markup Language (XML) form of the WPDL was published by WfMC. The new process definition format is called XML Process Definition Language (XPDL). This format is the same as WPDL except the medium is a XML document. With the recent interest in business process management, there are several standardization groups offering their own process definition languages. These groups include Business Process Management Initiative (BPMI), Object Management Group (OMG), IBM, Microsoft, and others. It is unclear what standard will ultimately be widely adopted. The danger with all the competing standards is the confusion created in the marketplace. IT practitioners not intimately involved with workflow standards will have a hard time deciding what all the standards are about. This may affect acceptance of BPMS in the marketplace. In a later section, we will discuss the different process modeling standards available. In this section, we will limit our discussion to XPDL and WPDL.

As a process definition language, XPDL contains process definition semantics that are understood by XPDL–compliant workflow engines. A workflow process is made up of sub-process (a separate workflow process definition), activities, participants, flow control, and transition. An XPDL workflow process could include another XPDL workflow process. The workflow process that is included in the calling workflow process is called a sub-process. This ability to include a sub-process is a powerful concept. It allows complex processes to be decomposed into a hierarchy of increasingly detailed processes. This not only aids in process reuse, it also reflects reality. For instance, the order-to-cash business process can be decomposed into order entry, order fulfillment, delivery, and billing sub-processes. Each of these sub-processes can be decomposed even further into more sub-processes.

An activity is work that has to be performed by a specific resource. There are two types of activities, manual and automated. A human participant performs manual activity. A system participant performs automated activity. An automated activity usually invokes another application component and receives a response. Another use of automated activity is for routing. The routing activity has no resource assignment; it is used to perform flow control. A flow control could be the implementation of an if–then–else statement in choosing the right activities to execute. A routing activity is the mechanism to implement flow control. We previously discussed sub-process. In XPDL, the mechanism to invoke a sub-process is through an activity. The activity would include the execution of the sub-process definition.

The participants in a workflow process could be an explicitly named human user, a role defined in an organizational structure, a position that is part of the organizational unit, or an information system. The direct assignment of a participant is the most straightforward. The participant of an activity is explicitly assigned using direct assignment. There is no additional logic needed to determine the appropriate participant for an activity during runtime. Another participant assignment mechanism is by role or position. In this scenario, the workflow engine references the organizational model with the role or the position specified in the workflow process model. The organizational model would contain the specific human participant assigned to the specified role or position. Using this mechanism, the appropriate human participant is not determined until runtime. The benefit of this approach is the extra level of abstraction between the role or position and the human participant. This helps mitigate organizational changes (e.g., employee promotions) that would affect the workflow model if a direct assignment mechanism is used. To handle a complex participant assignment scenario, dynamic and programmatic assignment logic can be used. Dynamic participant assignment uses the previous activities of the workflow to determine the correct participant. Another example is an activity to be processed by the supervisor of the employee who executed a previous workflow activity. The system determines during runtime the supervisor using the organizational structure. It routes the activity to the supervisor after the employee executes the previous activity. As the name indicates, programmatic assignment uses programming to determine the participant assignment. Using programmatic assignment, custom logic can be used to determine the participant assignment. The participants are defined in an organizational model that might not be part of the WfMS. For example, an enterprise organizational structure might be stored in a Lightweight Directory Access Protocol (LDAP) product. In this case, the workflow process model would contain references to the organizational model in the external product.

Flow control of the workflow tasks is the other element of the workflow process model. The sequence determines the routing information. There are four generic flow control mechanisms: parallel, sequential, iteration, and nesting. Parallel routing is branching in the workflow process such that multiple activities are performed concurrently. The decision for the branching could be conditional or concurrent. In conditional parallel routing, the process model specifies multiple branches at the point of parallel routing. Only the branches that satisfy predetermined criteria are undertaken. In concurrent parallel routing, all branches in the parallel routing are executed. In both conditional and concurrent routing, the branches could converge again to one single thread in a subsequent workflow step. Sequential routing is when one activity follows another activity and there is no branch in the workflow process. In sequential routing there is only one thread that is being executed by the WfMS. In contrast, parallel routing could have more than one thread that has been executed by the WfMS for a workflow process instance.

The other aspect of flow control is the iteration. This determines how many times an activity or a group of activities are to be executed. As long as a condition is met, a block of activities is repeated during runtime. The condition could be specified as a loop with an explicit number of iterations or by using a while-loop construct. In the simple loop scenario, the number of iterations is explicitly stated. The workflow engine will repeat the activity block until the number of iterations specified has been reached. Using the while-loop construct, the workflow engine will repeat the activity block until the condition specified returns false.

Transition is the last element of the workflow process model. It defines the criteria for moving to the next activity and it is usually represented as a line from one activity to the next in the graphical workflow process model. Unconditional transition is a transition that always occurs. There is no condition involved. Conditional transition is a transition that occurs only if the condition specified evaluates to true. If the condition evaluates to false, an exception branch could be specified for execution. Transition can be used to capture exceptions of a workflow process.

The workflow process model elements specified above are based mainly on XPDL. These elements represent the minimum semantic a workflow product should support. Despite the industry participation for WfMC, WPDL has not been implemented in many workflow products. Workflow vendors have traditionally chosen to implement their own process definition semantics. It is still useful to discuss WPDL and XPDL because it represents a generic workflow definition language and it contains features implemented in most workflow products. It is like the lowest common denominator of the workflow products.

Workflow Engine

The workflow engine is the runtime environment of the WfMS. The workflow engine takes the workflow process model from the process definition tool and enacts the workflow. This means it creates process instances of the workflow process based on a trigger it has received. The trigger for creation of a workflow process instance is usually an event. An event is a predefined circumstance the workflow engine is listening for. This could be the arrival of an email or the receipt of a leave request form. In an embedded WfMS, the trigger could be some status change of an application transaction. For example, the event purchase_order.create could trigger the purchase order approval workflow to be enacted. The purchase_order.create event is raised anytime a purchase order is created.

It is an event that is part of the application processing. Expanding on the purchase_order.create example, we can see the possibilities if workflow processes are directly linked to the available events the WfMS has been programmed to listen for.

When a workflow process instance has been created, the workflow engine manages workflow relevant data throughout the lifecycle of the workflow process instance. The workflow relevant data is used by the workflow process instance in its processing. The data could be used to determine state transition, participant assignment, and the various conditions that might be involved in the workflow process. The workflow relevant data comes from the process definition, applications that participate in the workflow process, or the workflow engine. WPDL and XPDL makes a distinction between workflow relevant data and application data. Workflow relevant data is the set of data that is available for the workflow process instance. Application data is data in the applications that participates in the workflow process but it is not available to the workflow process instance. Application data can be included as workflow relevant data. The mechanism for doing that is through an interface that links the application to the workflow engine. This is defined as interface 3 of the Workflow Reference Model. Another aspect of a workflow engine is it can communicate with another workflow engine. The workflow engines do not have to be the same product. Interface 4 defines the standard for passing data between different workflow engines..

Workflow Client Application

Workflow client application is another component of the Workflow Reference Model. Workflow client application is an application that requests services from the workflow engine. The services could include retrieval of a worklist generated by the workflow engine for participants to execute. An example of this is the integration of a workplace portal to a workflow engine. In this scenario, the workplace portal functions as the workflow client application. The workflow engine generates the work items assigned to specific users. The workplace portal retrieves the work items from the workflow engine and displays them to each user for action. This is beneficial when an organization wants one single portal for users to be performing work. The workplace portal could be the user interface for all the work items and emails from the various email and WfMSs in the organization. Because of its role in handling work items, the workflow client application would need to instantiate a workflow process instance, execute a work item, and update the worklist in the workflow engine as to the status of a particular work item. To provide interaction between a workflow client application and a workflow engine, the Workflow Reference

Model has specified interface 2 for the interactions between workflow engine and the workflow client application.

Invoked Application

Whereas the workflow client application requests services from the workflow engine, the workflow engine to perform work calls the invoked application. In a workflow process, the invoked application is a system participant. It usually performs a transaction as a result of the workflow process. An example is the purchasing requisition process. An online request form completed by a human participant might trigger the process. Once the workflow engine has received the purchase request form, the next activity in the workflow process is to create a purchase requisition in the backend ERP system. The workflow engine would then invoke the ERP system through interface 3 of the Workflow Reference Model. The workflow engine creates the purchase requisition transaction in the ERP system. We can consider the workflow client application as the front-end application that interacts with the users. The invoked application is the backend application that creates business transactions.

Administration and Monitoring Tool

The last component of the Workflow Reference Model is the administration and monitoring tool. This tool allows system administrators to manage the WfMS. A typical administration and monitoring tool allows an administrator to manage users, roles, and resources. If the resources are not part of the WfMS (e.g., LDAP to store organizational model), the administration and monitoring tool allows interaction to the LDAP tool. Other functions provided by the administration and monitoring tool are audit reporting, querying of process status, and updating active process instances. Workflow engines store all the events and they record updates to process instances in workflow logs. The administration and monitoring tool should be able to retrieve workflow logs for process instances that have completed and instances that are still in progress. These statistics provide data for process analysis, which can lead to process improvements. For process instances that are in error state, the administration and monitoring tool should be able to restart or terminate those instances.

Workflow Reference Model Interface 1

The Workflow Reference Model does not make assumptions about whether the various components of the WfMS are from the same vendor. In a heterogeneous environment, where the various components do not belong to one integrated product, Workflow Reference Model provides definitions for five interfaces to integrate the various components of the WfMS. Interface 1 links the workflow process definition tool to the workflow engine. The original data format for this interface was based on the WPDL. The process definition tool would export a WPDL file and the workflow engine would be able to import the WPDL file. The interface definition was later updated to use XPDL. This new format is extensible because of its use of XML. The extensibility allows different vendors to add additional information to the process definition. The additional information is useful for a workflow engine that can understand them. If the workflow engine does not support the additional information provided in the XPDL, the workflow engine can still use the process definition as long as the process definition tool supports the minimum set of requirements for the XPDL.

Workflow Reference Model Interfaces 2 and 3

Interface 2 of the Workflow Reference Model links the workflow client application to the workflow engine. It is a set of application programming interfaces (API) that the client application can invoke on the workflow engine. The client application is usually a front-end application with which a user would interact. Through interface 2, the client application can control workflow process instances, activities, and work items. The interface definitions include versions for the C programming language, Object Linking & Embedding (OLE), Microsoft Common Object Model (COM), and CORBA interface definition language (IDL).

Interface 3 connects the workflow engine to the business applications invoked during the processing of the workflow model. The workflow engine can use a set of APIs on third party applications. Interface 3 has been consolidated with interface 2 to form Workflow Application Programming Interface (WAPI). The functions provided by interface 3 include connection, disconnection, application invocation, status request, and termination of a running application. As with interface 2, the definitions of interface 3 include versions for C, OLE, and CORBA IDL.

Workflow Reference Model Interface 4

Interface 4 provides integration between heterogeneous workflow engines. This interface provides a set of APIs one WfMS can invoke on another. The functions provided by the APIs include instantiation of a workflow process, querying the status of a running workflow process instance, starting a workflow activity, and changing the status of a workflow instance. The first version of the interface 4 definition uses the Multi-purpose Internet Mail Extension (MIME) format for encoding the message that carries the request. It is an encoding protocol that allows a binary file to be enclosed in an email message. This means one WfMS would send an email message that encloses a request to another WfMS according to interface 4. The initial specification of interface 4 was not implemented in many commercial products. In the mid and late 1990s, many organizations were just beginning to experiment with workflow. There was little pressure on the vendor community for workflow interoperability. Using email as a transport medium for the implementation of interface 4 was specified initially by WfMC and was seen as less than ideal.[7]

With the advent of XML and open standards because of Web services, there has been strong interest in interoperability in the entire technology industry. This leads to the development of Workflow Extensible Markup Language (Wf-XML) by the WfMC in 2000. Wf-XML is a XML–based protocol that allows one WfMS to invoke functions on another WfMS through HyperText Transfer Protocol (HTTP). Essentially, it is the XML–based binding for implementing interface 4. The Wf-XML message contains three parts: transport, header, and body. The message transport is an optional section where the sender can specify characteristics such as security, processing model (batch, asynchronous, synchronous, etc.), and message identification. This section does not need to exist for the XML to be a valid Wf-XML message. The message header section contains the message type (request or response), whether response is required, language (e.g., English), and key to resources (e.g., the internet address of the process definition). The last section is the message body. It defines the parameters for a response to or a request of an operation.

Wf-XML expands on the functions provided by interface 4 to include three groups of operations one WfMS can request from another WfMS. The three groups are process definition, process instance, and observer. The process definition group contains the operation to create a process instance. This operation allows a WfMS to instantiate a process instance of a previously defined workflow process model in another WfMS. The process instance group contains operations to get process instance data and to change the state of a process instance. The observer group is for a WfMS or a system resource to be notified of a status change of a process instance. Currently there is only one operation, the change to the state of a process instance, defined in this group. An observer who has registered with a WfMS can receive notification when there is a change to the state of a process instance.

In 2004, the WfMC released version 2.0 of Wf-XML. With the wide acceptance of Simple Object Access Protocol (SOAP) as the XML protocol for Web services, Wf-XML 2.0 updated its message format to use SOAP.

The particular SOAP extension protocol that Wf-XML 2.0 is based on is the Asynchronous Service Access Protocol (ASAP). This sounds a little confusing, which, hopefully, should become clear after we discuss ASAP and Wf-XML 2.0.

Asynchronous Service Access Protocol (ASAP)

ASAP was conceived by another standards organization, the Organization for the Advancement of Structured Information Standards (OASIS), to serve as the protocol for long-running asynchronous Web service invocation. It is an extension based on the SOAP protocol. As stated in its name, ASAP protocol is specifically for asynchronous Web service, which treats the typical request and response operations in two requests, one request to start an operation and a separate request to communicate the result of the operation. Before the result of the first operation has been communicated, there could have been several requests to update the operation in progress. The ASAP protocol is suited for long-running processes that are subject to changes. Asynchronous Web service should not be confused with asynchronous messaging. Asynchronous Web service can utilize both synchronous and asynchronous messaging. The reason it contains asynchronous in its name is the asynchronous Web service operations are not synchronized. The requestor could send three requests. The receiver could respond to the second request, followed by the third request and finally the first request.

The ASAP specification describes ASAP as a protocol that can control and monitor the Web service that has been invoked.[8] This is accomplished by separating the interface that creates a process instance from the interface that updates and monitors the progress of a process instance. In ASAP, the requestor interacts with two entities: process factory resource (the creator of a process instance) and the process instance resource. The requestor in the ASAP model is also known as the observer resource. The process factory resource is typically the process server or the workflow engine. It is static. The process factory creates a process instance if that has been requested. A process instance is one lifecycle of a process definition. Therefore, a process instance is transient. The observer initiates the request to the process factory resource to create the process instance resource. When the process factory creates the process instance, the observer is subscribed to the process instance to receive state change notifications (e.g., notification when the process is complete). The observer could also communicate a send request to the process instance to check the status or to update the state of the process instance.

An example will better illustrate this differentiation. This example is illustrated in Figure 7.2. In a typical purchasing process, the customer

Purchasing asynchronous web service

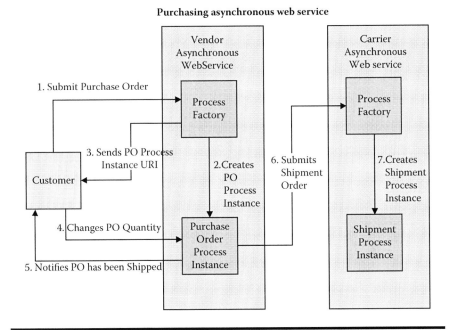

Figure 7.2   Purchasing process using ASAP asynchronous Web service.

sends the vendor a purchase order, and the customer could update and monitor the progression of the fulfillment of the purchase order. Modeling this scenario with ASAP, the customer sends an inquiry to the process factory (usually a process or workflow engine) requesting the definition of the purchasing process model. The customer, in this case, serves the role of the observer resource. The process definition tells the customer how to send a purchase order electronically that would invoke the vendor's process for receiving and fulfilling a purchase order. The customer then sends an ASAP message that instructs the vendor's workflow engine to create an instance of the purchase order process. Because the purchase order takes time to be filled, the process factory at the vendor returns a universal resource identifier (URI), which is the internet address for accessing the process instance, to the customer. The same time the purchasing process instance is created, the customer is registered as an observer to receive notification when the process instance is completed. After the customer receives the URI to the process instance, he or she can check on the status of the process instance. This is what the ASAP specification terms as monitoring. In our purchase order example, the customer could check whether the purchase order has been shipped. The customer could also request a change to the purchase order. In an example where the customer decides to order 100 units instead of 10, the customer would send an ASAP message to the URI of the process instance to make that update. Once the purchasing process instance is completed, the customer receives a notification that the purchase order has been shipped. If the transportation vendor also implements ASAP, this could result in a shipping process instance being generated by the factory resource at the transportation vendor. The customer could then receive notification to the status of the shipping process. We can see that, using ASAP, we could have process collaboration between different organizations that participate in a business process. The ASAP model does not deal with the implementation of the process definition at each of the participants. That is the job of the process server or workflow engine. Its task is to enable business processes that span more than one workflow engine or process server.

Workflow Extensible Markup Language (Wf-XML 2.0)

Just as ASAP is an extension of SOAP, Wf-XML 2.0 could be considered an extension of ASAP. Wf-XML includes features specific to the workflow engine and the process server. ASAP is a basic protocol that could be used for any asynchronous Web service. It is a generic standard that is not specific to workflow processes. Using Wf-XML 2.0, the requestor could request the workflow process definition in XPDL format. The requestor could also send an updated version of the workflow process to the server. ASAP is not specific on activities within a process. An ASAP completion notification is issued only when the entire process (or Web service) has been completed. Wf-XML introduces the concept of activity. A requestor could get the status of a particular activity and update the state of a particular activity within the process instance. In short, Wf-XML 2.0 adds to the ASAP model so the details of the process could be exposed and changed by a requestor.

The Wf-XML 2.0 model adds two resources to the ASAP model. In addition to the factory resource, process instance resource, and observer resource, Wf-XML 2.0 includes service registry resource and activity instance resource. The service registry is like the repository for metadata. The observer could request a process definition from the service registry resource. Also, the observer could add process definitions to the service registry resource. The interaction between the process definition tool and the workflow engine could be described as an observer interaction with the service registry. This interaction is similar to interface 1 of the Workflow Reference Model. The factory resource performs the same role as the factory resource in ASAP. It is used to create a process instance resource. The process instance resource in Wf-XML 2.0 has the added task of keeping track of the activities that are part of the process instance. An observer can request a list of all the activities that are currently active in the process instance. An activity is defined as a point when the process is waiting for an external resource to complete a task. According to this definition, each activity equates to an active activity in the workflow process model. The active activity could involve human participant or a system participant. Essentially Wf-XML 2.0 exposes the workflow process instance in a workflow engine to the outside world. A workflow engine that is compatible with Wf-XML 2.0 should expose its process instance and activities in the process through URI addresses that could be provided to an outside observer resource. An observer could register itself with the process instance. Once it is a registered observer, it can get the status of active activities and the process as a whole. It could also change the state of active activities and the process instance.

Using the purchasing example in our discussion of ASAP, Figure 7.3 describes the process using Wf-XML 2.0. The process definition tool at the vendor creates a new purchasing process definition. The process definition is exposed to the trading partner as a Web described through WSDL. A customer sends a Wf-XML 2.0 message to the vendor's factory resource to place a purchase order. The factory resource creates the purchasing process instance and registers the customer as an observer for the process instance resource. The customer wishes to get an update on the activities current in the process instance. The customer sends a Wf-XML 2.0 message to the process instance URI requesting a list of current activities. The process instance returns the list to the customer with the URIs of the current activities. In this example, the current activity is credit check. The customer sends a message to the credit check activity URI to get more information. The credit check activity returns stating vendor's credit analyst has to approve the transaction because the order value is too high. Sensing there might be a credit problem, the customer wants to reduce the quantity of the purchase from 100 units to 10. This is accomplished by sending the process instance URI a change of quantity. Assuming the rest of the purchasing process occurs without interaction with the customer, and once the purchasing process ends, the customer receives notification from the process instance resource that the purchase order has been filled and shipped. As in the ASAP example, the vendor could send an asynchronous Web service message to the transportation vendor to start a shipping process.

Hopefully the purposes and functions of ASAP and Wf-XML 2.0 are clear after our discussions and examples. The market of protocols and standards is rich in offerings. ASAP and Wf-XML 2.0 are two of many protocols that aim to address what is generically known as Web service choreography standards. The other notable Web service choreography standards are Business Process Execution Language for Web Services (BPEL4WS) and Web Service Choreography Interface (WSCI). Microsoft

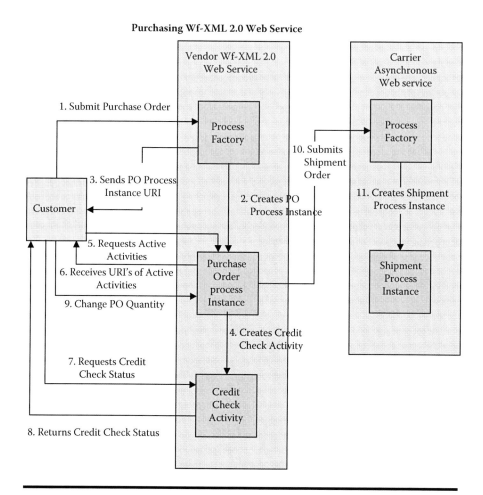

Figure 7.3   Purchasing process using Wf-XML 2.0 Web service.

and IBM started BPEL4WS. In 2003, OASIS was given control of the development of this standard. It is worth noting that OASIS has technical committees working on competing BPEL4WS and ASAP standards. The Business Process Management Initiative (BPMI.org) conceived the WSCI standard, which was turned over to the industry group World Wide Web Consortium (W3C) for industry acceptance. There is no lack of standards available right now. Currently there is debate raging within the industry on the technical merits of resource-oriented standards (i.e., ASAP and Wf-XML 2.0) versus RPC–oriented standards (i.e., WSCI and BPEL4WS). The technical details of the debate are beyond the scope of this book. The resource-based standards still use SOAP as the communication protocol. However, the XML that encodes the request or response points to other

URL for resources that participate in the request or response. This architectural style has been termed Representational State Transfer (REST) by Roy Fielding, the original author of the HTTP protocol, in his doctoral dissertation published in 2000.[9] ASAP and Wf-XML 2.0 are called REST–based standards because they return the resources as a URI to the observer. The various resources can be directly addressed using the URI assigned to each of them. WSCI and BPEL4WS could do that, but it is not in their standards.

Workflow Reference Model Interface 5

The last interface defined in the original Workflow Reference Model is interface 5 for workflow administration and monitoring integration to the workflow engine. The one concrete interface definition from WfMC is for audit data. In 1998, WfMC defined the Common Workflow Audit Data (CWAD) 1998 that specifies the data a workflow engine should capture for the various events in the workflow process. The definition is broken into four sections: process audit information, activity instance audit information, work item audit information, and remote operation audit information.[10] The process audit information specifies basic information (i.e., process instance ID, process instance state, user, etc.) that needs to be captured when a process instance is started or changed. The individual workflow engine can define additional attributes that are recorded (with old values before change and new values after change) and are available for transfer using interface 5. Both the activity instance audit information and the work item audit information specifications are defined similar to the process instance audit information. They both capture information when an activity instance or work item is changed and they allow the workflow engine to define additional attributes available to interface 5. The remote operation audit information section specifies data that should be captured when one workflow engine communicates with another workflow engine. The operations between workflow engines that need to be captured are start conversation, stop conversation, create process instance, change process instance state, change process instance attribute, get process instance attributes, process instance state changed, and process instance attribute changed. In each of these operations, the source and target workflow engines both need to record information exchanged and data changed.

A few vendors have implemented the original interface 5 CWAD specification. CWAD uses proprietary format that makes it less appealing for product vendors. Currently there is a WfMC technical committee defining the XML version of the CWAD. Not only can audit data provide information on who did what when, it can provide information used to improve process performance. In the realm of process simulation, audit data can provide the input used to perform the simulation. The result of these simulations can be used to tweak a design to achieve better process performance. Another less glamorous, but no less important, use of an audit log is for system recovery purpose. The audit log contains the state of all the work items and process instances. In the case of a system failure, the audit log provides complete data for the WfMS to recover to the state at the time of the failure.

In the years since the introduction of the Workflow Reference Model, many new technologies have been introduced. The interfaces first defined in the reference model have also been updated to reflect these new technologies. Figure 7.4 illustrates the Workflow Reference Model with the updated interface definitions. Though BPMS is now the buzzword and

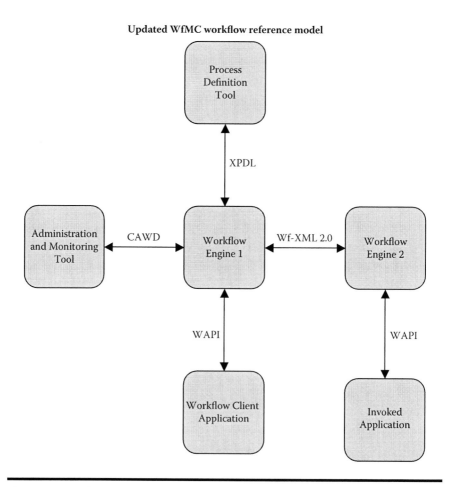

Figure 7.4   WfMC Workflow Reference Model with current interface definitions.

every vendor wants to describe its products, the Workflow Reference Model has laid a good foundation for several aspects of BPMS.

Differences between Workflow Management System (WfMS) and Business Process Management System (BPMS)

Now that we have discussed the typical WfMS using the workflow reference model, the natural question that arises is how is a WfMS different from a BPMS? WfMS, as stated by WfMC, exists to define, create, and manage workflows. The definition of workflow is the automation of business process that involves multiple participants, and results in documents and tasks to be passed from one participant to another. Looking back at Chapter 1, we defined business process as a standardized and coordinated flow of activities, performed by humans or machines, which can cross functional or departmental boundaries to create value to customers. The structured approaches to design, analyze, control, and improved business processes are called business process management. If we take the definition that BPMS is any system that enables the practice of business process management, we see that WfMS could very easily fall into that category. In our discussion of the workflow reference model, we see that the WfMS according to the model contains a process definition tool that helps business designers to design business processes. The audit data from the workflow engine could be used to analyze and improve the business processes. Once it has been enacted, the workflow process instance is a standardized flow of activities that has human and system participants. The administration and monitoring component of the workflow system provides some degree of control over the execution of the workflow process instance. From a high level, WfMS seems to satisfy the definition of a tool that enables business process management.

If that's the case, why do we have another category called BPMS? Instead of marketing their products as WfMS, why are workflow vendors all rushing to market BPMS? Though there is a certain amount of re-branding to the fashionable label for marketing purposes, from technical and functional standpoints, there are differences between BPMS and WfMS. In simple terms, we can consider BPMS as the next evolution of WfMS. BPMS adds robust application integration, application development, process analysis, and richer process simulation and modeling capabilities that traditional workflow systems are lacking.

The workflow reference model specifies interfaces 2 and 3, which are relabeled as workflow APIs, for application integration. However, these interfaces are offered in C and do not follow the prevailing component models such as J2EE, COM/.NET, or CORBA. WAPIs provide very limited functions when compared to the integration capabilities of enterprise application integration tools (EAI). These EAI tools offer integration through messaging, component interfaces, and Web services. Not only are there a variety of integration mechanisms, the EAI tools also offer graphical tools that ease the tasks of mapping from one application format to another. EAI is an integral part of BPMS. From a holistic top-to-bottom standpoint, BPMS offers critical data and application integration capabilities that are lacking in a typical WfMS. In the realm of process design and analysis, BPMS is supplemented with simulation and business intelligence components that enable continuous process improvements. Traditional WfMS does not offer tools that help in process design and analysis, aside from the basic process designer. Process simulation capabilities have only recently been introduced. When they are introduced they are included in BPMS or WFMS–relabeled–BPMS products. This is the same with tools for process analytics. Though WfMS contains audit logs, traditional WfMS does not provide the means to analyze this data for process improvement purposes.

In addition to these enhancements, BPMS is more flexible when reacting to organizational and process changes. The traditional workflow management systems have been criticized for their inflexibility. When they were introduced, workflow management systems were not envisaged as process solution development platforms. WfMS exists as an application to connect steps needed for a business process. In contrast, BPMS is envisioned as a platform for developing and executing process solutions. As a development platform, workflow is one aspect of BPMS. The other aspects are application integration, process analysis and design, and application development. With all these capabilities, BPMS constitutes a robust and independent process layer in the enterprise architecture that abstracts the business processes from the business applications. Taken by itself, workflow would be more susceptible to be influenced by changes in applications it is coordinating. The functions of WfMSs should play critical roles in any BPMS.

As with many developments in the technological world, a new technology, even if it is evolutionary, is marketed with a new name. The reason is mostly marketing and partly to distinguish it from the existing technologies. This applies to BPMS to some extent. BPMS is an evolutionary technology built with the foundations of WfMS and enterprise application integration systems. In the next chapter, we will look at the various types of process integration systems, discuss the ideal BPMS, and we will attempt to elucidate the various standards, competitors to the standards we described here, to support BPMS.

Notes

1. WfMC. 1999. Terminology and Glossary, 3rd Edition. Document Number WFMC-TC-1011. Workflow Management Coalition.
2. Allen, Rob. 2000. Workflow: An Introduction. Chapter 1. *Workflow Handbook 2001*. L. Fischer (Ed). John Wiley & Sons. New York. New York.
3. Leymann, F. and Roller, D. 2001. Understanding Workflow. *The Business Integrator Journal*. Fall. 24–31.
4. zur Muehlen, M. and Allen, R. 2000. Stand-Alone versus. Embedded Workflow — Putting Paradigms in Perspective. In *Excellence in Practice Volume IV: Innovation & Excellence in Workflow and Knowledge Management*. L. Fischer (ed). Lighthouse Point. Florida. 49–58.
5. Hollingsworth, D. 2004. The Workflow Reference Model 10 Years On. In *Workflow Handbook 2004*.L. Fischer (Ed). Future Strategies Inc. Lighthouse Point, FL. 295–312.
6. WfMC. Terminology and Glossary. 11.
7. Zur Muehlen, M. 2004. *Workflow-Based Process Controlling: Foundation, Design, and Application of Workflow-Driven Process Information System*. Logos Verlag. Berlin. 124.
8. Organization for the Advancement of System Information Standards (OASIS). 2004. Asynchronous Service Access Protocol (ASAP) version 1.0. Document Number wd-asap-spec-01. available at http://www.oasis-open.org/committees/asap/docs
9. Fielding, R. T. 2000. Architectural Styles and Design of Network-Based Software Architectures. Doctoral Dissertation. University of California at Irvine. Irvine, CA.
10. WfMC. 1998. Audit Data Specification. Document Number WFMC-TC-1015. Workflow Management Coalition.

Chapter 8

Different Types of Business Process Management Systems

In the previous chapters, we discussed various integration technologies. In this chapter, we will look into the Business Process Management System (BPMS) components and tools based on the previously discussed integration technologies. BPMS is the convergence of the various integration technologies that culminate in a process-centric information technology (IT) platform for delivering business process management solutions. The BPMS technology platform is process-centric because it employs a top-down approach to solution design, starting with the design of the business process. The BPMS platform provides the development capabilities to integrate applications and humans into the business process. Using its various components, a holistic business process solution, driven from the business process definition, could be architected using BPMS. In this chapter, we will look at the various types of BPMS products available in the marketplace. This segmentation is by no means exclusive. Most BPMS products evolved from other product categories, such as Extract, Transform, Load (ETL) tools, Enterprise Application Integration (EAI) tools and workflow management systems. The segmentation is based on these product categories. After we discuss the various BPMS types, we will discuss what the ideal BPMS product should offer.

Types of Business Process Management System (BPMS) Processes

Before we embark on the technological discussion, let's first revisit the definition of a process as it relates to BPMS. We defined the meaning of process previously as it applies to business processes. A business process is defined as a coordinated and standardized flow of activities performed by people or machines, which can traverse functional or departmental boundaries to achieve a business objective that creates value for internal or external customers. In the systems world, the meaning of process is more varied. Process, in the systems arena, does not have to involve people, and it might not achieve business objectives for customers. According to Delphi Group's *BPM 2002 Market Milestone Report*, BPMS processes are grouped into three types:

- System-to-system processes, which involve transfer of data structures across multiple applications and may contain many steps in their sequences
- Person-to-person processes, which are the most complex and most closely resemble the traditional definition of a business process
- Person-to-system processes, which involve human participants who initiate a system process for creating transactions

All three process types could be further subcategorized into simple or complex processes. A simple process, such as single-step integration, is one that has a short lifespan and does not involve management of the state of the process. The word instance in this usage means an occurrence of the process. For example, the process might be to create a sales order in the Enterprise Resource Planning (ERP), render the goods and services, and bill the sales order. An instance of that process would be all of the tasks associated with the creation of a particular sales order and its invoice. A complex process is one that has a long lifespan and involves state management of the process. What do long and short lifespan mean, and why would differentiation of simple versus. complex matter? The answer is in the state management. State management is knowledge about the current status, with knowledge of all of its variables and what has been done, of a process instance. The ability of BPMS to know the exact stage and data of a process at any given time is what allows BPMS to monitor, control, and manage processes. This ability differentiates BPMS from other integration technologies. A process with a short lifespan typically does not require process management, though a short process with human participants might.

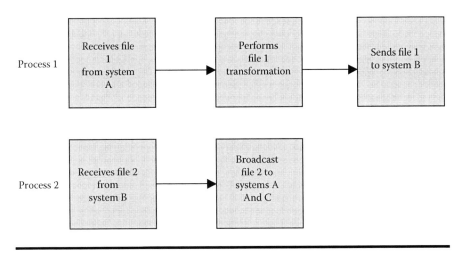

Figure 8.1   Simple System-to-System Processes.

System-to-System Processes

The first type is system-to-system processes. In a system-to-system process, data is transferred across multiple applications. System-to-system processes involve only applications and they could be simple or complex, depending on whether state management is required. Figure 8.1 shows two examples of simple system-to-system processes. System A sends a file to the integration platform; the file undergoes transformation by the integration platform and is sent to system B for further processing. System B sends another file to the integration platform, which broadcasts it to systems A and C.

An example of a complex system-to-system process could be to direct a store shipment for the retail industry. On receipt of a shipment drop-off message from a driver's wireless device, the integration platform would create a transaction in the ERP system for the sales order. The integration platform would create delivery and billing documents in the ERP system corresponding to the sales order. If the invoice is successfully created, the integration platform would send the invoice to the customer electronically. In Figure 8.2, state management is required to track whether the entire process is successful or if any error might reside in the process sequence.

Person-to-System Processes

A person-to-system process is a process initiated by human participant. After the process has been initiated, the process would go through one or more system steps. Typically, a person-to-system process involves a

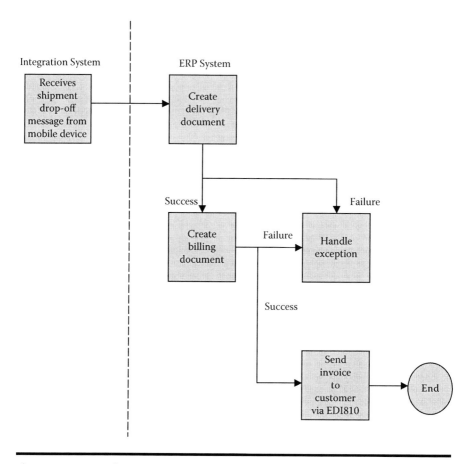

Figure 8.2 Complex System-to-System Process.

simple Web page that a human participant can complete. Once the Web page has been submitted, it creates transactions in the backend applications. An example of a simple person-to-system process is a front-end screen to an ERP sales order entry transaction. Instead of navigating through multiple screens to create a sales order in the ERP system, a simple Web page might be created for the user to complete. The Web page would contain all the necessary inputs that exist in multiple ERP screens the user needs to enter for his or her particular type of order. Once the Web page has been submitted, a transaction is created in the ERP system. The benefit of this process is simplified end user training and better information in the ERP because there are fewer chances for mis-entry of the information.

A complex person-to-system process involves more than one transaction or backend application. An example of a complex person-to-system process is a customer pick-up sale. In this scenario, we can extend the simple sales order process mentioned above to include performing goods issue and billing transactions in the backend ERP system.

When a customer picks up items from the warehouse, a clerk enters the relevant information into a Web page, as illustrated in Figure 8.3. Once the Web page has been submitted, sales order, delivery, and invoice transactions are created in the backend SAP system. The invoice could even be sent electronically to the customer's accounts payable department, or a direct debit could be processed against the customer's bank account. The orange node indicates a task that requires human action, the blue nodes are system nodes, the green is the end node, and the yellow node is a global exception handling node that captures all exceptions. Because there might be a possibility of failure of any of the transactions in the backend system, state management is needed to make sure the state of an erroneous process instance is captured.

Person-to-Person Processes

Person-to-person processes are the most complex and most closely resemble the traditional definition of business processes. In person-to-person processes, multiple people are involved collaboratively to complete business transactions. The human participants can belong to different organizations, and the processes are generally long running. Systems are typically involved in person-to-person processes. Because a person-to-person process involves more than one person, each of whom could take an indeterminate amount of time to complete his or her task, a person-to-person process requires state management. Thus, it is not possible to have a simple person-to-person process. The closest example of a simple person-to-person process might be email, if we can consider that a process. The sender writes the email and the receiver reads the email. An example of a complex person-to-person process is the credit line application process at a bank illustrated in Figure 8.4. A human applicant initiates this credit process. The application is validated for correctness and a credit report request is sent to the credit reporting agency. When the credit application has been validated, the application is approved, rejected, or labeled as requiring manual review. Once the application is approved, a credit line is given, and the customer account is updated.

Data-Centric Integration Product

Data-centric integration products focus on extracting, transforming, and transporting data mainly across database systems. What are the BPMS

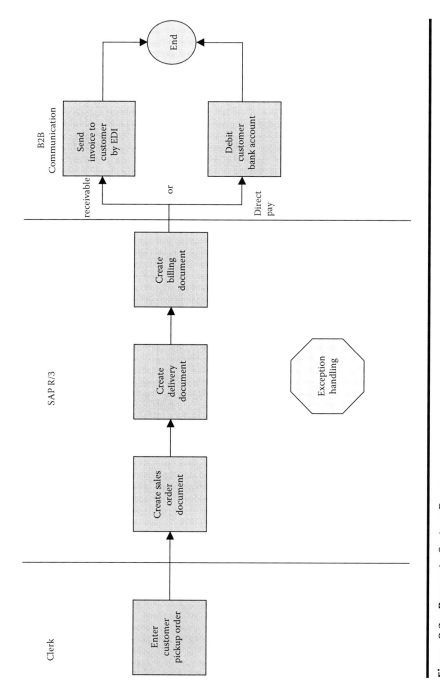

Figure 8.3   Person-to-System Process.

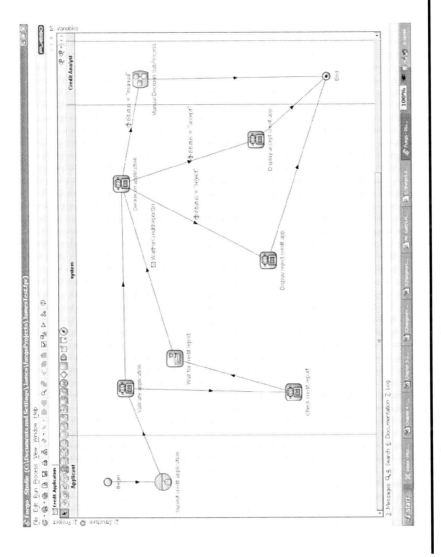

Figure 8.4   Complex Person-to-Person Process.

processes that data-centric integration products can help integrate? Data-centric integration products were originally created to transfer large amounts of data from multiple sources to a single destination. While functions have been added to allow data-centric integration products to integrate multiple source systems to multiple destination systems, this product class is limited to performing system-to-system processes. When movement of large amounts of data is required, data-centric integration products are the ideal tools. The metadata management features of some products in this class make them good candidates for enterprise data management. An enterprise data architect can store enterprise data models in the metadata repository of a data-centric integration product. Once these data models are in the repository, the metadata can be automatically created for the data architect to manage and maintain any changes to the enterprise data.

In terms of the BPMS processes described earlier in this chapter, data-centric integration products are best used to perform simple system-to-system integration. Functionally, system-to-system integration requires the ability to extract or to receive data in multiple formats from multiple source systems, perform transformation of the data, and to push the transformed data to multiple target systems in potentially multiple formats. Technically, system-to-system integration places the requirement to communicate with other systems in either real-time or batch processes, and the medium for communication can be via message, database driver, application programming interfaces (API) objects, or Web services.

Data-centric integration products have evolved from ETL products commonly used for data warehousing. As the name implies, ETL tools function to extract data from a source database, provide the capability to transform the source data to values and formats of the target database, and update the transformed data to the target database. ETL products were mainly used to load data from multiple online transaction processing (OLTP) systems to a data warehouse for analysis.

The databases of OLTP systems are built to perform transactions. OLTP databases store enormous amounts of data, most of which are not relevant for reporting, and these databases store data in different formats. To create meaningful reports using data from different OLTP systems, organizations need a central repository to store the relevant data of the various OLTP systems. The data warehouse was created to specifically bridge the reporting gap of multiple OLTP systems. The data warehouse consolidates the various OLTP data into a consistent database. Unlike the relational data model of an OLTP system, a data warehouse uses star schemas oriented to an organization's reporting requirements. A star schema is a set of tables in which one central table contains all the measures that an organization would be interested in. Examples of measures could be the total amount paid to vendors or the total sales amount. The central table is linked to dimension tables by foreign keys. The dimension tables contain the information to splice the measures in the central table. A dimension table might contain time period, products, or customers. With the dimension tables, it is possible to answer questions like the sale of a particular product in a particular time period. To enhance the performance of data retrieval, star schemas are completely de-normalized. Relational databases typically are normalized to reduce redundant data across tables. Because of the reduced amount of data that need to be affected, normalized databases have better performance for inserting, deleting, or updating records in the database. De-normalized databases, such as a data warehouse with star schemas, are optimized for data retrieval because they have fewer tables than normalized databases. In these respects, data warehouses are created to provide subject-relevant data, which are optimized for reporting.

As the mechanism to supply data to the data warehouse, ETL is an important enabler to the function of the data warehouse. A proficient ETL product should come equipped with database drivers to access all the major databases. This requires the ETL tool to be platform neutral. It should be able to connect to an Oracle database running on a UNIX server as easily as it connects to a Microsoft SQL Server running on a Windows server. The data access mechanisms provide the ETL product the ability to extract data from a source database and load data into a target database. Another feature of a proficient ETL product is its data transformation function. The most common data transformation method is a graphical transformation tool. The graphical transformation tool allows a data analyst or a programmer to graphically link fields of a source format to fields of a target format. To handle complex transformation and to translate field values, an ETL product provides pre-built transformation rules. For complex transformation requirements, the graphical transformation tool provides the ability for developers to program transformation rules. These transformation rules format the source data fields to the target and translate the field values from the source to equivalent values in the target format.

For specialized data transformation needs, such as rationalization of master data from multiple systems and conversion of legacy master data to a new system, ETL products contain data cleansing and profiling features. Data profiling allows the data architect to uncover patterns and metadata of any data set. The patterns and metadata that could be uncovered include the count of a particular value, format of fields in the data set, maximum and minimum length of data fields, and custom calculation rules. The statistics uncovered by data profiling helps the data architect to determine the quality of the data set. Using these data profiling statistics, the data architect can create data cleansing rules using the data cleansing feature of the ETL product. Data cleansing rules include eliminating duplicate records, correcting misspelled words, correcting address data, and custom rules for transforming free text fields. To support data cleansing and data profiling, ETL products are equipped with complex probabilistic matching rules to help in gathering statistics and correcting data errors. The data profiling and cleansing features are useful in ensuring the data quality from the source systems. Increasingly, data quality is viewed as a critical success factor in the implementation of data warehousing and enterprise system projects.

A key feature that ETL products provide is metadata management function. Metadata is the information or the data about data. This sounds like a circular definition. Essentially metadata should help answer what the data is, how it is collected, where the data resides, who needs the data, how often is the data collected, and what is the benefit of the data. Examples of metadata are the description and definition of an enterprise data element, the source and target systems that the enterprise data element connects to, and all the transformations the enterprise data element undergoes. Central to metadata management is the metadata repository, which could store all the metadata for an organization. The metadata repository allows the data architect to create an enterprise data model that all organizational systems have to map to, automatically capture metadata from imports of data models of existing organizational systems, and store metadata in standardized formats for sharing with external systems. Some ETL products provide graphical tools for the data architect to link data models imported from multiple systems. This linked model is useful in identifying the impact of an added system to the enterprise data model and the impact of data changes in one system to the rest of the enterprise systems. A graphical modeling tool eases maintenance of enterprise data management. From a data transformation perspective, the metadata repository is the location where each transformation rule and source-to-target data map is stored. Reporting metadata is another feature of the metadata repository. Business analysts and data architects could get logs and usage reports on each data extract, transformation, and load from the metadata repository. Supplemented with metadata management capability, an ETL product is capable of integrating databases and managing enterprise data standards.

New Generation of Data-Centric Integration Products

The traditional ETL products are used mainly to load data warehouse databases. Evolved from the traditional ETL products are the more advanced data-centric integration products capable of a wide variety of data-integration and application-integration functions. Because data warehouse does not require real-time data, the traditional ETL product is not event driven, and it uses scheduled jobs to perform its extract, transform, and load functions during run time. Data-centric integration products offer real-time data integration capability in addition to scheduled batch processing. To accomplish real-time processing, data-centric integration products either have a message queuing engine or contain connectors to message-oriented middleware. In real-time data integration mode, the message queuing engine listens for an event, such as creating a new transaction, to triggering the start of the data integration process. In cases where database changes are the triggering event, some data-centric integration products come equipped with tools for capturing data changes. These tools have a listener mechanism on the source database that can detect changes to specified database tables. Whenever an insert, update, or delete database operation is performed on a monitored database table, the listener mechanism captures the data changes and delivers the changed data to a message queuing middleware for transport back to the data-centric integration product. Once the data-centric integration product receives the message from the message queuing middleware, it transforms and loads the data into the target systems. Figure 8.5 illustrates the architecture for a typical data-centric integration product.

Another real-time integration mechanism that some data-centric integration products are providing is integration through APIs. In the past decade, application development has increasingly become polarized into using either Java or Microsoft technologies. Packaged applications developed using these two technologies usually come equipped with APIs for integration with other applications. For applications developed using Microsoft technology, the APIs are exposed as COM or .NET components. For Java-developed applications, the APIs are exposed as Java objects or Enterprise Java Beans (EJB). To enhance the real-time integration capability, some data-centric integration products have mechanisms to utilize the Microsoft or Java APIs of packaged applications. These mechanisms usually come in the form of a component repository to catalog the APIs of the packaged application. Once the APIs have been catalogued, they are available for the developer to include in the integration process design and execution. To ease the task of application development, some data-centric integration products go one step further by providing adaptors for specific applications. The adaptors enable the data-centric integration product to connect to the target applications with minimal additional development work.

With the advent of Web services, data-centric integration products also offer the ability to invoke external Web services or to externalize its functions to external systems as Web services. Instead of integrating

Generic Data-Centric Integration Product Architecture

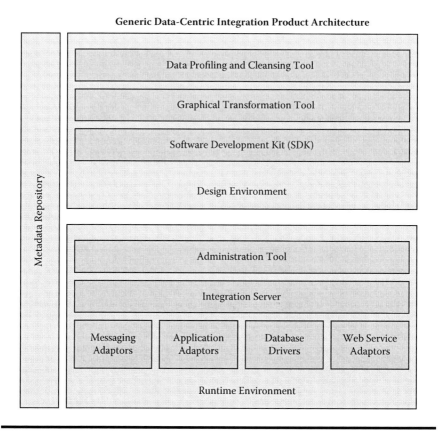

Figure 8.5   Architecture for a Typical Data-Centric Integration Product.

entirely at a database level, Web services allow integration through Web service–enabled APIs of the systems being integrated. With external or internal Web service directories, data-centric integration products have the services listed in the directories. The directories are, in effect, a set of expanding features available for developers to use for implementing data integration solutions.

Data-centric integration products lack the process management functionality required to handle long-running processes. In a simple data load process from an OLTP to a data warehouse, a process instance would be for a batch job of an ETL product extracting a data set from the OLTP, transforming the data set, and loading the transformed data into the data warehouse. In this scenario, minimal state management is necessary because the process is continuous and it is not difficult to correct errors and resume processing after error correction. In contrast, a process that spans multiple days, starts and stops, and contains several interlinked transactions would be much harder to manage. Without the crucial state management feature, data-centric integration products are not suitable at handling complex integration processes. We will discuss process management and state management functions in application-centric and process-centric integration products.

Application-Centric Integration Products

Instead of data-level integration, application-centric integration products have their integration focus on applications. Application-centric integration products are used best to implement system-to-system and person-to-system processes. These products have more robust application integration capabilities than the data-centric integration products. Adding a process engine allows the application-centric integration products to handle complex system-to-system processes. With development toolkits that come with an application-centric integration product, user interfaces can be built that allow human participants to engage in a person-to-system business process.

Just as data-centric integration products have their origin in ETL products, application-centric integration products have their origin in Message-Oriented Middleware (MOM). Mainstream application-centric integration products utilize the messaging backbone as the mechanism for enabling integration. What does MOM offer the application-centric integration product? The primary functions of MOM are to facilitate communication between disparate systems, through asynchronous messaging. All the MOM functions described previously are available in the application-centric integration product. Taken as a whole, MOM provides a robust and highly scalable foundation on which an application-centric integration product can function.

The basic functions of MOM are not enough for it to serve as an enterprise application platform. Despite all of its strengths, MOM is essentially a one-step transport tool. It allows an application to send or to receive messages from it. It does not allow for data transformation, metadata management, process management, or development of support functions that are essential for enterprise application integration, let alone business process management. To address these shortcomings, software vendors added functions on top of the MOM foundation. In this book, we will refer to these MOM–evolved products as application-centric integration products. Readers who are familiar with integration technology might know them as EAI products. We can broadly segment the traditional EAI architecture into three layers: messaging service, message broker, and process management. Figure 8.6 illustrates a generic architecture for application-centric integration products.

Generic Application-Centric Integration Product Architecture

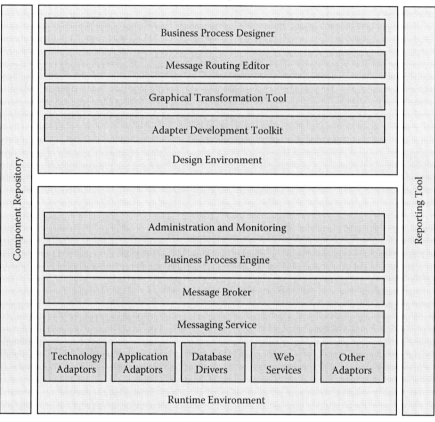

Figure 8.6   Application-Centric Integration Product Architecture.

Messaging Service Layer

The messaging service is the lowest layer. This is the traditional message-oriented middleware. It functions to transport the message using message queuing or publish-subscribe messaging protocols. In addition to communication protocols, the messaging service also provides the application-centric integration product with asynchronous transmission, guaranteed message delivery, and message prioritization. The messaging service has proven to be high performance because it allows for nonblocking and time-independent communication. The nonblocking characteristic enables the message sender to continue processing without receiving a response from the message receiver. This optimizes application processing performance. Using message queues enables the receiver to process the message at the time of its choosing. This time independence characteristic decreases the connection time between the MOM and the sender/receiver. Given the limited number of simultaneous connections, a decrease in the average connection time increases the number of connections the messaging service can handle. Some of the well-known messaging services are Microsoft Message Queue (MSMQ), Message Queueing (MQ) Series, and Java Messaging Services (JMS). In the past several years, JMS has emerged as the de facto messaging standard supported by major messaging product vendors. Readers can refer to Chapter 5 for more details on messaging mechanisms.

Message Broker Layer

On top of the messaging service is the message broker (see Figure 8.6). The messaging service provides the communication mechanism, while the message broker provides the controls for the message translation, transformation, and routing. The message broker comes with an event generator that can trigger a business process. Generating an event is the same as generating a message. When an event has been triggered, translation, transformation, and transformation rules can be designed to be invoked by the event. Translation of a message associated with an event is to translate the message from one format to another. An example of message translation is to translate a flat file into an Extensible Markup Language (XML) file. The application adapter usually does the role of message translation. We will discuss application adapters in the next section.

Message transformation is conversion of fields from a source file to a target file. Once a flat file has been translated into an XML format, the source XML file can be transformed into the target XML file. The transformation process maps fields from the source to the target schemas and converts the values of the source fields to values that the target application can understand. The transformation rules are designed using a graphical transformation tool, not unlike the tools used by mainstream data-centric integration products. In a typical transformation tool, there is a utility to allow a system analyst to define the source and target schemas. These schemas are usually in XML formats. After the schemas are defined, lines can be drawn to connect source fields to target fields. Specific rules can be embedded in each of the source-to-target connections. These rules can be as simple as assigning a constant value to a target schema field or to providing a conversion table lookup for converting values the target application can understand.

The message routing design is typically done using a message routing editor. This message routing editor allows the systems analyst to graphically define the steps a message should undergo after an event associated with the message has been triggered. The steps of a message flow are low level, when compared to the steps of a business process designer. A step might be to transform the message according to a transformation rule designed using the graphical mapping tool. This could be followed by a step to update an ERP system with the output of the transformation. To support reuse, the results of the design efforts (transformation map, message flow, and transformation rules) are stored in a component repository. Figure 8.7 illustrates an example of what a typical message routing might look like.

The illustration in Figure 8.7 looks similar to Figure 8.4, which is a process designed using a business process designer. Are there differences between a message routing editor and a business process designer? Message routing has been around since the introduction of BPMS and its business process designer. The original message routing editor is used to define the lifecycle of a message. This focus is different from a business process designer's, which focuses on the lifecycle of a process. The type of messages handled by the message broker, therefore the flows designed using message routing editor, does not require state management. That means the lifecycle of the message is short. The business process designer, in contrast, can be used to design long-running processes that involve multiple sources and process participants. In the application-centric integration product arena, the ability to handle a long-running process is a major distinction of whether a product is capable of BPM. So how long does a process have to be to be long running? There is no fixed definition. Generally, a short-running process executes in seconds, while a long-running process executes over an undetermined length of time. The long-running process could be an entire order-to-cash cycle, which could take weeks. The systemic implication is a short-running process does not require its state to be persisted. This is because the process finishes in a reasonable amount of time and its processing does not go into hibernation. In long-running process, system processing could be interrupted and restarted. This requires all the process data to persist for use when the processing starts again.

Hub-Spoke Message Broker Architecture

As the name implies, a message broker is a broker of information between applications. Most message brokers employ the so-called hub-and-spoke architecture. The hub is the message broker. The spokes are connected to applications by adapters supplied either by the application-centric integration product vendors or by third-party software providers. There are two types of adapters, application and technology adapters. The application adapters are developed specific to each application. An application adapter performs the role of translating the proprietary data from

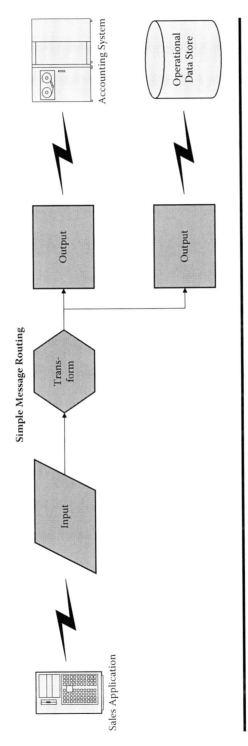

Figure 8.7   Example of Message Routing.

the application into the formats of the message broker hub. They are plug-in components that expose the application interfaces for the integration platform to use. This is done without custom programming. The adapter is considered the glue that binds an application with the message broker. On the one side, it understands the interface definition of the application. On the other side, it presents the interface definition to the message broker in the format the message broker can understand. For example, if an application can only be invoked via Remote Procedure Call (RPC)–style API, the adapter communicates with the application synchronously using RPC. The adapter communicates with the message broker using messaging. Complex application adapters go beyond data exchange. They can contain an event listener and event generator components. The event listener can receive an asynchronous message or an RPC call from the application to which the application adapter is connected. Once the event has been received, it is translated, and the translated message is sent to the message broker hub server for processing. The event listener handles inbound events to the application-centric integration environment. For processing outbound events to the connected application, the application adapter uses the event generator. The event generator can invoke an RPC or send an asynchronous message to the connected application. The adapter is under the control of the central message broker hub server. It performs the RPC request when instructed by the central hub. If the connected application can take requests directly from a messaging service, the hub server can directly send a message thus bypassing the adapter.

While application adapters allow different applications tied to the message broker to communicate, technology adapters allow applications of different technology platforms that are integrated by the message broker to communicate. Technology adapters are used when the applications to be integrated do not have published APIs. An example of a technology adapter is an adapter to access a Customer Information Control System (CICS) environment. CICS is an IBM transaction management tool that allows transaction processing in the mainframe. Applications monitored by CICS execute transactions. CICS programs are often built using Common Business-Oriented Language (COBOL) and do not have defined application programming interfaces. A developer can use the CICS technology adapter to build a specific application adapter to invoke a CICS transaction. Typically, a technology adapter comes with an application adapter builder. The adapter builder contains pre-built components that ease the task of building a custom application adapter by the developer. During run time, the application adapter built using the technology adapter can listen for events generated by the CICS application. The CICS event will trigger an inbound message from the CICS application to the message broker. The adapter can also invoke a CICS transaction when it needs to send a message to the CICS application.

In Chapter 6, we discussed the emergence of Java Connector Architecture (JCA). The JCA standard has significant implications for application-centric integration product vendors. Prior to the arrival of JCA, product vendors have to develop application adapters for every platform the application runs on. If the application runs on different variants of Java 2 Enterprise Edition (J2EE) application servers (such as IBM WebSphere and BEA WebLogic application servers), adapters have to be built specifically for each application server. JCA significantly reduces the work product vendors have to do. In application servers that implement the J2EE JCA standard, the application-centric product vendor only has to develop adapters for the JCA standard. These JCA–compliant adapters will work on every application server that supports JCA. However, JCA does not help with applications that run on non-J2EE platforms. An application that can run on both J2EE and Microsoft .NET environments will require two sets of application adapters from the integration product vendor.

One characteristic of the hub-and-spoke message broker architecture is it is inherently an asynchronous infrastructure. When married to the message broker, the application-integration products inherit an asynchronous foundation. Even if the application adapters used by the message broker hub communicates synchronously with the application, the communication from the hub to the adapter is asynchronous. This could pose problems during error handling. One example is an error experienced by one adapter in a transaction that involves simultaneous updates to multiple applications through application adapters. To maintain a two-phase commit in such a scenario, a mechanism has to be built that notifies the message broker hub of application update success from each application prior to the message broker issuing an update commit message to each adapter. Most mature message brokers have implemented mechanisms to support two-phase commit and transactional context. This has alleviated the challenges asynchronous communication presented for scenarios that require synchronous communication or global transactional context.

Figure 8.8 illustrates the various components of a message broker. The adapters for a message broker do not have to be distributed. In Figure 8.8, we can see that the Web service and database driver are centralized. Typically, in a message broker, an adapter engine runs the centralized adapters. When third-party adapters are used, most often they have to be run using the adapter engine provided by the third-party vendor. The hub-spoke architecture utilizes one central integration server (e.g., message

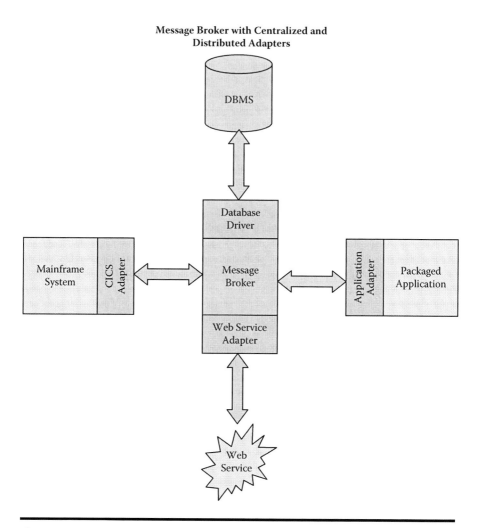

Figure 8.8   Message Broker Architecture.

broker server). The integration server performs the message routing, translation, and transformation. In the hub-spoke architecture, the integration server is where the bulk of the message processing takes place. In this respect, it could become a performance bottleneck in handling a high message volume. To circumvent the performance bottleneck, one mechanism is to create a federation of integration servers. Each hub would be connected to a set of applications. One hub is connected to another hub as if it is connecting to an application. Another alternative to the single point of failure issue with hub-spoke architecture is clustering. By deploying a cluster of hub servers, the messaging throughput can be increased.

Enterprise Service Bus (ESB) Architecture

In recent years, the concept of ESB has gained popularity. Sonic Software introduced the first ESB product in 2002 as an alternative architecture for application-centric integration products to meet the scalability challenge. In contrast to hub-spoke architecture, ESB architecture does not rely on a central server to perform most of the processing. ESB architecture contains a bus that transports the message from one ESB endpoint to another. An endpoint is an application.Typically, an ESB bus utilizes JMS as the messaging service. An endpoint is connected to the bus via a bus connector. An application can post data to the ESB bus and receive data from the ESB bus. The bus connector is like a small message broker. It contains the routing, transformation, and business rules that are relevant for the application it is connected to. It receives a message from the bus that is initiated by another endpoint. It can also send a message to another endpoint through the bus connector and the bus. The exchanged message contains its message itinerary. Based on the message itinerary, a bus connector knows what to do with the message after it has been processed. This architecture is also termed peer-to-peer. The message translation, transformation, and routing rules are designed centrally but can be deployed selectively to each bus connector. This keeps the bus connector lightweight. Because this architecture functionally acts like many small message brokers, the processing is distributed to the systems the bus connectors reside on. Figure 8.9 illustrates the ESB architecture.

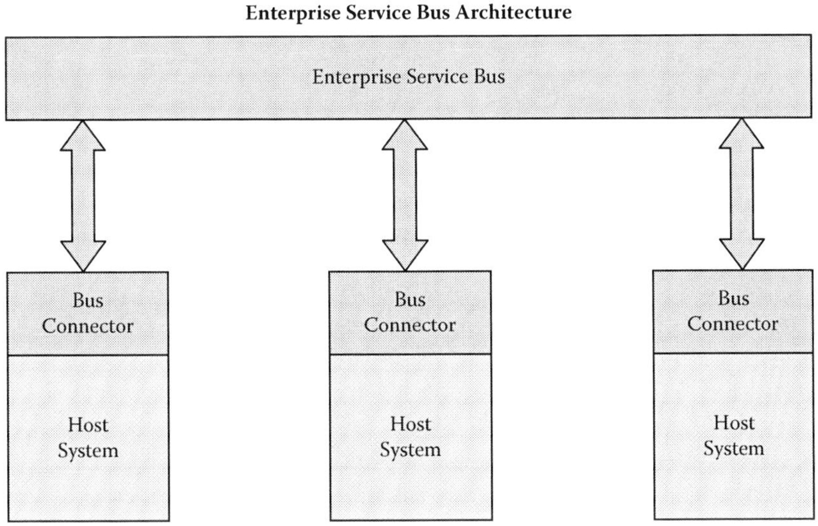

Enterprise Service Bus Architecture

Figure 8.9 Simplified ESB Architecture.

Currently there is considerable debate within the application-centric integration product segment on the virtues of hub-spoke and ESB architectures. The leading IT research firm, Gartner Group, predicts a majority of large enterprises will employ ESB by 2005.[1] In fact, Roy Schulte of Gartner Group coined the phrase ESB. Sonic Software was the first company to offer an ESB product. The marketing materials for ESB products stress that they are nonproprietary and standards-based. These standards include JMS for messaging service, Extensible Stylesheet Language Transformation (XSLT) for message transformation, and JCA and Simple Object Access Protocol (SOAP) (for Web service connectivity) for application connectivity. These are also the attributes of today's hub-spoke products. Although most message brokers started with proprietary connection protocols, they have evolved to include the standards such as JMS, JCA, and SOAP. Because the message brokers have a longer history, they also support not-so-widely accepted standards, such as Microsoft technology adapters and transformation capabilities for non-XML documents. The main difference between ESB and a message broker is their architectures. ESB relies on many lightweight servers (e.g., miniature message brokers) to accomplish message processing. The only thing centralized is the message bus, which is usually the JMS messaging service.

At this point, a message broker is clearly the more mature technology. It is inherently harder to manage transactions and ordering of messages while control is diffused across the network. When there is a central server, such as the hub in the hub-spoke architecture, ordering of messages from multiple origins to a single destination can be managed centrally. The same applies to a transaction that involves multiple messages from different applications. A message broker is currently easier to administer than ESB architecture. Instead of having to deploy designs to several ESB agents, hub-spoke architecture requires deployment only to the central hub server. Because ESB agents are like miniature message brokers, the amount of system administration work increases with the number of agents plugged into the ESB bus. Despite these shortcomings, which are related to ESB architecture's relative young age, there is growing consensus that application-centric integration products with ESB architecture will gain prominence in the future. New ESB products are offering functionalities that address the current shortcomings. A case in point is the Fiorano ESB architecture. Fiorano ESB includes a central ESB Enterprise Server that allows for centralized administration of the ESB environment. The central server also serves as component repository and state engine. The other components of Fiorano ESB architecture are the peer servers. The peer servers are the bus connectors. JMS is used to serve as the messaging service for transporting messages along the bus. Even though the debate is far from over, if past technology migrations are any guide, ESB architecture might benefit from the technology trend toward distributed processing.

Process Management Layer

Before the advent of BPMS, the message broker was the extent of the application-centric integration products. Of course, these products were known as EAI products in those days. To offer BPM capabilities, EAI vendors added process management and workflow layers on top of the message broker layer. The process management layer provides two important components: a business process designer and a business process engine.

Business Process Designer

All integration products with a process management layer have some sort of business process designer. We have already described the business process designer as a graphical tool, much like Microsoft Visio, that allows a business analyst to map out the business process. The design palette of the business process designer contains a set of services from the component repository that can be used in the process. Nodes in a business process model indicate activities or actions performed. The components could also be used as steps in the business process. After a business process design has been developed, the business process definition is also stored in the component repository. Most business process designers have the business process features listed in Table 8.1.

To integrate human participants, there needs to be a workplace portal where the human participants can execute work items assigned to them. There is also a need to determine which human participants receive which work items under what circumstances. The current offerings of most application-centric integration products do not yet have work list and user interaction portal capabilities. This is where application-centric integration products are trying to catch up with process-centric integration products.

The business process designer of most application-centric integration products are integrated with the data transformation tool provided by the message broker layer. If the business process designer supports the transform node, the data transformation tool would be used for designing the transformation map inside this node. Otherwise, the process designer calls the transformation designer to create a transformation map used by a business process activity. During run time, the business process engine executes the business process. Whenever there is a need for application

Table 8.1   Common Flow Controls for Application-Centric Integration Products

Subprocess	This is a call to another business process.
Loop	The business process executes the same steps within the loop until the exit condition has been reached.
Listen	Listening for events to start a process instance or start a different branch in the current process instance.
Decision	Decision node allows the process instance to choose which path to undertake based on predefined criteria.
Branch	Branching node creates multiple process threads. This is useful when the process needs multiple tasks or sets of tasks to be performed at the same time.
Activity	This is an activity in the process design. An activity could be request to a Web service. It could also be posting a transaction in the backend system.
Transform	This node transforms a message from source format to target format.
Exception	Exception node specifies how the process instance should respond when an exception occurs during process execution.
Wait	Wait node suspends the processing of the process instance until the wait condition has been fulfilled.
Join	The join node is where different branches can combine into a single process thread.

integration, the business process engine relies on the message broker to send and receive data from the target application.

Business Process Engine

The distinguishing feature of process management versus message broker layer is the ability to execute a long-running process. This is the minimum requirement for BPM. In terms of BPMS processes, traditional EAI products are capable of simple system-to-system processes and, with a custom development effort, simple person-to-system processes. The inclusion of state management sets the foundation for complex system-to-system, complex person-to-system and, with the help of workflow and portal components, person-to-person processes. State management is the heart of the business process engine. As stated previously, it keeps the content of the process instance at any point in time. The process instance could have a lifecycle of seconds or days. Typically, the business process engine executes the process instance and stores the state in the database. Once the state is needed again (e.g., when a process activity is acted on), the process instance retrieves the process variables from the database. The business process engine manages the retrieval of the process variables automatically to minimize using memory and system resources. In short-running process instances, process state information is stored in memory. Any system resources (i.e., thread, connection, etc.) remain active. Obviously, system resources and memory cannot be dedicated to long-running process instances and remain active throughout process instance lifecycle. The management of system resources and storage and retrieval or process state in the database is important to the performance of the business process engine.

Aside from business process execution, other functions performed by the business process engine include process version management, process instance monitoring, and process analysis. Process version management is the capability to execute different versions of the same process definition. This is done by attaching the version of the process definition to each process instance. Version management allows changes to be made to process definitions without affecting process instances that are being executed using the old process definition. Some BPMS products even provide the option to update running process instances to the new process definition. Without process version management, new process definitions cannot be deployed until all the running process instances have been completed or terminated.

Business Activity Monitoring

One of the new buzzwords related to BPM is Business Activity Monitoring (BAM). BAM is another phrase coined by Gartner Group.[2] It determines abnormal events in the process and creates alerts when predefined conditions occur. An example of a BAM alert could be a credit card that has been charged five times in the past hour. This might trigger an alert to the fraud prevention department to have a closer look. Another example of a BAM alert is when inventory is below a specified inventory level for merchandise at retail stores. This alert could trigger an automatic process to place a purchase order with the vendor for delivery of the merchandise. Implementation of BAM does not necessarily have to involve BPMS. However, the BPMS business process engine and the business process designer contain the design- and run-time tools that facilitate implementation of BAM solutions. The possibilities offered by BPMS could possibly render BAM obsolete as a product category.

As the run-time environment for executing BPM solutions, the business process engine contains the process data that allows process monitoring and analysis. Process monitoring is related to BAM. Receiving alerts about a process instance is one aspect of process monitoring. Another aspect of process monitoring is its ability to see the current state of every running process instance. Through an administration tool that comes with the business process engine, a system analyst could intrusively change the state of a process instance. This is useful for distributing workload among process participants. A manager at a support office could decide that participant A has too many work items in his or her queue. The manager could reassign some support requests from participant A's to participant B's work list. This capability exists in most workflow management systems and some application-centric integration products that have implemented human workflow in their process management layer.

With the availability of process data, the business process engine is the repository for process analysis. The process information allows a business analyst to determine the cost of a process. Based on the cost information, return on investment could be calculated for process improvements. The availability of process information is essential to continuous improvement management practice. Without process information, it is not possible to quantify current state and measure improvement. At the minimum, the business process engine should allow process statistics to be extracted for the analysis. Some integration products include a data mining function that allows a business analyst to discover correlations and opportunities for improvement.

Product Enhancement Strategies

In their attempts to build a process management layer on their application-centric integration products, several large vendors have purchased workflow companies. An example of the growth by acquisition was the purchase of Staffware by Tibco in 2004. Staffware has been a leader in the workflow product segment. When the BPMS market materialized, it has become a leader in the BPM market. The acquisition of Staffware will increase Tibco's penetration in the BPMS market. However, the challenge of integrating the Staffware process engine and Tibco's strength in application integration will not be easy.

IBM's BPMS strategy represents another product growth strategy. IBM has been a major player in the application integration market with Websphere Business Integration Message Broker. IBM also created one of the first commercially available workflow products, Flowmark, in the early 1990s. This product later evolved into what is now called Websphere MQ Workflow. By combining MQ Workflow, Business Integration Message Broker and other integration products in its product offering, IBM seeks to cover the BPMS product functions with a combination of products. This approach offers a wide range of capabilities to the customer, but it currently requires considerable effort to implement solutions using a combination of products. In the future, an integrated development and administration environment should ease the task of implementation.

The third strategy for application-centric vendors to implement process management is to develop enhancements to their application-centric products. SeeBeyond is a vendor that pursued this strategy. SeeBeyond is one of the early vendors to offer EAI products. Its latest product offering is the Integrated Composite Application Network (ICAN) suite. The ICAN suite includes SeeBeyond's mature eGate platform for application integration as well as ePortal for end-user workplace portal and eInsight Business Process Manager for the business process engine.

The different strategies have the same feature in common. The application-centric integration products are taking a bottom-up approach to reaching BPMS status. They add process management functions on top of an application integration (typically asynchronous messaging) foundation. This approach is different from the top-down approach taken by the process-centric integration vendors.

Operation of Application-Centric Integration Products

How does the business management layer interact with the message broker layer? Is there an overlap between the business process designer of the process management layer and the message routing editor of the message broker layer? Depending on segregation of functions, some application-centric integration products have eliminated the message routing editors that were part of the original message broker products. For example, Microsoft Biztalk Orchestration Designer (which is the business process designer for Microsoft's application-centric integration product) uses an integrated design environment for message routing and business process design. Message transformation is performed in the Biztalk Mapper component. The message map contains the transformation definition of a source message schema to a target message schema that can be defined. A transformation map can be assigned to the transform node in the business process designer. Similar to Microsoft Orchestration Designer, BEA WebLogic Workshop follows the approach of integrating business process design with message routing. WebLogic Workshop is BEA's business process designer for its application-centric integration product. Using the Workshop, a system analyst can embed integration into another application using Control Send and Control Receive nodes in the business process design. These node types can be configured to interact with an application using a variety of application integration mechanisms, including messaging.

Not all application-centric integration products have combined a business process designer with a message routing editor. IBM, for example, has retained Websphere MQ Workflow Buildtime as its business process designers and Websphere Business Integration Message Broker Message Flow Editor as its message routing designer. In the business process designer, an activity node can be defined to be executed by the Business Integration Message Broker Server. The activity node is assigned an input and output data format. In the message broker, the routing for the message related to this activity is specified. During process execution, the workflow run time passes to the message broker run-time environment the message for processing. After the message broker completes the message flow process, it returns a result back to the workflow run time if the business process design has requested a response. The benefit of separating message flow from business process flow is it offers an extra layer of abstraction. The business analyst can focus on the business process flow using the MQ Workflow Buildtime. When an application integration is needed, the systems analyst can design the integration using the Message Broker's Message Flow Editor. Separate design environments do present more complexity than an integrated design environment.

Because of their application integration origins, the application-centric integration products are very good at handling simple and complex system-to-system processes. Most of the application-centric integration products also offer application development toolkits that enable the creation of user interfaces for complex person-to-system processes. Now, most application-centric integration products do not have robust human workflow capabilities. Due to this deficiency, most application-centric integration products are not ideal for implementing complex person-to-person processes. This is where vendors are striving to improve. IBM is one vendor that has made notable progress in this area. In its MQ Workflow product, IBM already offers robust human workflow capabilities. In terms of functionalities, IBM's Websphere Business Integration Server offers the most capabilities of all the BPMS products. The challenge that IBM faces is to integrate the various products to provide unified design- and run-time environments. With the efforts vendors are spending to incorporate human workflow and workplace portal capabilities, by the time this book is published, it is conceivable that application-centric integration products could be sufficiently mature for implementing complex person-to-person process solutions.

Process-Centric Integration Product

The third class of integration products is process-centric integration products. These products have a wider origin than the previous two integration product classes. Some process-centric integration products evolved from workflow management systems. The switch from WfMS to BPMS is natural because workflow management systems already take the top-down process-centric approach to implementing business process solutions. Other products in this class are built entirely to tackle BPM challenges. These products do not have origins in workflow management systems. Regardless of whether the products have workflow origins or not, process-centric integration products share several characteristics. They have robust process design capabilities through a process designer that offers more functions than the ones offered by application-centric integration products. They have process modeling capabilities that include abilities to run a simulation against process designs. They offer workplace portal and work list capabilities that can present work items to the appropriate human participants for execution.

Compared to data-centric and application-centric products, process-centric integration products are better suited for implementing complex person-to-person business process management solutions. Process-centric products offer strong capabilities to integrate human participants into business process solutions. They also take a strong top-down approach to BPM. The business process designer is central to the functions of the process-centric products. In contrast, the application-centric products sometimes take a more cursory approach to the business process designer component. In terms of application-integration capabilities, the application-centric products most often have the edge. The application-centric products have focused on application-integration since their inception. They are more mature and offer more capabilities, if only because of the wide array of adapters they have developed. Figure 8.10 illustrates the components that make up a typical process-centric integration product.

The main components of process-centric integration products are the process designer, the simulation tool, the process engine, the human interaction tool (e.g., workplace portal), integration services, and the process monitor.

Process Designer

Like the application-centric integration products, process-centric integration products provide graphical process designer components. In general, the process designer components from process-centric vendors offer more functionalities than the ones offered by application-centric integration products. The designers of the process-centric products offer all of the process palettes listed in Table 8.1 for application-centric products. In addition, they offer the human participant, or interactive, process node type. Using the interactive node, work can be pushed to human participants via Web forms or other user interface views. Most process designers

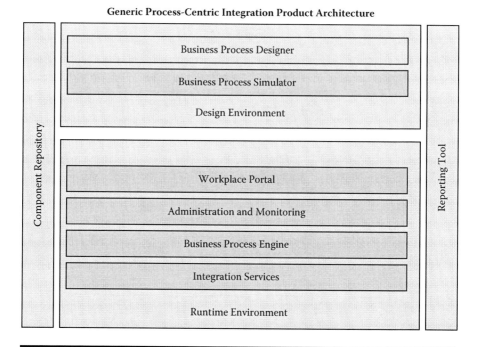

Figure 8.10   Process-Centric Integration Product Architecture.

from process-centric vendors offer form designers that allow interactive forms to be easily designed and published. The form designers function as bare-bone Web authoring tools for creating forms that are integrated with the process design. When these forms are deployed, the data entered by the users can be directly used in the process instance. Because these forms are executed in the same process server run-time environment, there is no extra integration work needed to integrate the Web pages and their associated server-side logic to the business process environment.

The business process designer typically supports two levels of view into the business process definition. The business process flow is the higher-level process definition created by the business process analyst. Under the activities in the business process flow are the specific integration instructions that can be added by a technical analyst. The two-level approach allows the business analyst and technical analyst to work off the same business process definition. In the process design palette, we talked about the design capabilities of the process flow layer. The technical design environment of the business process designer consists of the form designer, business rule editor, and transformation editor. Figure 8.11 illustrates the components of the process-centric business process designer.

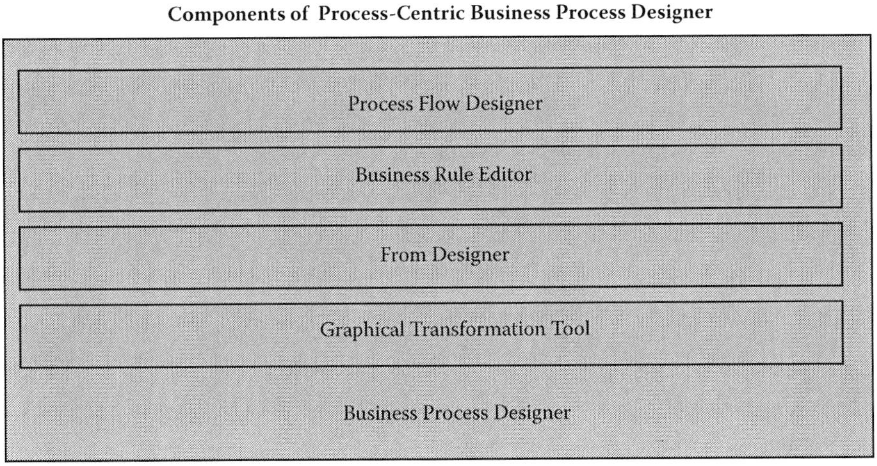

Components of Process-Centric Business Process Designer

Process Flow Designer
Business Rule Editor
From Designer
Graphical Transformation Tool
Business Process Designer

Figure 8.11   Components of Business Process Designer.

Most process-centric products take a component-based development view to enabling the lower-level technical design environment. In such a view, the process solution is an assembly of components and human interactions orchestrated by the business process definition. A component could be an application, a database table, transformation map, messaging service, Web page, etc. These components are available in a component repository used in a drag-and-drop fashion in the business process design. An external component, such as interfaces of a packaged application, is catalogued into the component repository by having its functions exposed in the format understood by the business process design. For example, the API of an ERP for creating a sales order can be catalogued in the component repository by having its EJB interface definition translated for the business process design environment. Once it exists in the component repository, the process design can use and invoke the API as if it exists in the business process environment. The business analyst and technical analyst do not have to worry about the complexity of making the actual RPC call across a network and across platforms. The business process engine and the component repository do the actual work. To use the components, the technical analyst can invoke the components using the business rule editor. The rule designer is a graphical tool that allows the business analyst to build rules with minimal coding. Some process-centric products do not offer graphical business rule editors, but they offer a programming environment that allows logic to be embedded in the individual activities of the business process flow. As we have seen in the previous section, application-centric vendors also offer a component repository. In general, process-centric products support more component types and places stronger emphasis on component-based design.

Extending on support for human interaction, the business rule editor is needed for role resolution and human participant assignment. It is rare that the same user performs process instances. Typically, there is a pool of possible human participants assigned work items. The challenge is in determining assignment of specific work items to the appropriate human participant. Role resolution and participant assignment is done by business rules created for this purpose. In the execution of the process instance, the business rule reads information from the process instance. These instance variables provide context for role resolution rules used by the process design to route the work items to the appropriate human participants. The role resolution rules could access directory services for organization structure information in its processing. Directories can be used to store users, roles, organizational structure, and access rights. There may be different organizational structures in the directory used for different purposes. For example, there may be an organizational structure for cost responsibility used to determine the approval hierarchy for purchase orders. Another organizational structure may exist for human resources. This human resource structure could be used for employee vacation approval and performance review processes.

The business rule editor goes beyond role resolution and detailed scripts for the activities in the business process flow. Business rules can be used to decide the transition from one task to another in the business process design. For example, a rule can be set up to say if condition A happens, then skip step 2 and go to step 3. The rule can be assigned to the transitions in the business process flow. Transitions are the lines that connect task to task in a business process definition. In products without a rule designer, code snippets could be created for each transition using the scripting environment. The last component of the business process designer is the graphical transformation tool. This is similar to the ones used by the data- and application-centric products. The graphical maps created by the transformation tool can be used in any activities of the business process flow that require them. In essence, they are components that can be catalogued in the component repository.

Process Modeling and Simulation

We mentioned in Chapter 2 that BPM is the convergence of process-focused management practices. The result includes heavy focus on continuous improvement through practices such as Six Sigma. To support the qualitative methodology such as Six Sigma, BPMS, as the enabling technology for BPM, needs to provide an integrated modeling and design capability. This means the ability to design a business process, simulate the design as if it has been deployed, tweak the design to improve weaknesses identified in the simulation, and repeat the design-simulate cycle before deploying an optimal process design. This is the direction most BPMS vendors, regardless of whether they have application-centric or process-centric origins, are headed.

Discrete Event Simulation

There are several different methods of simulation. The two most common are continuous simulation and discrete event simulation. In continuous simulation, the state changes as time progresses. One example is the volume in a fuel storage tank at a refinery. As there is constant movement of fuel into and out of the storage tank, the volume fluctuates with time. In discrete event simulation, the state does not change as time progresses; the state changes when an event occurs. Between the occurrences of events, the state of the system does not change in discrete event simulation. Business process is most suited using the discrete event simulation. As the name implies, discrete event means an occurrence of something at distinct point in time causes change in the state of the system or, in our discussion, business process. The occurrence of something could be a wide range of entities. If the model is for a business process, examples of events could be the arrival of a sales order, addition of a new employee, or an application for new driver's license at the driver licensing office. The event is measurable in real time. For example, the arrival of a sales order at 123rd second is a discrete event. In a discrete event simulation, an entity could enter the system and undergo multiple events before it exits the system. In short, discrete event simulation is the flow of an entity through the system while competing with other entities for limited resources throughout an entity's lifecycle in the system. This could correspond to the sales order entity as it traverses the order-to-cash business process. The sales order entity undergoes several events, such as arrival of sales order, fulfillment of the sales order, and billing for the sales order. In the process, the sales order entity has to be acted on by resources, such as order entry clerk, warehouse order processor, and billing clerk, before the order exists the system, in the order-to-cash process. This sounds like the business process definition. What is the difference between what we have described so far about discrete event simulation and business process definition? The difference is business process definition describes the business process and discrete event simulation is the computational activity of that business process definition. Simulation assigns randomness to the business process model. It can be used to determine how the business process model might perform as entities encountering events with random processing times traverse the business process model.

The key components of discrete event simulation are entity, event, activity, resource, queue, and priority rule. An entity is the traffic that goes through the system. In business process terms, an entity could be a sales order, a new customer, or a new employee. An event could be the arrival of a sales order, the loading start of the sales order, the end of loading of the sales order, etc. A pair of events could correspond to a business process activity. For instance, start and end loading events could constitute the loading sales order activity. Computationally, using activities is easier to implement than using events. This is because logic has to be inserted in the simulation to avoid generating an end loading sales order event before the corresponding start loading sales order event. An activity has a duration of service time rather than a point in time. The duration of the activity is based on a probability distribution. An example of a probability distribution could be normal distribution for the load sales order activity with a mean of 61 minutes and a variance of 12 minutes. In this discussion we will use the term event to denote the arrival of an entity into the system, e.g., a new sales order in the order-to-cash process. Subsequent events from the arrival event of a given process will be treated as activity. In a more rigorous setting, the activity would equate to a start event and an end event separated by a random service time. While an activity has a random service time that might follow the normal, or Gaussian, distribution, the probability of orders coming into the business process might follow a Poisson process. The Poisson process is widely used by statisticians to model random occurrences over time. The simulation model contains an event generator that generates events according to the stochastic process model the events employ. A stochastic process models the occurrences of random events over time using a probability distribution.

An activity requires a resource to provide a service to the activity. In the sales order entry activity, the resource would be the order entry clerk. Resources have attributes. These attributes could be working hours, working days, number of breaks, and break lengths. For example, the order entry department could have five workers working from 8:00 am to 5:00 pm. Each clerk works Monday to Friday. In a sophisticated simulation, we can even simulate the behavior of the worker. A worker could be simulated to take a certain number of breaks per hour, which would be modeled as events following a Poisson distribution. The break time might be modeled as a normal distribution. During the break, the worker would not be available to perform work. The more detailed the descriptions of the attributes, the more accurate the result of the simulation.

When an entity waits to be processed, it is in a queue. The queue contains entities, such as sales orders in our example, waiting to be serviced by an activity. The waiting time of a sales order depends on the service times of the sales order in front of it in the queue and the availability of resources. If an order entry clerk is taking a break from entering a sales order, he or she is not available to process the next sales order in the queue. The number of resources assigned to the activity also affects the wait time in the queue. If there are two order entry clerks, the wait time could obviously be less than if there is only one order entry clerk. In a business process with many activities, there is a queue for each activity. If the resource performing an activity has unlimited availability, there will not be any entities waiting in the queue for that activity. In today's world of clustered servers supporting an IT infrastructure, applications can usually be modeled with unlimited availability at the business process level.

Entities could have a priority rule assigned to them. For instance, orders from a company's largest ten customers could have a higher priority over orders from the rest of the customers. This priority attribute would force the sales orders with the higher priority to the front of the queue while sales orders are waiting to be serviced. There would also be a probability distribution assigned to the occurrence of high priority orders that might be different from other orders. Discrete event simulation also utilizes control elements. These control elements could be conditionals, Booleans, or other transition-related controls. The control elements correspond to the transitions in the business process model.

Benefits of Business Process Simulation

As we can see, the business process model that is defined using a business process designer is not much different from the discrete event model. In order for a simulation to be executed, the business process model needs to be enhanced with attributes for probability distribution, resource availabilities, queues, and event generators. With these attributes, the simulation engine can generate events and compute how the business process will perform according to the attributes assigned to the business process model. The outputs obtained from running a simulation include wait times, throughputs, and resource utilizations. The simulation can also compute the business process cost when costs are assigned to the resources involved in the business process. Most current process-centric integration products have varying levels of simulation capability. In the future, all enterprise-level BPMS should have process simulation capabilities to validate the business process designs.

Process-Centric Process Engine

The process engines for the process-centric integration products are similar to the process engines of the application-centric products. These process engines manage the state of the business process instances and supervise the execution of all of its interactions. Different versions of a business process design can exist in the process engine. When a new version has been introduced, the administration tool determines whether the new version should only apply to new business process instances or also to the existing business process instances. The process engine also manages the components in the component repository. In this respect, the process-centric process engines differ from application-centric engines. There is no message broker layer directing the interaction of the application integration. All the application integration work is performed through services provided by the application-integration components in the component repository. For instance, if an application involved in the business process takes requests by messaging, the process management engine could invoke a JMS component if that is what is designed in the business process design. If the business process definition defined in the process designer calls for interaction through MQ messaging, the process engine could invoke the application through IBM's MQ Message Broker.

So how are using integration services different from utilizing a message broker? By utilizing services catalogued in the component repository, the process-centric product is not tied to a specific application-integration mechanism. The process-centric product could use any application-integration services or products as long as these services and products can have their functions catalogued in the component repository through component introspection. The business process designer provides all the data required by the integration component. The integration component performs the task of getting the data to and from the application it is connecting to. The integrated design environment of the business process designer provides message flow and transformation, and the process engine manages them. In essence, the integration components, whether they are JMS, Java Database Connectivity (JDBC), Web service, third-party message-oriented middleware, or an API of the application being connected to, serve a function similar to the adapters of the application-centric integration products.

Integration Services

There are different approaches to implementing the integration services. Some process-centric vendors, such as Filenet, utilize the integration functions provided by the application server that is powering their process-centric products. Integration components come in the form of JMS provided by the J2EE application server, custom developed Java components, third party adapters that come in the form of Java components, and Web services. This approach allows for extensibility of application integration capabilities by purchasing packaged adapters or integration to an application integration product.

Other process-centric vendors utilize component introspection and self generation of the component bindings to catalog components into the component repository. Vendors taking this approach, such as Fuego and Intalio, offer a flexible mechanism toward application integration. Introspection of components means the APIs of an application, if it can be exposed using an established component model, can be added to the component repository without additional programming. Introspection is not limited to APIs of business applications. Adapters, database drivers, messaging services, and any program built using established component models can be introspected to use in the design and run-time environment of the process-centric products. In the process of introspection, the process-centric product creates the translation and binding to the foreign component so it can be invoked by the process-centric product. An application integration product can even be catalogued if it can expose its functions through APIs. In case the run-time environment of the integration component is different from the run-time environment of the process engine (e.g., the process engine might follow the J2EE model while the integration component follows the .NET model), the process engine provides a mechanism that bridges the two different component models and allows an automated introspection of the .NET integration component into the component repository. The quality of the technology bridge dictates how good the performance and stability of application integration capability provided by the process-centric product. Different vendors will undoubtedly tout different approaches as being better. Now, it is difficult to say empirically which integration mechanism is more cost-effective, offers higher performance, and provides more stability.

Process Monitor and Workplace Portal

The other components of process-centric products are the process monitor and the workplace portal. The process monitor for process-centric products serves the same purpose as the process monitor for application-centric products. Because we already described the process monitor in the previous section, we will not spend time on that. The workplace portal presents the tasks for the human participants to complete. They usually present these human tasks as Web forms into which human participants can input data. Most workplace portals support single sign-on (SSO) and configurable styles for the customer to implement its corporate Web style for consistent look and feel. The next stage of development for the workplace portal is to enable integration to enterprise portals. The process-centric workplace portals only serve the function of delivering work items to the end users. They are not designed to function as enterprise portal products. Consequently, they lack content management, personalization, and collaboration. With the growing use of enterprise portals, most corporations are demanding a single entry point for their employees to perform work and find information. Corporate enterprise portals serve that purpose. The challenge is for process-centric products to be able to push work items to the enterprise portal products that customers might implement. The other alternative is to provide an enterprise portal product as part of the BPMS offering. This alternative carries a high development cost and risk of alienating customers that have already implemented enterprise portal solutions. In the next section, we will discuss the BPMS trend and what the future BPMS product might look like.

Future BPMS Developments

From our discussions of the various BPMS products, we can see that application-centric and process-centric products are further along the BPMS development path than data-centric integration products. Technically, data-centric integration products should not be considered relevant for BPM because of the lack of state management. They do offer features, such as data cleansing, data management, and metadata repository, that should be included in future BPMS products. As for application-centric and process-centric products, the segmentation provided in this book is not exclusive and is based mainly on the origin of the products in each category. As the BPMS technology matures, the line between these two product categories will become more blurred.

Future Business Process Management System (BPMS) Product

What features should a future BPMS product contain? In this writer's opinion, the ideal BPMS product is not only an application, it should also serve as the platform for an enterprise to design, develop, execute, and supervise business processes. The future BPMS product should provide full support for all three BPMS processes we described earlier in the chapter. Figure 8.12 shows the components in a BPMS product.

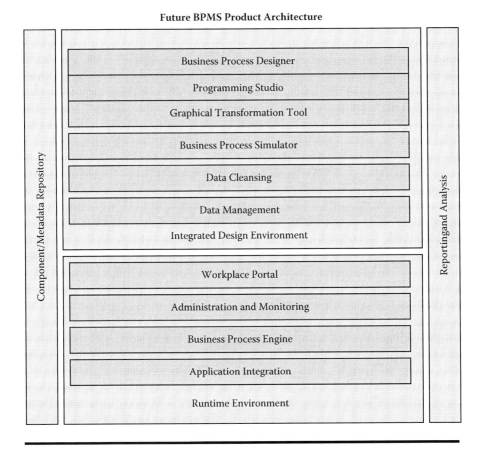

Figure 8.12   Example of Future BPMS product.

Design Environment Features

In the design arena, it should have the capabilities to model and simulate business processes. These capabilities already exist in the process designer and the simulator components of most BPMS products. In the development area, the ideal BPMS product should offer an application design environment that allows technical analysts and programmers to develop components. The components could be designed using object-oriented, procedural, or other programming languages. The programming language does not matter as long as the BPMS product can execute it natively and follow an established component model. What is required in the ideal BPMS product is an integrated design environment (IDE) that contains the various design pieces needed for implementing process management solutions.

The ideal IDE should be multilayered, componentized, and team oriented. The top layer of the IDE should be the business process designer in which the business analyst can model the business processes. The business process model created using this layer can be used as the basis for further technical development and process simulation. Under the business process layer should reside the application development layer. The development layer should contain a programming studio used to embed detailed logic for each of the nodes in the business process design. This programming studio should be capable of being invoked from the business process design or independently to develop components. The programming studio should allow for the development of application components and should contain features that enable Web service, Web, and XML developments. Another important feature of the programming studio is the development of Web pages or other user interface views to interact with human participants. The forms developed using the programming studio should be embedded in nodes of the business process design that require human interaction. When the process is executed, the user interface views can be deployed to solicit user input.

In summary, the ideal programming studio should be similar to Microsoft Visual Studio .NET or the Eclipse development environment. Unlike Visual Studio or Eclipse, the programs and user interface views of the programming studio are embedded in the business process design and deployed within the BPMS run-time environment. When a developer needs transformation service, it can invoke the graphical transformation tool to design the transformation from the source to the target formats. The results of the design and develop efforts should exist in the component repository that can be used by all the other tools (i.e., business process designer, programming studio, graphical transformation tool, etc.) in the IDE. The idea of component repository is essential. It allows different types of components (whether business process, integration service, transformation maps, Web services, etc.) to be catalogued and reused. The component repository is also the conduit to directory services, role determination rules, and organizational structures. These organizational-related services are critical for automatically routing work to the appropriate human participant when the business process design is executed by BPMS run time.

What is described here is a design and development environment that is more involved than the most sophisticated application development environments. Why is it necessary for the BPMS IDE to have all these features? The answer is BPMS is a process development platform. It is not simply an application or an application development platform. For BPMS to play the role of the process management layer in the enterprise architecture, it requires not only the traditional application development tools but also the process design tools. Many BPMS products in the market today advertise programming-free implementations. Obviously, the IT implementation nirvana is to eliminate the need to develop custom programs. Unfortunately, the technology to get to automatic generation of programs based on a pure graphical design environment is still a long way off. One example of this nascent technology is the Object-Process Methodology (OPM) developed by Professor Dov Dori of the Technion Israel Institute of Technology. Professor Dori has developed a novel product, OPCAT, which aims to achieve a purely graphical implementation of a process solution using three building blocks: object, process, and state. The main theme of OPM is as follows:

> "Objects exist, and processes transform the objects by generating, consuming, or affecting them. States are used to describe objects, and are not stand-alone things."[3]

Based on these three building blocks, any process can be modeled as a series of hierarchical object process diagrams. Technologies such as the ones based on OPM are still in research stages. Even if they come to fruition, they still do not address the question of how to integrate existing systems and applications.

Figure 8.12 shows data management and data cleansing components in the design environment we have not discussed. These two components are contained data-centric products. If data-centric products are not relevant for BPMS, why are we including its two components? The answer is the need for master data management. We have placed heavy emphasis on processes in this book. To make any process function successfully, it is necessary to have the correct data in the system. Without accurate data to support the processes, it does not matter how efficiently the business processes are executing. The result of incorrect data will invalidate the result of the business processes. One of the main points most corporations face is the quality of their master data. Master data is data that does not frequently change and is relevant for business transactions. Master data includes customers, vendors, products, etc. Typically, master data quality is the best when an organization has just implemented a new enterprise information system, such as an ERP system. EIS implementations include master data conversion tasks, which if followed rigorously, ensure master data has been rationalized across all business applications. After the EIS implementation has gone live, the quality of master data usually degrades over time. This is especially true if the ERP application does not replace all applications that require master data. In such scenarios, master data has to be interfaced and synchronized across the business application in the enterprise. To preserve the accuracy of master data, what is needed are processes and tools that enable the management of master data. If the requirement is to design a process to create master data involving multiple functional departments and several enterprise applications, the current BPMS products can perform such processes. However, such a process might create duplicate records among the enterprise applications and not allow linkages be made between a master data record in one enterprise application to the same record in another enterprise application. This is an area where data management and data cleansing components can help. The data management component, or content management as some called this feature, allows the linkages between master data records in different applications to be linked for reporting and data maintenance. A data cleansing component can detect whether a new record is a duplicate. If there are duplicates, the data cleansing component contains rules for merging duplicates. With the data management and data cleansing components in the design environment, the BPMS product can manage business processes as well as the data needed to support the business processes.

Run-Time Environment Features

There are varieties of architectures that exist to support BPMS. It is not possible to definitively say which architecture is better than another. In this discussion, we will describe the features of the run-time environment and not discuss whether the run-time environment should be based on a message broker, ESB, introspected integration components, or another architectural choice. Broadly speaking, the future BPMS product run-time environment should contain the business process engine, process monitoring tool, workplace portal, process analytics component, and application integration capabilities.

The business process engine is the heart of the BPMS. As we discussed a few times previously, the business process engine should execute the business processes. This includes the ability to execute multiple versions of a business process design. Because we will not be discussing architectural choices, the business process engine also supports the human and application integration. In terms of human integration, the business process engine manages the work items and work lists for human participants. For application integration, the business process engine allows the business processes to interact with other applications using messages, File Transfer Protocol (FTP), database drivers, Web services, RPC–style synchronous calls, and adaptors. Regardless of which application integration architecture is included for the BPMS product, it needs to provide exception handling and restarting capabilities in case a business process instance encounters an error during the application integration step. The exception handling mechanism should allow the process instance to be restarted at the point of failure and continue with the rest of the process execution.

The process monitoring tool and workplace portal components have been discussed in the previous sections. One requirement a future BPMS product should provide in its workplace portal component is integration to an enterprise portal product. We touched on this in our discussion of process-centric integration products. There are several ways to integrate a BPMS workplace portal into a third-party enterprise portal product. One method is through alliances between BPMS vendors and enterprise portal vendors. This method can provide tight integration but it requires the BPMS vendors to choose strategic enterprise portal partners. The choice of partners could affect the market acceptability of a BPMS product. Another method of third-party enterprise portal integration is using established standards for exchanging work items. One standard is the Workflow Management Coalition (WfMC) Workflow Application Programming Interface (WAPI) definition. The enterprise portal product can retrieve work items by calling BPMS using WAPI. When a work item has been selected from the enterprise portal, WAPI takes the user into the BPMS run-time environment. The downside of using WAPI is the integration between BPMS and enterprise portal is not as tight as a packaged integration resulting from strategic partnership of BPMS and enterprise portal products. Using WAPI could also require more custom development work for a customer implementing a BPMS product.

The last piece of the BPMS run-time environment is the process analytics component. Current BPMS products, regardless of whether they are process centric or application centric, all offer some form of reporting capability on process instances. Reporting on processes is an essential requirement for enterprises that have adopted BPM. Without accurate and versatile reporting capabilities, BPMS organizations do not have the necessary information to continually evaluate and improve their business processes. Therefore, the future BPMS product should provide very robust reporting and analysis capabilities through data warehouse and data mining functions. This means the process data should not only be in the database for the business process engine, it should also reside in a data warehouse. Ideally, the data warehouse should be part of the BPMS product. If this is not possible, then the BPMS vendor should provide tight integration to an external data warehouse. Data mining and analysis capabilities should also be provided. Through packaged Online Analytical Processing (OLAP) or custom OLAP data cubes, users should be able to analyze the process metrics in any fashion they desire.

Business Process Management System (BPMS) Trends

The current trend in the enterprise technology arena is the emergence of the application platform suite. This strategy is being pursued by such companies as SAP (NetWeaver platform), IBM (IBM Websphere platform), BEA (WebLogic platform), and Oracle (Application Server 10g). The application platform suite is bundled offering application serve, enterprise portal, business intelligence, BPM, application integration, and development support services. These major software companies have the pieces necessary for BPMS. Some of them, particularly IBM, have done remarkable jobs of integrating these pieces into the BPMS platform. The application platform suite is a powerful force in the marketplace. It offers customers one-stop shopping for their development needs. This strategy also offers customers reduced cost for bundled functionalities, technology roadmap from established major software vendor, and common system administration tasks because of a common platform.[4] Once a customer decides on an application platform suite, the customer is tied to the technology vendor.

What does this leave for the pure-play BPMS vendors? The outlook is not as bad as it seems. As a group, pure-play BPMS products offer more capabilities than the application platform suites vendors do. The gap is narrowing as the major software vendors integrate the various offerings they have. The functionality advantages offered by pure-play vendors should exist for a few more years. For customers who already have application servers and are looking to plug in BPMS, the pure-play vendors might be more attractive. As the BPMS technology matures, larger software companies will probably acquire some of the niche BPMS vendors.

Notes

1. Winkler, C. 2003. Early Riders. *ComputerWorld.* June 11, 2003.
2. Schwartz, E. 2003. Is BAM a scam or a score? *InfoWorld.* July 3, 2003.
3. Dori, D. 2002. *Object-Process Methodology: A Holistic Systems Paradigm.* Springer-Verlag. Berling. 5
4. Chang, J. 2003. The Current State of BPM Technology. *Business Integration Journal.* March. 35–38.

Chapter 9

Business Process Management System (BPMS) Standards

The following is a scenario that has happened repeatedly in the technology world. When a new technology comes onto the scene, vendors rush to offer products using that technology. Each first-mover vendor offers its own features and taxonomy. Customers comparing two products using the same technology have a hard time making the comparison. Some features offered by the products might be similar but most will be different. Complicating the matter is the names each vendor uses. The different taxonomies of features and concepts add another layer of confusion. At this stage, each product is considered a proprietary solution.

As the technology takes hold and the market for the technology grows, different forces converge to create standards. First-mover vendors who have established a reasonable market presence would want their products and taxonomies established as standards. Once a proprietary solution has been declared as a standard, the product vendor could gain a competitive advantage by offering a standard-compliant product and could even guide the future development of the standard to be inline with the release plans of its product. Customers are another force behind the drive for standards. With standards, customers will have an easier time evaluating products. The establishment of standards also confers the notion of nonproprietary. This notion implies that multiple products are available conforming to the standard. Customers are more likely to purchase standard-conforming products because they have the choice of switching to another product that conforms to the same standard. Vendors who are not first movers in the marketplace are the third force that would benefit from standards. Compared to first movers, these new entrants do not have market penetration and mature products. These new entrant vendors can benefit from the marketplace's recognition of the standards and gain a potential competitive advantage by marketing their products as open rather than proprietary solutions. With all these forces in the marketplace, groups of vendors collaborate to offer standards.

At this stage, instead of individual proprietary solutions, the marketplace is filled with a smaller number of standards. While this situation is less confusing for customers who are trying to make product selections, the risk of losing solution portability remains for the customers. The nature of new technology makes for a risky venture for customers as well as vendors. The fast-changing pace of technology means a new technology might be obsolete before it has a chance to gain market traction. Start-up vendors, usually the first movers in a new technology, go out of business with regularity. In this respect, solution portability is important for the customers. If the standard supported by the product vendor does not become obsolete, the customers can port their solutions to another product in case the original product vendor goes out of business. However, if the standard becomes obsolete, both customers and product vendors will be affected negatively. The customers are stuck with solutions that might not be portable to a prevailing standard. Vendors who comply with an obsolete standard lose competitive advantage and have to revise their products to the prevailing standard. Thus, in a marketplace with competing standards, choosing the right standard is important to both the vendors and customers.

Development of Business Process Management System (BPMS) Standards

The generic scenario for new technology development can be applied to the Business Process Management (BPM) technology environment with a few twists. Business Process Management System (BPMS) is developed to support BPM management practices. It is a technology that is pushed by management practices and not a pure technology-based innovation. Because BPMS is not a technology-based innovation, many products in this category evolved from other product classes, specifically workflow and application integration. We discussed the various product origins in the previous chapter. Aside from products that evolved to the BPMS product category, there are also products that were specifically created to meet the requirements of BPM. Summarizing our discussions in Chapter 8, the BPMS product segment contains products with no origins, products that evolved from workflow management systems, and products that evolved from application integration systems. Not surprisingly, the origins of the BPMS products influence the development of BPMS standards. We can broadly define three competing sets of BPMS standards based on the product origins: workflow, application integration, and new products. Vendors that offered BPMS products not based on previous product offerings offer the last set, new products. All three sets contain standards for business process definition and business process interaction. Business process definition standards specify how the business processes should be designed. As examples, process definition standards contain semantics for activity types, transitions, sub-processes, etc.

The process interaction standards define how process definitions can be invoked and process participants can collaborate on the execution of the business process using Web services.

Business process interaction standards are effective for business processes that traverse enterprise boundaries as well as those that function within one enterprise. These process interaction standards provide the specifications for a client to communicate with a BPMS through Web services. The client can be another BPMS, an external business partner, or an internal application. The client can invoke a new process instance, update an existing process instance, and query an existing process instance on a remote BPMS server. In this chapter, we will discuss the standards from Workflow Management Coalition (WfMC), Business Process Management Initiative (BPMI), and Organization for the Advancement of Structured Information Standards (OASIS). Table 9.1 lists the standards offered by each of the three standards groups. World Wide Web Consortium (W3C),

Table 9.1   BPM Standards

	Business Process Definition	Business Process Interaction
WfMC	XPDL (XML Process Definition Language)	Wf-XML 2.0
OASIS	BPEL (Business Process Execution Language)	BPEL (Business Process Execution Language)
BPMI/W3C	BPML (Business Process Modeling Language)	WSCI (Web Service Choreography Interface)

the official standards body for the World Wide Web, has also accepted the business process interaction standard submitted by BPMI, Web Service Choreography Interface (WSCI). There are many more standards than the ones proposed by these three groups. These three sets of standards are representative of the various product origins, and they have garnered the most attention.

The first set of standards evolved from the Workflow Reference Model offered by the WfMC. Interface 1 of the reference model was updated to use Extensible Markup Language (XML) and became XML Process Definition Language (XPDL). The XPDL standard is the WfMC's specification for business process definition. Similarly, interface 4 of the reference model was updated to use Simple Object Access Protocol (SOAP) and became Web service–enabled. The reincarnation of interface 4 became Workflow Extensible Markup Language (Wf-XML) 2.0, which is the WfMC's specification for business process interaction.

Business Process Execution Language for Web Service (BPEL4WS) represents the BPMS standard from traditional application integration vendors. It is the fusion of two different standards, Web Services for Business Process Design (XLANG) from Microsoft and Web Services Flow Language (WSFL) from IBM. Microsoft designed XLANG for business-to-business (B2B) and application integration processes for its Biztalk Server product. IBM designed WSFL for its Message Queueing (MQ) Series Workflow product. The two technology companies decided to merge their standards in 2002 to create BPEL4WS. This standard has since been endorsed by other companies such as BEA, SAP, SeeBeyond, and Siebel. To help legitimize BPEL4WS as an industry standard, Microsoft and IBM gave up control of BPEL4WS by submitting the standard to OASIS for further development. OASIS renamed the standard to be Web Services Business Process Execution Language (WS-BPEL) and created the BPEL Technical Committee to refine this standard. The terms WS-BPEL, BPEL, and BPEL4WS all refer to the same standard. In our discussion, we will use the term BPEL.

The third group of standards is from the BPMI.org. Intalio, a start-up company that has no previous products before its BPMS offering, spearheaded this organization in 2000. The BPMI consortium currently has about 200 member companies, including SAP, BEA, and Sun Microsystems. It is interesting to note that several technology companies participate in rival standards organizations. This is undoubtedly to spread the risk of choosing the wrong standards. BPMI offers three standards: Business Process Modeling Language (BPML), Business Process Modeling Notation (BPMN), and Business Process Query Language (BPQL). Originally, BPML was the specification from this consortium for business process definition. In 2002, Intalio, Sun, BEA, and SAP submitted Web Service Choreography Interface (WSCI) as their business process interaction specification to the W3C. The W3C acknowledges receipt of WSCI as a W3C note for discussion purposes. As a W3C note, WSCI serves as a main input to the W3C Web Services Choreography Working Group for formulating W3C's Web services choreography specification. W3C is the official standards body for the World Wide Web (WWW) and its specifications are highly regarded by the industry. The organizations that submitted WSCI to the W3C are also the organizations behind the BPML specification. This group of organizations envisioned WSCI as the process interaction standard and BPML as the process definition standard. However, the division of work between BPML and WSCI is blurry. Enhancements have been made to BPML that allow BPML processes to be exposed as Web services and for BPML processes to invoke Web services.

Overview of the Process Definition Standards

In this section, we will investigate the features of XML Process Definition Language (XPDL), BPML, and BPEL. These standards are all XML-based. This is to be expected because emergence of XML as the technology of formatting data has transformed the way data is exchanged. XML is structured so a tag describes each piece of data it contains. This means a recipient application can look for the data it needs from the XML document by the tags. The XML document could contain tags that are not to be used by a recipient application as long as the XML document contains the required tags. This is attractive for communication between multiple applications that have application-specific data needs. The fact that XML is structured allows human users to read the XML document. XML parsers can parse any XML document so the descriptions provided by the tag and data are displayed in a readable format for humans. Besides being structured, XML is an open standard that is platform-independent. XML data is stored in a text file. Because it is in plain text and does not use any binary data, an XML document can be understood by any platform, whether the platform is UNIX, Windows, Mac, etc. Another major benefit of XML is it is Web enabled. XML is closely related to HyperText Markup Language (HTML). There is already huge infrastructure and support for HTML in the marketplace. The existing investments can be leveraged to use XML. As enterprises migrate toward internet-based technologies, XML becomes a natural choice as the format for exchanging information between organizations.

XML Process Definition Language (XPDL)

XPDL is deeply rooted in the workflow technology. It is based on the Workflow Process Definition Language (WPDL) published by the WfMC in 1999. WPDL was designed as an interchange format to allow two WPDL–compliant BPMS products to exchange process definitions. The vision was for the process definition to be executable by another BPMS that can import the WPDL process definition, once a WPDL definition has been exported. In 2002, WfMC published a replacement specification for WPDL in XPDL. The major difference between XPDL and WPDL is XPDL is in XML-format while WPDL is not. However, XPDL is not a simple conversion of WPDL to XML. XPDL contains the specification for Web service support that is not present in WPDL.

XPDL contains several elements in its meta-model for process definition. Figure 9.1 illustrates the major elements of a XPDL meta-model. On an individual process level, the highest-level element is the workflow process definition, which encapsulates the business process definition and information about the business process (such as creator, date created, etc.). The workflow process definition is made up of activities and transitions. An XPDL activity is defined as a self-contained unit of work that is to be processed by resources (including humans) or computer applications.[1] The activities are the basic building blocks of the process definition.

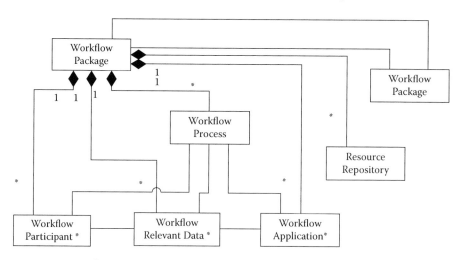

* entities can be redefined in the Workflow Process

Figure 9.1   XPDL Meta-Model. (WfMC. 2002. Workflow Process Definition Interface — XML Process Definition Language. Document Number WFMC-TC-1025. p. 13. copyright@2002 Workflow Management Coalition.)

What we just described can be called an atomic activity. As we will see when we discuss BPML and BPEL, XPDL is different from the other two standards in that it uses only two types of atomic activities. An atomic activity is either normal or relevant for the application. The difference between the two is an application-relevant atomic activity invokes an application function while a normal activity involves human interaction with no work performed by an application.

Aside from the atomic activity, activities can belong to three other groups: subflow, block, and route. A subflow is an activity that invokes another process definition. The subflow activity contains the input parameters from the parent process to invoke the child process, or sub-process. The child process returns results to the subflow activity through output parameters. The concept is similar to a function call in procedural programming. In the execution of subflow, the data in the parent process might not be available to the subflow. All data relevant for the subflow has to be sent from the parent process using the subflow invocation input parameters. Block activity is a set of activities linked by transitions that are executed. The differences between block activity and subflow activity are subflow activity can be executed asynchronously in a separate thread and subflow activity invokes a separate process instance that can have its own set of data independent from the parent process instance. In block activity, all of the data defined for the process is available to the activities in the block. Route activity is used for routing. The route activity is a dummy activity used to model a complex cascading transition condition. The example given in the XPDL specification is using route activity to specify if–then–else transition requirements.

An activity is linked to another activity by transition. The transition specifies the from activity, the to activity, and the condition that has to be fulfilled from the transition to occur. The transition can use the script language specified in the package to define expressions for a transition condition. Using transition, it is possible to perform a split and join. A split models the situation where multiple outgoing transitions are possible for an activity. A join models the situation where multiple incoming transitions are possible for an activity. Both a split and a join can be further qualified by AND and XOR restrictions. An AND split is a situation where the multiple threads of activities are executed, one for each transition that evaluates to true. An XOR split is a situation where only one thread out of the many possible transitions is executed. The first transition that evaluates to true in an XOR split is executed. XOR is an exclusive execution of many possibilities while AND is an inclusive execution of all the transitions that evaluate to true. Similarly, the same concepts apply to a join behavior. An AND join is a situation where all the incoming transitions have to be true for the activity to be executed. In contrast, a

XOR join executes the activity if one of the many incoming transitions evaluates to true. In the transition condition, exceptions can be specified. When an exception condition has been met, the transition goes to the activity associated with the exception condition. Similarly, a default to activity can be specified to which that transition would go when the transition condition is not met.

Other than workflow process definition, activity, and transition, other XPDL elements are package, application, participant, and workflow-relevant data. The element application refers to an information technology (IT) application that is invoked by an activity in the workflow process. The application definition contains the invocation parameters for invoking an application. A participant is assigned to an activity as the executioner of the activity. The participant can be a person, group of people, or an external IT application. Any participant in a workflow process has to be defined using the participant element. Workflow-relevant data is the set of data used in the workflow process definition. The workflow-relevant data can be passed from one activity to another, and the data can be used to determine conditions for activity transitions. XPDL specifies a set of data types that should be supported. A package consists of multiple workflow process definitions. This is a logical grouping that associates the process definitions with the sets of participants, applications, and shared data. Instead of defining sets of participants and applications for each workflow process definition, a package allows one set of participants and applications to be shared by the workflow process definitions within the package. At the package level, the scripting language used for the building expressions can be specified. Some specified scripting languages include javascript and vbscript. XPDL does not specify the syntax supported for each scripting language. This can create a compatibility problem when XPDL process definitions are exchanged between different BPMSs.

One XPDL feature that is worth mentioning is elements workflow process and activity contain attributes that can be used for simulation and cost calculation. Workflow process has attributes for waiting time, working time, and estimated time. The activity element contains attributes for average cost, waiting time, working time, and time estimation. Using these attributes, simulations can be built. Also, cost can be calculated for each process instance.

Business Process Modeling Language (BPML)

Whereas XPDL is a graph-structured language, BPML is a block-structured language. A graph in computer science is a set of nodes connected to by arcs. A directed graph, which is what XPDL is based on, is a graph where the arcs have direction. The arcs and nodes can have labels attached to them. There is an entire academic discipline that focuses on graph theory. Using graphs, it is possible to model a myriad of situations. One of the most widely known is using graph theory to calculate the traveling salesman problem. The problem is to find the cheapest cost for a roundtrip itinerary that involves a set of cities.

Block structured is a programming construct that uses blocks. A block is a logical grouping of code. The block can contain its own data declaration. One block can be nested in another block. When a block is nested, it can access the data declared in the parent block. Block-structured program operates procedurally in a top-down fashion. The blocks can be executed recursively in loops. Basically, any modern procedural language, such as C or Pascal, can be considered a block-structured language. Object-oriented programming builds on the concepts of block-structured language to include such features as inheritance and polymorphism. Most programming languages supports block-structured features. Graph-structured language is easier for humans to understand. Graph-structured language is less constrained than block-structured language. While it is possible to translate a block-structured flow into a graph-structured flow, it is not always possible to translate graph-structured flow into a block-structured flow.[2]

In terms of modeling elements, BPML uses the following elements: package, activity, process, context, signal, property, schedule, and exception. Figure 9.2 illustrates the high-level BPML meta-model. BPML package equates to an XPDL package. The package contains the process definitions and information shared by the process definitions in the package. This information includes namespace, properties, features, etc. We will define property in a following paragraph. Features listed in the package inform a BPMS that it needs to support the features listed to be able to process all the process definitions in the package. BPML does not provide a specific set of features. It allows a BPML package to list the features by name and by universal resource identifier (URI).

BPML defines an activity generically as an element that performs a specific function.[3] There are simple and complex activities. A simple activity is an atomic activity that fits the definition above. Unlike XPDL, which only has application and normal atomic activities, BPML is more granular in that it provides ten simple activity types. The list of simple activity types are listed in Table 9.1. A complex activity is composed of other activities. With the complex activity construct, it is possible to create a complex activity from other complex activities and simple activities. Activities can be grouped in an activity set. A complex activity can contain one or more activity sets. In such a situation, the complex activity needs to select the activity set to execute. A complex activity type choice waits for an event to be triggered to execute the activity set associated with the

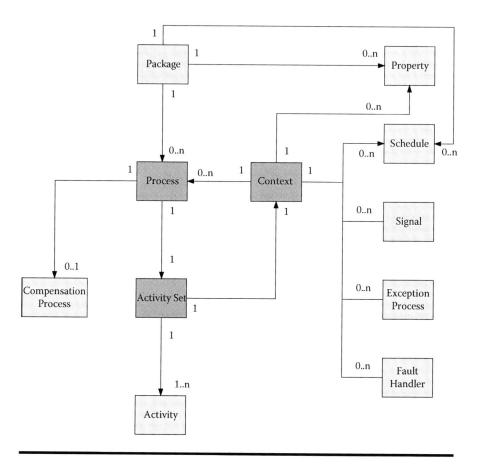

Figure 9.2   BPML Meta-Model.

triggered event. Complex activity type switch evaluates a condition to determine which activity set to execute. The choice and switch activity types are the only two that involve a choice between multiple activity sets. The other complex activity types are associated with one activity. The definitions of complex activity types are listed in Table 9.2.

The activities in the activity set shares the same context. The context is a BPML element that defines the environment for executing the activities. It is a container for the related activities. Data, or properties in BPML, can be defined specific for a context. Aside from properties, a context definition can contain exception processes, processes, schedules, signals, and fault handlers. The processes specified in the context definition are nested processes. These nested processes can be instantiated only in the instance of that context definition. When a child process is created, the child context inherits from the parent context. The child context also can include local definitions not included in the parent context.

Table 9.2 BPML Activity Types

Simple Activity	Description
action	This activity maps sends or receives messages. It maps incoming messages to input parameters and output parameters to outbound messages. The operations performed by this activity can be mapped to a Web service operation.
assign	Updates property with new value.
call	Starts a process instance and waits for the process instance to complete processing.
compensate	Reverts the work performed by process instance being compensated.
delay	Waits for a specified amount of time before proceeding with process execution.
empty	This is a dummy activity that does nothing.
fault	Throws a fault in the processing context.
raise	Issues a signal to be processed by matching *synch* activity.
spawn	Starts a process instance without waiting for the process instance to complete before proceeding.
synch	Waits for a matching signal before proceeding with processing. It behaves like an event listener.
Complex Activity	
all	Executes all the activities in the activity set in parallel.
choice	Executes one of the many activity sets it contains based on matching event.
foreach	Executes the activities in sequential order multiple times based on selection expression.
sequence	Executes the activities in the activity set in sequential order.
switch	Executes one of many activities it contains based on condition.
until	Executes the activities in sequential order multiple times until a condition has been met.
while	Executes the activities in sequential order multiple times while a condition has been met.

In BPML, a process is a type of complex activity. It has its own definitions. A process can contain a context definition, an instantiating event, parameters, an activity set, a persistence flag, and a compensation process. The instantiating event definition contains information on how a process can be instantiated. The instantiating event can be an incoming message, an action activity, or a signal. Parameters definition specifies the inputs for instantiating a process instance and outputs provided by the process instance. The process definition can contain the activity set it is executing, whether the process should be persisted, and the compensation process to revert back work associated with the process. The persistence flag means the process instance state data should be kept and be retrievable after system failure or after the process instance has completed.

A property is like variable of other programming languages. A property has a name and a property instance has a value. This is similar to a variable name and the value of the variable. A property instance is contained in a context instance. Thus, properties are instance variables that belong to a context and can be used by all activities in the context. When compared to XPDL, the property is similar to the workflow relevant data. BPML specifies that BPML–compliant BPMS should support expressions built using XML Path Language (XPath). The values in the properties can be changed using the assign simple activity. A signal is used to coordinate the execution of activities. A signal belongs to a context. A signal is raised by the raise simple activity. To catch raised signals, BPML uses the synch simple activity. The synch activity listens for a named signal that has been raised. Once the matching signal has been detected, the synch activity proceeds with processing the signal instance. In a way, signals are like events that are generated and handled. Activities can also listen for signals to start their processing. Signals cannot cross a context boundary.

BPML has a specification for a schedule. The schedule triggers events based on time. This is similar to a job scheduler. A schedule instance can invoke only one process instance at any time. A schedule instance is akin to a step in a batch job schedule. Another specification contained in BPML is exception handling. An exception process reacts to exception signals or an input message for termination of processing. In addition to exception process, BPML specifies a fault handler to handle situations when an activity cannot complete successfully. In a fault situation, an exception signal has not been explicitly raised. Fault handlers are associated with context definitions. When an activity does not complete normally, it can abort with a fault. The fault handler handles the fault generated in the context. The compensation process is related to exception process and fault handler. A compensation process is a process that reverts effects of the parent process. BPML does not have a specification for its own transaction protocol. It assumes BPMS products sharing the same BPML process package will use the same transaction protocol (BTP, X/OPEN, etc.).

How does BPML relate to Web services? One of the most important BPML activity types is the action activity. This activity is used to receive and send Web service requests. When the action activity is used, it references a WSDL port type and a WSDL operation. In the case of invoking a Web service, the action activity could also contain the location of the Web service. In situations where inbound messages could belong to one of many context instances in a process instance, the action activity can utilize the correlate feature of WSDL and pass on the value so the message could be associated with the correct activity instance. Because BPML process can be instantiated by an action activity, the BPML process can be exposed when the action activity references an incoming WSDL operation and port type.

Business Process Execution Language (BPEL)

BPEL is the merger of two separate standards, Web Services for Business Process Design (XLANG) from Microsoft and Web Services Flow Language (WSFL) from IBM. XLANG is a block-structure language, while WSFL is a graph-structured language. Because of its two different roots, BPEL is a block-structured language that allows for graph-structured constructs. This is done using a flow activity type. In addition to a process definition language like BPML and XPDL, BPEL also provides a process interface as Web services for other systems to invoke, update, and query running BPEL process instances. BPEL is both a process definition and a process interaction standard. In this section, we will discuss the process definition aspects of BPEL.

The main elements of BPEL are process, activity, partner link, compensation handler, fault handler, event handler, and correlation set.[4] Figure 9.3 illustrates the high-level meta-model of BPEL. The process is the highest level entity in BPEL. In contrast to XPDL and BPML, there is no package element that binds resources and other shared entities to BPEL process definitions. There are two types of processes: abstract and executable. An abstract process is used to define a business protocol. The example given in the BPEL specification is to think of the abstract processes as the business processes a buyer and a seller would execute in a business protocol. The two abstract processes would be linked by partner links and they would exchange protocol-relevant messages.[5] Abstract process can be used to govern the sequencing of an executable process. In a B2B scenario, the abstract process would define what messages can be exchanged during which stages of the B2B process. Another way to look

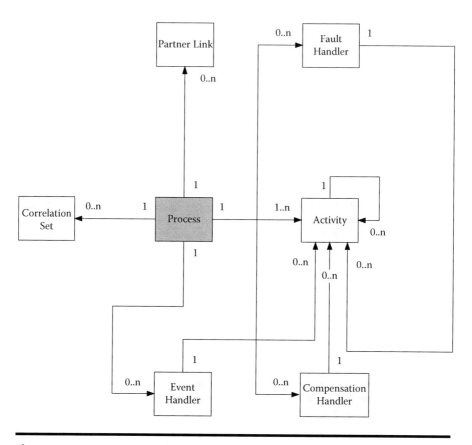

Figure 9.3 BPEL Meta-Model.

at an abstract process is it does not specify the internal computations of the business process. This means it cannot be used for data field assignments. The internal definitions of the buyer's and seller's business processes are hidden. Only the parts of the buyer's and seller's business processes that require cross-enterprise interaction are modeled in the abstract process. In terms of Web service, abstract process defines the interfaces for a Web service, whereas an executable process is a complete specification for the Web service. An executable process is similar to a process in XPDL and BPML. The executable process describes the exact behavior of a business process. This executable process can be implemented and transported between different BPMS products. At the process level, process wide attributes can be assigned. Some of these attributes include query language and expression language. A query language can be used to query the process attributes and the states of activities in the process. The default query language for BPEL is XPath. An expression language can be used to include Boolean, deadline-based, duration-based, and assignment expressions. As with a query language, the default expression language is XPath.

As in XPDL and BPML, a BPEL process is made up of activities. There are two types of activities: basic and structured. A basic activity is analogous to an atomic activity in XPDL and a simple activity in BPML. There are three basic activities for communication purposes: receive, invoke, and reply. The receive construct allows the process to wait for a message to arrive. Using the receive activity, processing is blocked until the message arrives. The reply activity is used in response to the receive activity. It is a reply to the message that has been received by the receive activity. The invoke activity allows the business process to invoke a Web service operation on a port type offered by a partner. The partner does not have to be an external business partner; it could be an internal application that has been exposed as a Web service. The other basic activities are assign, throw, exit, wait, empty, compensate, and rethrow. The definitions for each of these basic activity types are provided in Table 9.3.

A structured activity is an activity used for control flow. According to BPEL specifications, "structured activities prescribed the order in which a collection of activities take place."[5] We can roughly equate BPEL structured activity to BPML complex activity and XPDL block activity. BPEL structured activities can be composed of other structured activities as well as basic activities. The six BPEL structured activities are sequence, while, switch, pick, flow, and scope. The sequence activity contains a series of activities that are processed sequentially. The while activity executes a series of activities multiple times. The iteration stops when the condition associated with the while activity has been fulfilled. The switch activity contains several branches; each branch is associated with a condition. The first branch that has its condition fulfilled is executed. If no branch condition is fulfilled, an otherwise branch can be specified and executed within the switch construct. The pick activity listens for a set of events. The pick construct contains a branch for every event it is listening for. When an event occurs that matches one within the set, the branch matching the event is processed.

The flow structured activity is used for concurrent processing of activities and to synchronize activities. There is a link construct that is used with flow to link activities within the flow. The use of flow and link allows graph-like control flows to be designed. Within the flow activity, several activities can be concurrently processed. The activities can be nested within the flow activity. Also, the activities within the flow can be synchronized with the link construct. The link is somewhat similar to the transition in the graph-structured language. A link has to have source activity and a target activity. The source activity can contain a transition condition while

Table 9.3 BPEL Activity Types

Basic Activity	Description
assign	Updates the variable values.
compensate	Reverts work completed normally by a process instance. Can only be invoked in the fault or compensation handler.
empty	This is a dummy activity that performs no work. It can be used to synchronize concurrent activities.
exit	Terminates the execution of the process instance.
invoke	Initiates a request/response or one-way request to a partner port type. It is a Web service call.
receive	This activity blocks processing until a matching message has been received. Receiving a message can instantiate a business process.
reply	This activity sends a response message as a result of a corresponding *receive* activity.
rethrow	Rethrows a fault that has been encountered by a fault handler.
throw	Generates a fault during execution of a process instance.
wait	Suspends processing for a specified period of time.
Structured Activity	
sequence	Executes activities in sequential order.
switch	Selects one of many branches to process based on condition.
while	Repeats an activity or activities while a condition holds true.
pick	This activity listens for a set of messages and it initiates processing when the first message it listens for has arrived.
flow	Allows one or more activities to be performed concurrently. Can use *link* construct to link activities within the flow activity.
scope	Allows activity to be defined with its own nested variables, exception handlers and compensation handler.

the target activity can contain a join condition. The equivalence between flow and graph-structured language is not complete however. BPEL places restrictions on using the link construct. For example, a link cannot cross a boundary of a while activity and the source activity cannot be preceded by the target activity. Thus, BPEL allows an acyclic graph, in which the nodes cannot go into a loop. The scope activity is the last structured activity. The scope activity defines the execution boundary for the activities it contains. It can be used to specify the boundary for a fault handler, a compensation handler, and a transaction boundary.

The partner is a BPEL element used to define any party that interacts with the BPEL business process. Some examples of partners are customer, vendor, shipper, internal Web service–enabled application, etc. Each of the partners interacts with the process through partner link type. A partner link type is a set of related Web services and the roles that participate in these services. For example, the partner link type transportation link might contain two roles, shipper and carrier. The carrier role contains the WSDL port type to receive a shipping order. The shipper role contains the WSDL port type for the carrier to contact the shipper. In a BPEL process, the process can specify what role the owner of a business process performs for each partner link type. Once the partner link is included in the process, the process can use all of the Web services included by the WSDL port type. For example, using the receive activity, a BPEL process for the carrier to handle a transportation order might receive a request from a Web service operation defined in the partner link type definition. The partner link is the connection of the BPEL process with internal and external Web services. In the receive activity, the input variable would correspond to the XML document received by the Web service.

BPEL contains two related mechanisms for error handling: compensation handler and fault handler. The compensation handler reverses the state changes caused by the activities within the compensation scope. The scope is the name of the scope structured activity that is given to the compensation handler. The fault handler is used to handle exceptions raised by the throw basic activity or as a fault response when from an invoke basic activity. The fault handler contains a catch construct used to specify activity to perform for each fault. In BPEL, fault handling is defined as the reversal of work performed within the scope that raised the fault. Consequently, the compensation handler is always invoked as part of the fault handler. The BPEL compensation handling does not cross business process instances, and it does not apply to situations requiring coordinated compensation among distributed participants. Contrary to the fault handler being used for abnormal scope behavior, the event handler is normal processing. The event handler is used to handle events that have arrived to the business process. An event handler is associated with a scope. The scope might be the general business process instance scope or nested scope within the business process instance. In the event handler, actions and activities can be specified for the arrival of each event. An event could be a request that requires a response or it may be a one-way asynchronous event that requires no response.

BPEL recognizes that messages being exchanged sometimes require data from previous messages. Thus, it provides a correlation set element to relate the data between the different messages belonging to the same scope. As an example, the correlation set could be a sales order instance. The correlation set might contain values for customer number and customer order number. A correlation set can be specified for invoke, receive, and reply basic activities. The message associated with these activities will carry the properties defined for the specified correlation set. Correlation set and partner link are useful for Web service interaction. A Web service could take a request from several different partners and make several concurrent process instances. Using correlation sets allows the messages to be routed to the correct process instance the Web service is processing.

Comparing XML Process Definition Language (XPDL), Business Process Modeling Language (BPML), and Business Process Execution Language (BPEL)

Recently there has been significant interest in academic circles regarding BPMS standards. Just as several technologies converge to form BPMS, academic segments studying the various technologies converge on the BPMS field. Technology standards are manifestations of the fundamental features of the different implementations of a particular technology. The study of standards is useful because it provides objective analysis of the strengths and weaknesses of the standards. This sort of analysis helps to guide the industry in standards development and adaptation. The relative merits are not the only factor in the ultimate survival of a standard. Other factors like the clout of the vendors supporting a standard and the marketing of a particular standard also affect the ultimate market adaptation. Nevertheless, academic research into standards comparison is helpful to educate and inform the industry.

To study standards, there needs to be a framework for the comparative analysis. One of the frameworks is based on a collection of workflow patterns. Van der Aalst et al. compiled a list of workflow patterns in 2000 to serve as framework for comparing the various workflow management systems that were on the market at the time.[6] After BPMS standards are published, this framework has been used to analyze several of the popular standards. Some of the BPMS standards that have been analyzed using the workflow pattern framework include XPDL, BPML, and BPEL. We will explore the differences van der Aalst et al. noted in their studies. These patterns originate from the workflow management system world and they represent control flow features that are useful for process modeling. Because control flow represents only a portion of the standard specifications, we will also investigate the differences in meta-model, support for human participation, transaction support, exception handling, and cross-enterprise collaboration.

Meta-Model Comparison

Looking at the meta-models of XPDL, BPEL, and BPML, we can see they share several similar elements. At the highest level, XPDL and BPML both utilize the concept of a package. This element is missing from BPEL. A package allows definitions to be shared by different process definitions. The package concept is useful in reducing duplicate definitions used by multiple processes.

XPDL contains the application element not present in BPEL and BPML. The XPDL applications defined in the package definition could be used for an application activity. An application definition contains specific call parameters to an external application. An example of the call might be check order status. In the process definition, the activity names the application it wants to invoke and passes the application actual data for the parameters the application invocation needs. The inclusion of application abstracts the activity definition from the invocation to the application. This means if the application for the invocation is changed to another platform or the invocation mechanism is changed (e.g., from synchronous API call to Web service), the definition in the activity will not be affected. BPEL assumes all interactions are through Web services. It contains partner links and port types to define the communication requirements for invoking and receiving Web services. The BPEL partner link is associated with WSDL definitions for the various Web services. BPML also uses Web service for application interaction. The Web service communication is defined through WSDL. A BPML action activity can be used to receive or invoke a Web service. The action activity references a WSDL through the port type attribute. The WSDL contains information to execute the interaction. BPEL and BPML use WSDL for integration with internal and external applications, while XPDL uses the application element to define mechanism for application integration.

The activity element is present in all three standards. XPDL uses atomic activity, BPML contains simple activity, and BPEL has basic activity types.

In contrast to the numerous simple and basic activities, XPDL specifies two atomic activities. A XPDL atomic activity could be relevant for human interaction or application action. BPML and BPEL definitions of activity are more granular. For example, BPML contains different activities for assigning property values, invoking Web service, raising faults, compensating work done, etc. Similarly, BPEL contains different activities for receiving Web service, replying to a Web service request, invoking a Web service, assigning variable values, etc. With the more granular approach, BPEL and BPML are more expressive and they are better suited for detailed process definition.

In terms of the higher-level activity, XPDL has block activity, BPML contains complex activity, and BPEL uses structured activity. Because XPDL is a graph-structured language, it does not support looping constructs such as the while activity of BPEL and BPML. However, because XPDL is graph structured, it does not need to have specific activities to perform a looping operation. It can employ a cyclical transition until a transition condition has been reached. XPDL uses block activity to execute a sequence of activities. In his paper comparing XPDL, BPEL, and BPML, Shapiro observed that most features of BPML complex activities can be modeled using XPDL block activities.[2] In another paper comparing BPEL and BPML, Mendling and Müller noted that BPML complex activities can be mapped to BPEL structured activities. The BPML activities foreach and until have no direct equivalence in BPEL. However, BPEL can use the while activity to express the foreach and until BPML features.[7]

BPML uses context to define the processing boundary. BPEL uses scope for the same purpose. The concept of processing boundary is not present in XPDL. This deficiency in XPDL impacts its ability for error handling and compensation process. On the other hand, XPDL provides a participant element that has no direct equivalence in BPEL and BPML. In terms of similarities, BPEL and BPML are more similar to each other than they are to XPDL.

Human Participation Support

With the participant element, XPDL provides direct support for assigning a participant to a process activity. The participant can be a role, organizational unit, human, or system. The participant is the actual entity that executes the process activity. In the participant definition, an external reference can be included that points to an organizational model or resource repository. Neither BPEL nor BPML provide support for participant assignment. Thus, XPDL is more suited to modeling person-to-person processes than BPEL and BPML.

Transaction Support and Error Handling

Both BPEL and BPML provide definitions for processing boundaries. BPEL has scope and BPML has context. It is possible to delineate the transactional context across multiple activities within a process definition using context or scope. In transaction processing, BPML context and BPEL scope define the transactional context in the process definition. The activities in the process definition communicate the transactional context to the applications involved in the activities. All the applications involved in the transactional context would have to use the same transaction protocol. The available protocols include Business Transaction Protocol (BTP) from OASIS, WS-Transaction from IBM, Microsoft, and BEA and XA from X/Open. The transaction protocol actually implements the two-phase commit. BPEL and BPML provide the context for the transaction protocol to manage the transaction. XPDL does not have an equivalent element to BPEL scope and BPML context. Thus, it would require extended attributes to implement transactional support using XPDL.

The error handling mechanisms are similar between BPML and BPEL. Both contain a fault handler construct. Both also provide a compensation mechanism to revert data back to the state prior to an error. XPDL does not provide a construct for a compensation mechanism nor does it provide any explicit error handling mechanism. The closest XPDL attribute for exception handling is the deadline attribute included in the activity definition. The deadline attribute defines the length of time in which an activity has to be active before a deadline exception is raised. On raising the deadline exception, an exception transition can be followed that leads to other activity or subflow.

Cross-Enterprise Collaboration

BPEL is a specification that is well suited for cross-enterprise collaboration. It is designed to use WSDL and Web services for all kinds of application and cross-enterprise interactions. Using BPEL, specific partner interactions and correlation of sequence of messages in a cross-enterprise process can be defined. In a business process, a business partner can invoke Web services defined in the BPEL process or receive Web service invocations. Thus BPEL is as much a process interaction standard as it is a process definition standard.

BPML also aims to be a process interaction standard as much as a process definition standard. BPML leverages WSDL and Web services for application and partner interaction. Compared to BPEL, BPML is not as detailed and structured for facilitating cross-enterprise collaboration. There is no correlation set concept in BPML that exists in BPEL. The feature closest to the correlation set is the BPML correlate function, which helps to link an incoming message to the correct activity of process instance. This is different from the BPEL correlation set, which links all of the messages of a Web service conversation. This is useful because a Web service can hold several concurrent conversations. Furthermore, BPML simply assigns the URI of a WSDL for interaction with a business partner. BPEL provides many more implementation details in its use of partner link.

In contrast to BPEL and BPML, XPDL does not provide much support for cross-enterprise collaboration. It is more of a static model for describing the business process definition. It does not provide the mechanism to receive a request or an incoming message. It can be extended to invoke an application using a Web service. However, that requires implementation-specific extended attributes to be defined. According to the WfMC Workflow Reference Model, the purpose of XPDL is process definition. Wf-XML is specified for process interaction. Process interaction not withstanding, XPDL, as a process definition language, has not embraced the service-oriented approach as much as BPEL and BPML have. Using a Web service requires implementation of an external reference. In contrast, BPEL and BPML require a Web service to be used for an application and for partner interactions.

Control Flow Comparison

The workflow pattern framework that Professor W. M. P. van der Aalst, of the Technische Universiteit Eindhoven, devised is helpful in understanding the expressiveness of a process definition language. Van der Aalst et al. published three articles describing BPEL, BPML, and XPDL, respectively, in terms of the workflow pattern framework.[8–10] In this section, we will look into the various patterns that are included in the framework. Table 9.4 contains the descriptions for the 20-workflow patterns in the framework. Table 9.5 illustrates support for these workflow patterns by BPEL, BPML, and XPDL.

The analyses performed by van der Aalst et al. show interesting results. They found XPDL to be the least expressive of the three process definition standards. Comparing XPDL specification to several workflow management systems, they found that XPDL specifies the intersection of features provided by these workflow management systems rather than the union of features. While BPML and BPEL support deferred choice workflow pattern, which chooses one of several alternative paths based on arrival of an event, XPDL does not support this pattern. Related to the lack of an error handling mechanism, XPDL does not support cancel activity and cancel case patterns in the workflow pattern framework. These two patterns allow activity or process instance to be terminated.

Table 9.4 Workflow Patterns

Workflow Pattern	Description
Sequence	Activities are performed sequentially; subsequent activity is started after the previous activity has completed.
Parallel Split	A point in the process where the processing splits into two concurrent branches.
Synchronization	A point where multiple branches converge in the process into one processing thread.
Exclusive Choice	One of several branches is chosen based on condition.
Simple Merge	Several alternative branches that are not executed in parallel converge without synchronization.
Multi-Choice	Based on a decision, several branches are selected and executed in parallel.
Synchronizing Merge	Several paths converge into one path and one processing thread. Some of the paths are active and some are not active. The activity, after synchronizing merge, performs only after all paths arrive at the point of synchronizing merge.
Multi-Merge	The convergence of multiple branches without synchronization. The activity after the point of multi-merge gets executed for every active branch converged.
Discriminator	Waits for one incoming branch to complete before starting a subsequent activity. It does not until after all the incoming branches arrive; then it resets for activation again. This is useful in a looping situation.
Arbitrary Cycle	Repeatedly visits any point in the process without restriction on number, location, and nesting. This flow control is more arbitrary than the entry and exit points provided by *while* construct.
Implicit Termination	Process is terminated when there is nothing left to be performed. There is no need for an explicit process termination activity.
Multiple Instances without Synchronization	Multiple instances of an activity are created and run in independent threads.

Table 9.4 (continued)   Workflow Patterns

Workflow Pattern	Description
Multiple Instances with Prior Design Time Knowledge	Multiple instances of an activity are created and synchronized before performing a subsequent activity. The number of instances to be created is known during design time.
Multiple Instances with Prior Runtime Knowledge	Multiple instances of an activity are created and synchronized before performing a subsequent activity. The number of instances to be created is known at some point during runtime.
Multiple Instance without Prior Runtime Knowledge	Multiple instance of activity are created and synchronized before performing a subsequent activity. The number of instances is not known until after all the required instances have been created.
Deferred Choice	Several branches exist at a point in the process. The choice of which branch to execute is not made until the arrival of an event.
Interleaved Parallel Routing	A set of activities is executed in arbitrary order. The sequence of activities to execute is decided at runtime. The decision for follow-on activity is made after an activity has completed.
Milestone	An activity is executed after another activity (the milestone) has completed and a follow-on activity to the milestone activity has not started.
Cancel Activity	Terminates processing of an activity instance.
Cancel Case	Terminates processing of a process instance.

Source: Wohed, P., van der Aalst, W.M.P., Dumas, M., and A.H.M. ter Hofstede. 2003. Analysis of Web Services Composition Languages: The case for BPEL4WS. *22nd International Conference on Conceptual Modeling (ER 2003).* Volume 2813 of *Lecture Notes in Computer Science.* Springer-Verlag. Berlin. 200–215.

Given the close resemblance of BPML and BPEL we discovered thus far in our discussion, it is not surprising to find that BPML and BPEL are similar in their support for the workflow pattern framework. Because BPEL also uses construct derived from graph-structured language, it is slightly more expressive than BPML. Using flow and link constructs, BPEL can easily express multi-choice and synchronizing merge workflow patterns, while BPML has to rely on extensive workarounds to implement these patterns.

Table 9.5 Support for Workflow Patterns by BPEL, BPML, and XPDL

Workflow Pattern	BPEL	BPML	XPDL
Sequence	X	X	X
Parallel Split	X	X	X
Synchronization	X	X	X
Exclusive Choice	X	X	X
Simple Merge	X	X	X
Multi-Choice	X		X
Synchronizing Merge	X		X
Multi-Merge		X/-	
Discriminator			
Arbitrary Cycle			X
Implicit Termination	X	X	X
Multiple Instances without Synchronization	X	X	X
Multiple Instances with Prior Design Time Knowledge	X	X	X
Multiple Instances with Prior Runtime Knowledge			
Multiple Instance without Prior Runtime Knowledge			
Deferred Choice	X	X	
Interleaved Parallel Routing	X/-		
Milestone			
Cancel Activity	X	X	
Cancel Case	X	X	

Note: X/- means partial support for the pattern.

Source: Van der Aalst, W.M.P. 2003. Patterns and XPDL: A Critical Evaluation of the XML Process Definition Language. QUT Technical Report FIT-TR-2003-06. Queensland University of Technology. Brisbane, Australia.

Summary of Process Definition Standards Comparison

Based on the comparison, we can generalize that XPDL is better suited for modeling processes that contain non-Web services application interactions and nonsystemic participants (e.g., humans). BPEL and BPML are better integrated to Web services and can easily expose processes as Web services. The tight integration to Web services makes BPEL and BPML more suitable for modeling processes involves cross-enterprise interactions. As Web services have become the technology of choice for implementing cross-enterprise business process integration, BPEL and BPML are more suitable for modeling these processes than XPDL. XPDL provides attributes that are useful for simulation and cost calculations. These attributes are useful for optimizing process design and measuring the costs associated with a particular business processes. With regard to implementation, BPEL and BPML offer key exception handling and context capabilities that XPDL does not provide. If BPEL and BPML do not enhance their standards with specifications for human participants, their relevance for BPM is limited to system-to-system processes. XPDL provides the most comprehensive features for designing complex person-to-person processes. As they stand right now, all three process definition standards have room for improvement.

Overview of Process Interaction Standards

In the previous sections, we discussed process definition standards. In reality, it is hard to distinguish between process definition standards and process interaction standards. Several standards embody both process definition elements and process interaction protocols. The best example of a comprehensive process definition and interaction standard is BPEL. Not only does BPEL offer control flow elements to define business processes, it has rich semantics for defining Web services interactions. For our discussion, we will define process interactions standards as those standards that allow entities (external partners or internal resources) to interact with a business process through Web services. The current technology trend is to use Web services and implement service-oriented architecture. This architectural approach allows organizations to leverage existing infrastructure and utilize widely adopted internet technologies. Furthermore, the architectural allows inter- and intra-enterprise communication. Therefore, Web service and service-oriented architecture (SOA) have been adopted as the technology basis for most process interaction standards. Before we discuss the process interaction standards, we will delve a little into SOA and the Web services stack.

Service-Oriented Architecture

Service-oriented architecture is the new buzzword in the IT field. It evolved from the concept of application programming interface (API). The API exposes an application's function to the outside world through an established component model and a service contract (e.g., interface definition language). We refer to componentized APIs as component interfaces. The concepts of components and interfaces are discussed in Chapter 6.

The component interface service contract guarantees an invoking client will receive output in a predefined format if the specified inputs have been received by the application. The service contract is central to component-based architecture. In component-based architecture, software components are assembled to create a software solution. The assembly of components is done by integrating the services of individual components through their interfaces. The software solution could be a composite component made of an interwoven set of components. The component functions are clearly documented through an interface definition language thus eliminating the need to tamper with the internal component code. SOA is the fusion of component-based architecture with Web services. Instead of using RPC–style communication, SOA uses SOAP over HTTP as its communication medium. The Web service definition language has replaced the component interface definition language. Another aspect of component interfaces is the interface repository. This has been replaced by service registries such as Universal, Description, Discovery, and Integration (UDDI).

Is SOA simply a replacement for API–based architectures? The answer is no. SOA allows both inter-enterprise and intra-enterprise communication, whereas API–based communication is generally limited to intra-enterprise scenarios. In the past, architectures that used APIs for application communication had a hard time passing through firewalls of external enterprises. SOA uses HTTP, which is a protocol most firewalls allow to pass through. SOA also relies on technologies (i.e., HTTP and XML) that have been widely adopted by organizations. API–based communication requires the invoking client and the receiving target to use the same component model (i.e., CORBA, J2EE, .NET, etc.). The component model requirement and the difficulty of communication through a firewall using RPC–style communication render API–based communication effective only for intra-enterprise scenarios.

Supporters for SOA are envisioning it as the unifier of the different application integration mechanisms. In a typical organization, it is not unusual to find applications built using various technologies including COBOL, Java, COM, CORBA, etc. These application technologies are tied to incompatible component technologies. Implementing SOA would mean the entire core functions of these applications are exposed as compatible Web services. There is no longer the headache of making a COM component talk to a CORBA component. The wholesale technology shift toward Web services means even older technologies, such as COBOL applications, can be made to expose its functions as Web services. Leveraging existing infrastructures by upgrading them to be Web services–compatible is one of the great attractions of SOA.

Web Services Stack

What are the main ingredients of SOA? SOA is an architectural approach that places heavy emphasis on Web services. All of the functions offered by applications and external partners are in the form of Web services. In this Web services-centric world, there needs to be a hierarchy of different protocols to enable SOA. There is no consensus on the definitive Web services stack. Figure 9.4 offers a generic stack.

The lowest level of the Web services stack is the transport layer. Key concepts of SOA are to build, using widely available standards and to leverage the internet. With this guiding philosophy, the transport layer of the Web services stack uses widely accepted internet protocols. The most

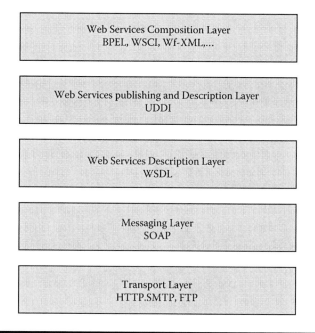

Figure 9.4 Web Services Stack.

common support for the transport layer is HyperText Transfer Protocol (HTTP). Other internet protocols, such as Simple Mail Transfer Protocol ((SMTP) (email)) and File Transfer Protocol ((FTP) (file transfer)), are supported to a lesser extent. All three of these application-level transport protocols use Transmission Control Protocol Internet Protocol (TCP/IP) as the underlying network protocol.

Above the transport protocol is the messaging layer. The messaging layer specifies the application message formats and encoding rules for Web service request-and-response messages. The industry has standardized on SOAP as the messaging layer. SOAP messages are created as XML documents and they can be carried using internet protocols such as HTTP, Multipurpose Internet Mail Extensions (MIME), and SMTP. In addition to carrying the message and encoding rules, SOAP also contains the ability to execute a RPC–like call on the Web service that is taking the request.

A SOAP message encodes a Web service request or response. To prepare the SOAP message, the Web service participants need to agree on the message content that a requester should provide and the message content that the receiver should return to the requester. The Web service requester also needs to know how to invoke a Web service. The Web service description layer provides this information. There is growing acceptance of using Web Services Description Language (WSDL) as the standard for the service description layer. The WSDL document describes the address to find the Web service, the input data required to invoke the Web service, the output data the Web service can expect to provide, and whether the Web service supports one-way invocation or response–response invocation.

Now we have the Web service and the description of the Web service, the next step is to find the appropriate Web service. This is the job of the Web service publishing and discovery layer. This layer is akin to the yellow pages for Web service. It is a registry of Web services that can be searched. There are several Web services directories available. The most widely used directory is probably the UDDI directory. It is envisioned that, in the future, applications can be automated to search UDDI for the most appropriate Web service in its application execution. After the Web service has been located using UDDI, a future application can retrieve the WSDL for the Web service and dynamically generate the SOAP message for Web service invocation using the information from the WSDL document. Once this vision becomes reality, the world of computing will be composed of intelligent agent applications that can automatically interact with each other through Web services.

With the layers of the Web services stack that we have discussed thus far, we can now search and invoke Web services. The actions are limited to independent Web service invocations. In the business process collaboration arena, seldom does one business process involve only one contact between business partners. Another mechanism is needed to manage a string of Web services communication that belongs to one conversation or business process instance. This is the job of the Web services choreography–orchestration layer. There is a distinct difference between choreography and orchestration. Choreography defines the rules and agreements governing Web services interactions among collaborating business partners. There is no central point of control. It does not define a process from the perspective of a participating business partner. Orchestration, on the other hand, has a central point of control. An orchestration model defines the Web services interactions of an executable business process from the perspective of a participating business partner. Because of the differences, some industry pundits have used the term Web services composition layer to describe the orchestration–choreography standards. Regardless of whether it is orchestration or choreography, the Web services composition language defines rules that govern business process collaboration. These rules include the sequence of messages allowed, correlation of the messages that belong to one business process instance, transaction and exception handling, and definition of partner roles. In the next sections, we will investigate some of the more prominent Web services composition languages.

Web Services Choreography Interface (WSCI)

The development of WSCI illustrates the extent of standards proliferation. Intalio, BEA, Sun, and SAP submitted WSCI to W3C in 2002. WSCI is the primary input for the W3C's Web Services Choreography Working group. The WSCI standard has an overlap to the BPML standard. Both WSCI and BPML share similar elements. Intalio provided significant input to the development of both standards. In fact, the first draft of BPML included the WSCI specifications. Unlike BPML, which focuses on the process definition, WSCI focuses on interaction of Web services to support a process. These interactions are realized through message exchanges. WSCI is a specification to define the message exchanges between Web services. WSCI does not address the business process that generates the Web services interactions.

There are nine concepts outlined in the WSCI specification document: interface, activity, process, property, context, message correlation, exceptional behavior, transactional behavior, and global model.[11] The interface describes the behavior of a Web service. An interface can contain multiple WSCI processes. A WSCI process is a detailed behavior. For example, the interface OnlineStore might have the processes PlaceSalesOrder and CreateNewCustomer. A WSCI interface can only contain process definitions, and the process is the basic unit of reuse. A WSCI process is composed of activities. An atomic activity is the basic unit in WSCI. The most common atomic activity is an action. An action can be request–response invocation of a Web service, a request-only invocation of a Web service, instantiating a process, sending a notification, etc. An action is bound to some WSDL operation and it contains the role of the participant that performs the action. Using the OnlineStore scenario, an action of PlaceSalesOrder might be ReceiveSalesInquiry. This ReceiveSalesInquiry contains the role OnlineStore because the online store is the one doing the receiving of sales inquiry. The ReceiveSalesInquiry is also bound to a WSDL operation that defines the Web service receiving sales inquiries. A complex activity is composed of atomic activities and other complex activities. The complex activities used for control flow are all, sequence, choice, foreach, and switch. The definitions of these complex activities are the same as the complex activities in BPML with the same names. The other WSCI elements shared with BPML are property and context.

Message correlation is an important aspect of WSCI that is not in BPML. WSCI message correlation is a construct that allows a Web service to distinguish the various conversations it is participating. A Web service constantly receives messages and sends messages. There might be several different business partners that might interact with an OnlineStore Web service. These business partners generate several simultaneous process instances that the Web service has to manage internally. To help the Web service manage the stream of messages that belong to different process instances, the message correlation definition is carried by all messages that need to be correlated. BPEL has a similar mechanism in place for BPEL process instances to identify messages that are part of the process instances.

Like BPEL and BPML, WSCI contains specifications for exception and transaction handling. The WSCI exception handler can react to a fault related to an action, to a timeout situation, or a fault related to the receipt of a message. The exception handler is specified to a context. Transaction behavior is implemented using the transaction element. This element specifies the context of the transaction, and it can be used to include a compensate activity. The compensate activity reverts back a completed transaction for whatever reason.

Other than message correlation, a difference between WSCI and BPML is the global model. The global model describes the Web services interactions through participants, interfaces, and message exchanges. The global model is a documentation tool to depict the high-level overview of a WSCI interaction model.

At this point readers must be wondering about the differences between BPML and WSCI. The primary difference is philosophical. WSCI is used to model Web services interactions as part of a process definition, while

BPML is used to model process definitions that exist behind the interacting Web services. WSCI aims to view the interactions from all the different participants' perspectives, while BPML implements the process definition for one participant. In this manner, BPML process definitions are private in that other process participants cannot see them. BPML process definitions can expose its functions as Web services. These services are then defined by WSCI as interfaces for interacting with participants. In other words, WSCI defines the public portion of a BPML process definition. The designers of WSCI and BPML envisioned complementary roles when they designed these two specifications. Figure 9.5 contains an illustration from the original WSCI specification that will help explain how WSCI can be used.

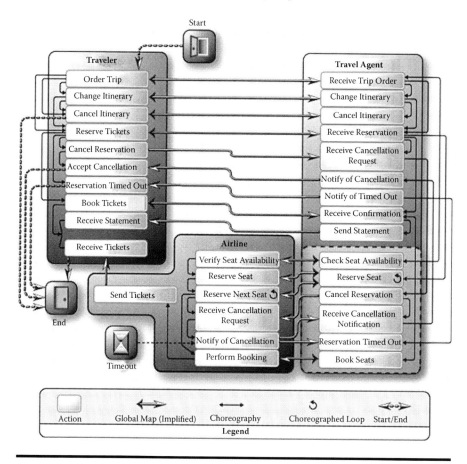

Figure 9.5 WSCI Travel Booking Example. (Copyright © 08/2002 World Wide Web Consortium, (Massachusetts Institute of Technology, European Research Consortium for Informatics and Mathematics, Keio University). All Rights Reserved. http://www.w3.org/Consortium/Legal/2002/copyright-documents-20021231)

In the travel booking example illustrated in Figure 9.5, we see there are three participants in the overall process: traveler, airline, and travel agent. The illustration shows the interface exposed by each participant. For example, the travel agent process is made up of a series of action activities that are linked by the control flow elements. The action activities are only those steps in the travel agent's travel booking process exposed as Web services. They do not represent the entire business process. There might be activities that involve internal employees and applications in the travel agent process. These private activities are not captured by WSCI. The concept of exposing only public activities using WSCI applies to the processes for the traveler and the airline. The WSCI model captures the message sequence, message correlation, and the linkage of partner action activities. For example, the traveler's cancel_reservation action activity is linked to the travel agent's receive_cancellation_request action activity. All the activities shown in Figure 9.5 are linked to WSDL operations. We can think of WSCI as an extension of WSDL for choreographing the interactions of Web services described by the WSDL.

WSCI contains significant overlap with BPML. BPML has a more complete set of atomic activities. WSCI primarily relies on action atomic activity. BPML contains ten simple activities, including action activity. BPML specification contains detailed discussions on defining processes, various activities, and expressions. WSCI is more scant when it comes to discussions of these aspects. This is understandable because of the philosophical focuses of these two specifications. However, WSCI contains many of the elements present in BPML. It is theoretically possible to design rudimentary process definitions using WSCI, even though this is not the purpose for which WSCI is designed.

Workflow Extensible Markup Language (Wf-XML) 2.0

Wf-XML is the WfMC specification for Web service interaction. Wf-XML serves to expose a process definition to the outside using Web services. An external party can retrieve a process definition, change the process definition, invoke a process instance, and change a process instance using Wf-XML. Unlike BPEL and WSCI, Wf-XML does not provide syntax for atomic or complex activities. Instead, it allows a requester to retrieve any active activities in the process instance. Based on the requester's processing logic, any active activities can be updated. Wf-XML specifies operations that a process consumer can use to interact with a process provider. In terms of object-oriented programming, Wf-XML specifies a list of methods that all objects (XPDL processes) should support. There is extensive discussion of Wf-XML 2.0 features in Chapter 7.

Comparison of Business Process Execution Language (BPEL), Web Service Choreography Interface (WSCI), and Workflow Extensible Markup Language (Wf-XML)

These three specifications approach business process interactions in different ways. A BPEL process defines the business process from one business participant's perspective, such as a vendor's sales process, using Web services. One process step or activity might be to create a sales order in the backend ERP system. BPEL would use the invoke activity to invoke the ERP system's CreateSalesOrder Web service. Using a Web service extends the activity to interaction with external parties. In the same BPEL sales process definition, the customer would interact with the process through a partner link. The BPEL process would be exposed as a Web service for the customer to place a sales order. In this sense, BPEL provides the mechanism to define both a private process definition and expose the process as a Web service to other business participants.

As we have seen in the previous section, WSCI takes more of a spectator view for Web services composition. As a choreography language, WSCI facilitates process interactions by providing message exchange. WSCI is implemented on top of WSDL and it is tightly bound to WSDL. This means the collaborating Web services have to implement WSCI in a choreography process. If an organization uses BPML to define business processes, the outside world does not know how to interact with the business process. To interact with the outside, the BPML process definition has to be tied to a Web service. When a message is received from a business partner through a Web service (for example, receive sales order), the Web service sends a message to the BPML to instantiate a BPML process instance. BPML does not generate the Web service, but the Web service is bound to an action activity in the BPML process definition. On the other side, the Web service is bound to WSCI definition for exchange Web service messages. In other words, WSCI contains the public portion of the business process definition that is defined using a process definition language such as BPML. Technically, WSCI does not require a process definition. WSCI is bound to Web services through WSDL. WSCI is tied to a process definition language only if the business process is exposed using WSDL. If a process definition is bound to a Web service, the WSCI choreography definition has to be synchronized with the process definition. The synchronization includes context, messages, transactions, etc.

The differences between BPML and WSCI should be more transparent after the above discussion. Whereas BPML requires WSCI for process interaction, BPEL contains the semantics to interact with business partners. Wf-XML approaches process interaction differently than both BPEL and WSCI. Wf-XML contains no construct for message correlation, transactional context, or compensation. In Wf-XML every process, activity, and resource is assigned a URI when it is activated. This means when a XPDL process instance is instantiated, the requester receives a URI for that process instance. Anytime an activity in the process is activated, the requester can receive the URI for that activity. Thus, there is no correlation issue. The requester can send a message referencing any URI to change state (data values) or get state information of a process instance or active activities. Wf-XML also uses a process factory entity to create process instances. BPEL and WSCI create a process instance depending on an activity in the process definition tied to the WSDL operation.

What are the benefits of Wf-XML compared to BPEL and WSCI? For Wf-XML, the SOAP message contains the details of a request. Using Wf-XML does not require having separate WSDL operations for ChangeSalesOrder and RequestSalesOrderData. Whether the SOAP message is to change or request sales order data, it is received by the same URI. Using BPEL and WSCI, change and request sales order data would be different operations in the Web service. These two different operations would require two different WSDL ports. The requester using BPEL and WSCI would have to know the different WSDL ports to which to send messages of different operations. The disadvantages of Wf-XML are it does not contain any specification for exception handling, context, or compensation that might be required in process collaboration.

Summary

What is the current state of the standards war? Because of the support of technology heavyweights and detailed specifications, BPEL is emerging as the standard that is likely to succeed. As a process definition standard, BPEL is more complete than BPML. To provide support for human participants, IBM is augmenting BPEL with its own extensions. WSCI could emerge as part of a W3C Web services choreography specification. Being the standards body for the World Wide Web, any W3C specification will likely gain industry support. XPDL is a workflow-centric standard. It does not depend on Web services for application integration. This might be a positive, because most legacy applications will probably not be Web service–enabled. However, XPDL lacks crucial constructs for exception handling and transactional processing. The Wf-XML 2.0 standard is in its infancy. WfMC boasts it has over 300 members. This sounds like good news for Wf-XML 2.0 acceptance. However, WfMC standards in the past have not found wide adaptation by vendors. If experience is any guide, the betting is against Wf-XML being implemented to any significant degree. At time of writing this manuscript, the standards war is ongoing and will probably remain so for the next couple of years.

Notes

1. WfMC. 2002. Workflow Process Definition Interface — XML Process Definition Language. Document Number WFMC-TC-1025. Workflow Management Coalition.
2. Shapiro, R. 2002. A comparison of XPDL, BPML and BPEL4WS (Version 1.4). http://xml.coverpages.org/Shapiro-XPDL.pdf.
3. BPMI.org. 2002. Business Process Modeling Language. Version 11/13/2002.
4. Dubray, J-J. 2003. WS-BPEL. http://www.ebpml.org/bpel4ws.htm
5. Andrews, T., Curbera, F., Dholakia, H., Goland, Y., Klein, J., Leymann, F., Liu, K., Roller, D., Smith, D., Thatte, S., Trickovic, I., and Weerawarana, S. 2003. Business Process Execution Language for Web Services Version 1.1. BEA, IBM, Microsoft, SAP, Siebel.
6. Van der Aalst, W., ter Holfstede, A., Kiepuszewski, A., and A.P. Barros. 2003. Workflow Patterns. *Distributed and Parallel Databases.* 14:1. 5–51.
7. Mendling, J. and M. Muller. 2003. A Comparison of BPML and BPEL4WS. *Proceedings of 1st Conference Berliner XML-Tage.* R. Tolksdorf and R. Eckstein (Eds). 305–316.
8. Wohed, P., van der Aalst, W.M.P., Dumas, M., and A.H.M. ter Hofstede. 2003. Analysis of Web Services Composition Languages: The case for BPEL4WS. *22nd International Conference on Conceptual Modeling (ER 2003).* Volume 2813 of *Lecture Notes in Computer Science.* Springer-Verlag. Berlin. 200–215.
9. Van der Aalst, W.M.P., Dumas, M., ter Hofstede, A.H.M., and Hohed, P. Pattern-Based Analysis of BPML (and WSCI). 2002. QUT Technical Report FIT-TR-2002-05. Queensland University of Technology. Brisbane, Australia.
10. Van der Aalst, W.M.P. 2003. Patterns and XPDL: A Critical Evaluation of the XML Process Definition Language. QUT Technical Report FIT-TR-2003-06. Queensland University of Technology. Brisbane, Australia.
11. Arkin, A., Askary, S., Fordin, S., Jekeli, W., Kawaguchi, K., Orchard, D., Pogliani, S., Riemer, K., Struble, S., Takacsi-Nagy, P., Trickovic, I., and Zimek, S. Web Service Choreography Interface 1.0, 2002. http://www.w3.org/TR/wsci

Chapter 10

Business Process Management Implementation Methodology

In Chapter 2, we briefly discussed the process management lifecycle. In this chapter, we will expand on the concepts in Chapter 2 and focus on the essential elements needed to successfully implement a business process management (BPM). We will discuss the steps an organization seeking to implement BPM can perform. BPM is simply not a technology proposition. We will take a holistic view and look into organizational, functional, and technical aspects of implementing BPM.

Lessons from Business Process Reengineering (BPR)

BPM management practices owe their origins to previous management practices. Two influential management practices are Total Quality Management (TQM) and BPR. The latter is more relevant because of BPM's reliance on technology as a key enabler. While BPR had a large following among large organizations, it achieved mixed results as discussed in Chapter 1. Several factors contributed to BPR implementation failures.

Several of the factors are related to the BPR enabling technologies. To help formulate a BPM implementation methodology, it is helpful to learn from the BPR lessons.

In their formulation of BPR management concepts, Hammer, Champy, and Davenport discussed the implementation of BPR at a high level. The marketplace relied on project methodologies designed by various consulting firms and ERP companies. These methodologies are based on the traditional systems of engineering methodologies. There are typically four phases. The first phase usually involves an analysis of the current state. This includes understanding the current business processes, mapping these processes to the applications that support them, and documenting any unique requirements that need to be addressed. Areas of opportunity are also identified. The next phase is designing an Information Technology (IT)–centric solution for the future state. The reason it is IT–centric is the current business processes are compared to the business processes of the Enterprise Resource Planning (ERP) system that is to be implemented. The ERP system essentially provides the best practice business processes the organization should adopt. In cases where there are gaps, workarounds or custom solutions are designed. At the end of the design phase, the project should have written design specifications for how the system should be configured and what customized solutions should be built. After the design phase comes the development phase. During this phase, systems are configured to the design specifications, customizations are developed, and organizational changes are enforced. The last phase is the deployment of the solution. The deployment phase involves testing the systems and processes and training the users. The phases are dependent and sequenced. Each phase usually takes one month to six months. At some point in the design phase, business requirements are frozen, because future business changes are difficult to include in project scope. This methodology is typically called waterfall, presumably for its relative inflexibility to revisit completed phases and start work on a subsequent phase prior to completion of the current phase. As most ERP projects are complex and time consuming, they force the businesses to freeze their business processes until the projects have been implemented. The freeze could take from three months to one year, depending on the length of the project. This is obviously hard for businesses to stomach because most industries face changes much more frequently than the imposed freeze periods. This is one of the major drawbacks of the ERP waterfall implementation methodology.

Another common problem of ERP and other IT–enabled business change methodologies is the lack of emphasis on change management. Lynne Markus and Robert Benjamin published an excellent article, "The Magic Bullet Theory in IT–Enabled Transformation," on this topic in 1997.[1]

In their article, the authors describe the common belief that the IT solution is the magic bullet that always finds its target. Because the bullet always finds its target, IT specialists do not feel the responsibility for ensuring that users are adopting the technology solution. Senior managers also take comfort in knowing the bullet is always on target, and they turn the projects over to the IT specialists, who also serve as the convenient scapegoat if the projects fail. The point the authors want to make with the magic bullet theory is most projects do not follow change management practices. In most IT–enabled business process change projects, the users are assumed to be docile, submissive beings who always succumb to the magic bullet. In fact, the authors say users are anything but. They know how to dodge the bullet by finding faults with the IT solution. They may use the solution but still fail to reach management's intended results, and they also may fight back by blaming IT and questioning the value of IT. The authors suggest two change management alternatives. The first alternative is based on an organizational development theory they call the IT change facilitator model. While everyone should share the responsibility for change, this model calls for change facilitators to be part of the change effort. The change facilitators should be neutral to any proposed solution and serve to empower the business users and IT to arrive at a solution. The second alternative that Markus and Benjamin propose is the IT change advocate model. In this model, the change advocates are people within the organization who have visions for the future and can influence people to these visions. Change advocates are usually charismatic people who know how to affect people to change. Markus and Benjamin conclude their article by recommending that IT specialists and line managers adopt and embrace change management practices. After all, it is usually the people, not the technology, that decide whether business change projects will succeed or fail. They follow with the second recommendation that all organizational members involved in business change projects should learn and practice change management skills.

Readers who have experienced IT–enabled business change projects would probably agree with Markus and Benjamin's comments on the importance of change management and the lack of it in most projects. This is relevant to BPR and other IT–enabled business process projects. This is validated by a study of BPR projects, discussed in Chapter 1, that found process transformation and social design as two of the top three stages for achieving project success based on a survey of BPR participants. Change management should be the number one priority of any IT–enabled business change implementations. The change management team must have a direct relationship to the executive champion of the project, and its members must be influential senior managers who are respected within the business. Ideally, change management team members should engage in all process designs. In the design phase, they actively engage the business to understand their concerns about proposed process changes, and they collaborate with process team members to design processes that will be easier for the employees and the corporate culture to adopt. If there are disagreements, they are the facilitators to resolve any conflicts and issues. In addition to process work, change management specialists should be engaged in designing organizational changes that facilitate the changes accompanying the business change implementations. The role of change management is to make sure the changes are tolerated, if not well received, and accepted by the organization as a whole. This goes a long way to ensuring the success of the project. It has often been said that IT–enabled business change, especially ERP projects, are all about people and much less about technology and systems. Technological issues are a lot easier to overcome than people issues. While broken systems can be replaced, it is a lot harder to replace an organization that is resisting the change. Unfortunately, the role of change management has been reduced to user training and project communication in most business change implementations. This project methodology deficiency is probably due to the systems engineering origin of most IT–enabled business change methodologies. The end product of systems engineering does not involve humans after all.

The third most common complaint about IT–enabled business change projects is the lack of executive ownership. IT project managers who do not represent the business usually manage ERP projects. Projects managed by IT managers could give the perception that the projects are IT–driven. This perception automatically raises resentment from the business. Even on ERP projects that are managed by senior managers from the business, there is usually a considerable gap between project management and executive management. This slows down the issue escalation process when tough cross-functional issues, such as transfer price and product costing, have to be addressed. The ideal setup is to have either the Chief Executive Officer (CEO), President, or another senior executive of the corporation be the project champion. Project management should have a direct relationship to the project champion. Issues are resolved with the full participation of the steering committee, which includes the project champion and the various business stakeholders.

Business Process Management (BPM) Implementation Methodology

The complaints discussed above are not only relevant to BPR and ERP implementations. These are common complaints that are relevant to any

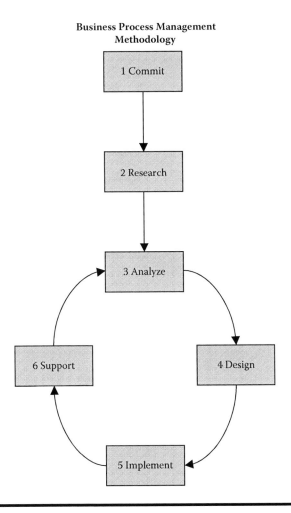

Figure 10.1   BPM Implementation Methodology.

technology-enabled change projects. Undoubtedly, most lessons from BPR or any other technology-enabled change practices will be relevant to implementation of BPM. In the following sections, we will discuss a generic BPM implementation methodology that contains commit, research, analyze, design, implement, and support phases.

Figure 10.1 illustrates the various phases of BPM methodology. During the commit phase, the organization commits to process management through organizational alignments and strategic direction. The research phase is for the organization to determine existing business processes, research, and select a process management product (e.g., Business Process Management System (BPMS)), and prepare for business change. The next four phases form an iterative cycle for implementing a process management project, focusing on one or a small set of processes identified in the research phase. The analyze phase starts the cycle with the project team, project charter, and the current process performance metrics. In the design phase, the to-be process is optimized and architected. Any necessary organizational adjustment and employee reward metrics are made during this phase. The process solution is built and tested, and users are trained during the implement phase. The end of implement phase marks the go live of the process solution. The last phase of the cycle, the support phase, is to measure the new process for comparison to performance goals and perform the project closeout with lessons learned. From the process perspective, the support phase does not stop. The new process will be continually monitored and controlled using BPMS. However, the process management implementation team can focus on new tasks or projects after project go live and a period of go live support. Because this is not a book on project management, we will discuss the BPM methodology on a high level. In formulating this generic methodology, we incorporate generally accepted project management practices, change management practices, lessons from ERP implementations, and practices from TQM and Six Sigma methodologies. The blending of these practices is made to take advantage of BPMS features. Hopefully, readers looking to implement BPM and BPMS will find this methodology useful as a starting point for their implementation plan.

Phase 1: Commit

Once an organization has decided to adopt BPM practices, the organization has to be committed to this decision. Too often business improvement initiatives are pet projects initiated by executive management that never receive the proper executive attention and organizational support they need to be successful. What usually happens is a project team will be formed to implement the business improvement initiative. The executive sponsors take a hands-off approach, and their only involvement is in occasional project status briefings. It is up to the project team to engender culture change, suggest organizational adjustments, design the business improvements, and implement the business improvements. This approach might work in an organization that has a change-friendly culture and has the organizational framework already in place so major reorganization is not necessary. In a change-friendly organization, the scope of the business improvement project is usually small and most issues do not require executive decisions.

Business change projects in organizations not accustomed to change are risky undertakings. Some projects fail because of the overwhelming resistance from the organizations to adopt the business changes the project teams want to implement. There will always be resistance in organizations. Most people are happy with status quo; this is general human nature. We adopt ideas quickly, and we loath to adjust the ideas we have adopted. That is probably why children learn faster than adults do. As human beings, once we are set in our ways, we do not want to disrupt those ways and have to rearrange our lives. Thus, it takes effort, sometimes external motivation, and time to prepare humans for change. This extends to all organizations made of humans. Implementing a project in an organization that has not been properly prepared for change carries the additional burden of having to introduce the concept of change to the organization. This undoubtedly will create tremendous organizational upheaval, which means additional risk to the project.

Major organizational alignment is best done outside the scope of a business improvement project. By organizational alignment, we are referring to changes in organizational model, such as from a functionally oriented to a process-oriented model. This kind of organizational change is a complex endeavor that deserves dedicated attention from executive management. Even if all the executives agree on the alignment, there will often be strong resistance from senior managers reporting directly to executives. These senior managers will fight with teeth and nails to protect their turf and positions. It takes conviction and planning to convince the senior managers and business unit heads to the necessity for organizational alignment.

Therefore, in our BPM methodology, we introduce the commit phase to address the larger strategic, cultural, and organizational aspects of the major business change initiative. This is the phase in which the organization makes a serious commitment to BPM from the top-level executives. We divide the tasks into two major groups: set strategic direction and effect organizational alignment. Figure 10.2 illustrates the tasks that need to be accomplished during this phase.

Set Strategic Direction

There is usually a champion for every business change initiative. The champion is the person who pushes for the business change initiative. In the case of BPM, that champion should be the CEO. BPM, implemented throughout the organization affects so many departments, that only the person overseeing the various departments, typically the CEO, has the

Phase 1 Commit—Overview

Participants
  • Executive Management
  • Process Czar

Set Strategic Direction

  • Unite executives to support BPM initiative
  • Include process management as management guiding principle
  • Link strategic business goals to BPM

Effect Organizational Alignment

  • Adjust organizational structure to be compatible with process management
  • Appoint an executive to be the process czar
  • Implement process management organizational unit with process implementation office, process support office, and process managers
  • Articulate employee reward strategy based on process performance

Figure 10.2   Tasks for Phase 1 — Commit.

influence to generate support in the executive ranks. Before they can convince others, the executives must first be convinced themselves. This paraphrase of a quote from Thomas Carlyle is appropriate for any situations that call for persuasion. Prior to embarking on business process, organizational executives have to buy into BPM as a management practice. Despite the common belief humans possess individuality and make independent decisions, the reality is other people of higher perceived stature or influence, influence most of us. Employees on the lower portion of organizational hierarchy look to their executives for guidance. Unity at the top of the organization illustrates determination for the BPM initiative from the executive ranks. The show of determination and unity can help persuade employees to support the new initiative.

After the executive ranks agree and support BPM initiative, the next task is to cultivate an environment that is conducive for BPM. This can be initiated by setting process management as a guiding principle for the organization. The effect of a guiding principle is it will impress, on the management levels, that executives see process management as a key management practice for achieving strategic goals. This will likely generate attention and develop support from the senior management and mid-level management levels.

Another method to engender organizational support for a BPM initiative is to tie the initiative to strategic goals. Strategic goals are important to steering the organization toward a clear destination. When they are passionately communicated throughout the organization, they can galvanize the employees with a sense of purpose and soften resistance to changes associated with the business initiative. It serves the BPM initiative well to set strategic goals that use the business process as the key enabler. A strategic goal might be to achieve 10 percent productivity improvement per year by continuously improving the business process. At the very least, this sort of pronouncement should prepare the organization for the BPM initiative. Any business change initiative requires enormous amounts of communication. Most people do not register the information given to them the first time. As humans, the more mature we become, the more times information needs to be reinforced for our minds to accept the information. It is important for the organization to hear from the executives on the process management strategic direction and the goals that BPM will enable the organization to achieve. This information needs to be reinforced multiple times, either by executive management or by other management levels.

As we mentioned previously, there are often challenges in converting senior managers to embrace any initiative that changes the organizational structure. It is never good to mandate certain behaviors. People can be influenced and mindsets can change when a case for change is successfully built and precisely communicated. There are books written on how to influence and change organizational mindsets.[2] These books present approaches that could help any organization deal with business change. It might also help to present a sense of urgency for change. Business changes swiftly. There are mergers, acquisitions, and changes in business environments. Given these dynamics and the centrality of processes in dealing with these dynamics, executive management has to present a clear case for change to deal with the urgent business challenges.

Effect Organizational Alignment

Aside from strategic direction, the organization should commit to BPM through a process-focused organizational structure. In Chapter 2, we discussed various process-focused organizational structures. Most organizations are organized along functional departments. It is extremely painful for an organization to change to a pure process-based organizational model. In the pure process-based organization, there are no functional departments. Every employee is part of a process unit. While this organizational model might react quicker to changes in business processes, it also creates duplicate functions within different process units. Thus, there is productivity loss from this redundancy. Not to mention the business risks and organizational turmoil a functional organization faces while it is undergoing transformation to a pure process-based organizational model. A popular alternative is a matrix, or network, organization that retains functional departments, but it also contains process units that interact with the functional departments. Employees in a matrix organization have direct or indirect reporting relationships to functional departments and process units. Although a matrix organization requires more managerial attention and communication, it is probably the preferred organizational model for organizations not familiar with process-focused management practices.

Just as departments have department heads and business units have business unit leaders, processes should have process leaders. A senior executive should be in charge of the business processes. This leader should serve as a process management czar who oversees process management activities. To help establish credibility, this process czar should report to the CEO. Processes do not know departmental or business unit boundaries. Having a senior executive as the process czar ensures there is enough political clout to manage the business processes effectively. Serving under the process czar are a process implementation office, a process support office, and process managers. We will discuss more about these subunits in our discussion of the research phase. At a high level, the process implementation office is responsible for implementation of process management projects and maintaining knowledge relating to the implementation of these projects. The process support office is responsible for monitoring, controlling, and reporting on processes. Process managers are the process owners who are responsible for the performance of business processes. In this phase, the process implementation office should be created and ready for operation at the beginning of the research phase. In the next phase, the process implementation office will participate in product selection and cataloging of current business processes. After process management projects have been implemented, the process support office should be ready to control and measure these processes.

People behave the way they are measured and compensated. Employee compensation strategy is an important factor for making process management work. During the commit phase, an employee compensation strategy that takes into account process performance should be formulated. Obviously, this can only be stated at a high level because no process management projects have been implemented at this stage. The formulation and broadcast of process-based performance evaluation serves to attract attention to the BPM initiative from employees. The more attention employees pay to the BPM initiative, the easier it is to communicate the benefits of the BPM initiative. Communication is the key to winning support.

Phase 2: Research

The commit phase requires work from the executive management level. After the executives set the strategic direction and initiated the organizational alignment, the next set of tasks falls on the process management organizational unit and senior managers. While executive management planted the seeds for BPM, much work remains to be done. In this phase, we divide the tasks into three major groups: prepare organization for change, determine current business processes, and establish process management technology infrastructure. Figure 10.3 illustrates the tasks belonging to these major groups.

Phase 2 Research—Overview

Participants

- Process Implementation Office
- Change leaders
- Subject matter experts from the business units

Determine Current Business Processes

- Catalog existing business processes
- Identify core business processes
- Prioritize business processes for process management implementations

Establish Process Management Technology Infrastructure

- Organize product selection committee
- Conduct product selection competition
- Establish process management technology group
- Start to build process management framework

Prepare Organization for Change

- Establish training program for change leaders
- Establish training program for process design techniques and BPMS design tools

Figure 10.3   Tasks for Phase 2 — Research.

Determine Current Business Processes

Once the organization is committed to BPM, one of the first process management tasks is to determine the current business processes. This can be done by the process implementation office. Even organizations that are not process-focused have business processes. Maybe that is not the phrase people are used to. Processes are steps that workers follow to conduct business. In nonprocess focused organizations, the processes might end at the departmental boundary. Once the task has been handed to another department, the previous department is no longer concerned with the outcome. Understanding of current business processes is critical to BPM. First, this exercise would help identify unique business requirements to the organization or the industry the organization belongs to. Without surveying the current processes, these unique requirements might be left out. Second, organizations accumulate knowledge as they evolve. In the growth of an organization, processes might become needlessly complicated because old methods of doing things were never challenged. Some processes might have evolved to be exemplary, efficient, and confer competitive advantage. Again, without canvassing current processes, these exemplary processes might have been neglected. Third, one of the benefits of process management is to measure process performance and improvements. Improvements cannot be measured unless current processes are identified and their performance measured. To catalog current processes, process implementation team members should interview all the functional departments and all the business units within the organization. We will refer to members of functional department and business units simply as the business. This tedious work will require numerous meetings with the business. During the interviewing process, the business should be asked to rate the importance and throughput of the processes they are describing. It is helpful to create a database to capture processes from various units and organize them by major groupings such as order-to-cash, purchase-to-pay, product development, marketing, etc.

After all the current business processes have been cataloged, the next task is to determine which of these processes are core to the organization. Core processes are those that are critical to competitive advantage or that create the most value. Obviously, value is hard to quantify at this point because no process performance analysis has been performed. However, with inputs from the business and senior management, core processes can be subjectively determined. Do core processes have to be current processes? Core processes are most likely existing business processes. There might be strategic initiatives that will confer competitive advantage and require new processes to be designed and implemented. In such situations, these new processes will be core once they are implemented. From a cost perspective, there are benefits to include these new, yet-to-be implemented, processes in the list of core processes and implement them as part of the process management initiative. There are risks associated with this approach because the process management initiative is only beginning at this stage. However, after several projects have been completed through the Analysis, Design, Implement, and Support (ADIS) cycles, these risks are mitigated.

With existing business processes cataloged, they can be prioritized for implementation. The first process to be implemented should not be overly complex or critical. In conservative organizations, it might be prudent to start with a process that is not a core process and not overly complex. The process management implementation methodology and BPMS technology infrastructure will mature over time. The choice of a noncore process will not seriously impact business if there are implementation problems. Furthermore, it is important to the BPM initiative that the first project be successfully implemented. After the organization has one or a few successes with BPM projects, the implementation priority list should be given to core processes. This process list is by no means static. As the business environment changes, new processes can be added and the prioritization can change.

Establish Process Management Technology Infrastructure

The next set of tasks is related to the technology aspect of BPM initiative. A BPMS product selection committee should be established to choose the right BPMS product for the organization. Ideally, any one department does not conduct the process of choosing a BPMS product. Everyone will be affected by the BPM initiative and will use the BPMS product directly or indirectly. The product selection committee should be composed of representatives from the process management unit, IT, and the various functional departments. The selection committee can canvass existing literature for products that are likely fits for the organization. Once the pool of likely products has been established, vendor candidates should be invited to give demos. Most of these product presentations should be taken with grains of salt. With constant news of technological advancements and scientific progress, we have been conditioned to believe in the illimitable capabilities of technology. For those of us in the IT field, undoubtedly comments such as why can't it do that, and it should be easy right, have been heard many times from business users annoyed when desired features were not available. IT is like the magic bullet we described previously. We have been conditioned to think of technology as capable of doing anything. Because this perception of technology is widespread, product vendors have to hype their wares to meet the market perception. After one vendor starts the hype, all vendors have to participate to compete. It is a rare occasion when a product vendor willingly admits to the shortcomings of its product. The purpose of vendor product presentations should serve to provide information of high-level product features. The more technical-savvy members of the product selection committee should be encouraged to ask tough technical questions to help draw the line between hype and reality.

In a marketplace where product hype is common, how should organizations make intelligent decisions on a product? A good method is to hold a competition for the various product vendors. The competition could be a process solution bake-off. The competing product vendors will be given the same process and the same technology infrastructure to prove the capabilities of their products. The business process chosen for the competition should not be complex, but it should cover at least two applications that need to be integrated, and two human tasks that need to be performed. It's a good idea to have employees embedded with each team if the product vendors allow for such practice. This will broaden the organization's understanding of BPMS products. The duration of the competition might take anywhere from three days to four weeks. In evaluating the prototypes from the various competing teams, the implementation time should be taken into consideration along with features and fulfillment of the business process. Implementation time gives a good indication of how easy or how difficult it is to implement solutions using a particular BPMS product. Depending on the potential size of a BPMS contract, it might be possible to ask the vendors to foot some or all of the costs for the product competition. It is still a good investment even if the organization has to pay the costs for the product competition. It is far cheaper to spend money for proper product selection than for the implementation and rework costs due to an unfit product.

With the selection of a BPMS product, there needs to be a technology group to support this product. This should fall under the responsibility of the process management technology group. This technology group should be responsible for maintaining the servers, databases, and system landscape associated with the BPMS product. The logical department to manage the process management technology group is the IT department. Most system administration tasks require the same skills regardless of the product. The IT organization already has the knowledge base to adapt to the maintenance of a BPMS product. Because this organization will be supporting the process management initiative, it is prudent to align the process management technology group to support process management projects. In the next phases, the process management technology group will need to provide dedicated systems administration support to the process management project teams.

With the BPMS product selected and the BPM initiative well underway, the task can be started to build a process management framework. The framework is a set of items and services that will be used in building a process management solution. These items include a meta-data model, an organizational model, implementation methodology, and standards. The meta-data model is particularly important because it includes the enterprise data model. There needs to be a consistent data model used throughout the organization to describe such information as customer, vendor, sales order, purchase order, business process performance, etc. Ultimately, data is the basis of information. If every business process is defined using its own set of data, it will be difficult to compare the same data from different processes. Thus, the establishment of an enterprisewide meta-data model is important. At this stage, no processes have been implemented. It is not reasonable to expect a meta-data model that can cover all the future processes to be implemented. The more comprehensive the meta-data model can be devised at this point, the easier it will be for process management projects. The other model is the organizational model. This model reflects the reporting hierarchy of an organization. Numerous people in the organization use most business processes. The goal of the organizational model is to expedite process management projects when the processes in these projects need to assign work to specific members in the organization. An example is the approval of a purchase order. The process design can use the organizational model to indicate the approval work item should be routed to the manager of the employee placing the purchase order. Standards and implementation methodology are the other components of a process management framework that should be developed. Implementation methodology is not unlike what we are describing in this chapter, except it is much more detailed. The methodology should specify the phases, participants, roles, and responsibilities, testing procedures and specific tasks of a process management project implementation. The contents of analyze, design, implement, and support phases described in this chapter would be contained in a process management project methodology. The methodology would serve as a guide for process management project implementations. In support of the project methodology are standards. These standards could be naming conventions, forms (e.g., functional design form, technical design form, etc.), process metric definitions, and training templates. The standards will ensure that projects are documented using the same mechanism and that the outputs from different projects are consistent.

Prepare Organization for Change

In the previous section, we discussed the process management unit and the process czar. The process implementation office is akin to the project management office we find in project-based organizations. The subunit determines which processes to improve, implements process management projects, devises implementation methodology, and serves as the knowledge center for process management. One of the BPM practices is continuous improvement. The process implementation office is the arm that executes process improvements. The benefits of the project office have been widely discussed in the management press. Their functional roots and relationships limit project teams within functional departments. Furthermore these functional project teams do not have the experience to deal with cross-functional integrations, and they lack a support organization that provides methodology and implementation knowledge. The role of the process implementation office is to provide a home for process management implementation teams. This office maintains the standards for implementation and the network for implementation team members to learn from each other. The implementation office decides which processes to improve based on the process performance gathered by the process support office.

Another important function of the process implementation office is to provide education on business process and business change. In recent decades, the change management discipline has garnered attention in the business management world. It is well established that effectively managing change and cultivating change leaders within the organizations are important for the business change initiative. Change leaders serve to influence others within the organization to adapt to the new business environment. Some people naturally adapt to change more readily than others do. These people are the candidates to be the change leaders. The ideal change leader candidates should also be respected members within the organization who can exert influence on others. The role of the process implementation office is to provide training for these change leaders on the value of the business change and how to create an organizational culture that is friendly to change. These change leaders should be returned to their functional departments to influence others to accept the process management. They also serve as a pool of change agents who can participate in process management projects, which we will discuss the analyze phase. After change leader training, the process implementation office remains their link to learning about process management projects. This way the change leaders will stay connected to the process management and the cycles of change even when they are not involved in process management tasks.

Aside from providing change agent training, the project implementation office should be responsible for providing training to the process implementation team members. These individuals are responsible for managing, designing, and developing process management projects and solutions. The training should cover process management implementation methodology, process design methodology, and BPMS product training. Because maintaining an internal training capability is expensive, some of these training activities will probably be outsourced. It is a good idea to maintain an internal capability at least for the project implementation methodology. As an organization completes the process management projects, it gains more knowledge about how to best implement these projects. This knowledge is part of the organization's intellectual property and should be transformed into enhancements to the project implementation methodology. Internal training is a good way to disseminate that knowledge.

Phase 3: Analyze

The next four phases form the outline of a process management project. Each process management project contains a cycle of these four phases. Once a project has been completed, the process implementation office can start a new project and a new cycle involving these four phases starts again. Analyze is the project planning and process analysis phase. The inputs to this phase are the process to be implemented chosen by the process implementation office and an estimated project completion date. Once an objective has been set, the project team should be formed. In this phase, the project team should develop a project charter and analyze the existing processes covered by the project scope. We will discuss the project team setup, project charter, and process analysis in this section. Figure 10.4 shows the tasks that should be completed during the analysis phase.

Assemble Project Team

A project team should at least have the following components: project management, business change, development, and technology support. Figure 10.5 shows the various teams in the project.

Project management is responsible for the overall success of the project. The best command setup is to have one project manager so responsibility is not diffused. The project manager's responsibilities include creating the project plan, coordinating the various teams within the project, eliciting project stakeholder participation, and engaging the project steering

Phase 3 Analyze—Overview

Participants

- BPM project team
- Steering committee
- Project stake holders

Assemble Project Team

- Include change leaders and core team members from the business into project team
- Create project steering committee
- Engage project stake holders

Deliver Project Charter

- Define process problem, project scope, implementation objectives, roles and responsibilities, high-level project plan and project assumptions
- Obtain approval from steering committee and stake holders for project charter

Perform Process Analysis

- Gather process data for existing processes within the project scope
- Analyze data to determine performance of existing processes
- Document current process challenges

Figure 10.4   Tasks for Phase 3 — Analyze.

committee. Stakeholders are any parties that are affected by the process management implementation project. They could include managers from departments affected by the process management project, the IT department because it has to support the systems, and users who have to learn new ways and technology to conduct business. The stakeholder committee is made of senior managers of business units that will be impacted within the BPM project scope.

The business change team is the driver for the business process design and organizational alignment. This team should be composed of change leaders, core team members, organizational design experts, and process design experts. The change leaders should provide leadership to the business change team and they should serve to influence the affected business units into adapting changes being implemented by the process management project. Core team members are representatives from the business units who can provide knowledge on how the current processes

BPM Project Structure

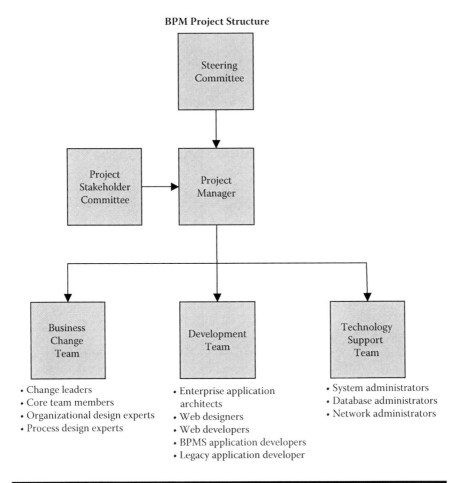

Figure 10.5   Example of Business Process Management Project Structure.

are performed. These core team members should be highly regarded and trusted within their organizational units so they can provide a positive communication link from the process management project to the business units. It is important for the core team members to believe in the process management initiative. Skeptical core team members communicating negative feedback to the business is detrimental to the change management process. What is the difference between core team members and change leaders? Core team members are usually people closer to the work. They have a good understanding of the operational aspects of their section of the business. Change leaders are usually higher up in the organizational hierarchy. Their role is to lead business change and to interact with middle- and upper-level managers.

The other resources in the business change team are subject matter experts, including experts in organizational design and process design. Organizational design experts have the responsibility of analyzing the organizational structure from a process performance optimization perspective. Sometimes the organizational design analysis leads to organizational structure modifications to provide best process performance. Changes in organizational structure usually entail changes in jobs and roles. Defining roles and responsibilities of jobs affected by process management is another task that organizational design experts have to tackle. In addition to these, organizational design team members help to define process performance goals and employee rewards for achieving process performance goals. Just as organizational design experts look to optimize performance from an organizational perspective, process design experts analyze the current business processes within the scope of the process management project, and they redesign the business processes using BPM principles. Process management experts are trained in process design methodologies, and they are trained in using the business process design and simulation tools of the BPMS product. The primary responsibility of the process management experts is to take the inputs from the other team members and utilize scientifically rigorous process design techniques to devise the best business processes within the scope of the project.

Supporting the business change team are the development and technology support teams. The development team constructs the programs required to support the process management design. BPMS vendors advertise their products as being capable of automatically generating code, with some vendors going as far as advertising programming-free solutions. The reality is development is still needed using any kind of BPMS product. The automatic code generation ability is generally limited to simple forms, interface proxies, simple interface transformations, and component stubs. Developers are still needed to implement complex business rules, user interfaces, and component interfaces. The development team should include Web designers, Web developers, enterprise application architects, application developers who are trained in using the application development tool of the BPMS product, and developers with experience in the applications that are part of the process management project scope. These development roles are needed in the development team. Individual developers might be able to satisfy more than one role. Thus, the number of development team members might be less than the number of roles. There is a distinction between Web designer and Web developer. The Web designer prepares the look and feel of a Web page, while the Web developer programs the server-side logic that controls the Web page. The enterprise application architect designs the component model of the process management project scope. The architect is responsible for making sure the components within the process management framework are leveraged for reuse and that new components are designed with future reuse in consideration. Another responsibility of the enterprise application architect is to ensure all components follow enterprise process management standards. Most of the applications in a process management scenario might not provide adequate interfaces to satisfy the requirements of the process management solution. Application developers knowledgeable about these existing applications should be part of the development team to ensure these applications can be properly integrated in the BPMS product.

The last team in the process management project is the technology support team. This team performs system administration tasks and system performance optimizations. For large-scale projects, a dedicated technology support team is essential to the success of the project. In such projects, any delay in the project timeline can have a large financial impact. A fully staffed and dedicated technology support team can ensure that technology related issues do not contribute to project delays. Regardless of project size and whether the dedicated technology support team is part of the project, there needs to be a previously agreed on service response time between the technology support team and the other project teams. This service level agreement should take the heightened support needs during the critical phases of the project into consideration.

Project Charter

With the team assembled, the next set of tasks revolves around the creation of the project charter. The project charter is the basis for the existence of the BPM project. It contains the process problem, project scope, implementation objectives, roles and responsibilities, high-level project plan, and assumptions. The concept of the process management project charter is similar to the project charter from the Six Sigma methodology. The process problem states the current business process (or lack of business process) and the business challenges are a result of the current state. The project scope is the scope provided by the process implementation office to initiate the project. Various teams should collaborate to determine the implementation objectives. These objectives include anticipated benefits as a result of the project. The benefits are high-level benefits that will be more detailed as the project engages in the design phase. Any assumptions made to reach the anticipated benefits should be stated in the project charter. Finally, the charter includes the roles and responsibilities of all parties involved and a high-level project timeline. Roles and responsibilities extend from those of the project team to the project stakeholders, the business users, and the steering committee. The project timeline included in the charter is a high-level timeline that will be tweaked during the design phase. This timeline is an estimate based on experience with previous projects of similar scope. The timeline might turn out to be unrealistic as the project team finishes the design phase. At that point, the detailed project plan should be submitted to the steering committee for approval with any changes in dates.

The main purpose of the project charter is to serve as a communication to all parties affected by the project. The steering committee and project stakeholders will sign this project charter. Once the project charter has been authorized, it serves as the mandate the project team can use to justify the project's existence and actions. By involving the stakeholders, the business will signal its commitment to the project.

Process Analysis

In preparing for the project charter, the project team needs to perform an analysis of the current processes in the project scope. High-level information about the existing processes has already been gathered during the research phase. The process analysis expands on the information previously collected. The primary goal of process analysis is to determine the performance of existing processes. The data to perform process analysis might not be easy to gather because there might not be consistent and readily available data for the current processes. If a process involves applications that contain transactional logs, these logs can be used to determine the activity duration. Sometimes when transactional logs are not available, the analysis would have to be done using indirect measurements such as dividing total transactions in a given period by the number of full-time equivalents for that period. Other techniques for process measurement include direct observation and interviews. One of the jobs of the process implementation office is to devise techniques and tools for enabling current process analysis. Other than process performance measures, the project team should also determine current process challenges while performing process analysis. Using the performance measures and information on current challenges, realistic project goals can be drawn. The results from the analysis are used as inputs to the project charter.

Phase 4: Design

The design phase is when the project kicks into high gear. The primary goals of this phase are to design the best process management solution and to build a prototype that validates the feasibility of the design solution. Figure 10.6 shows the tasks for the Design phase.

Phase 4 Design—Overview

Participants
- BPM project team
- Project stakeholders

Optimize Business Process Design
- Conduct workshops to obtain business inputs
- Draft design alternatives
- Use simulation to pick the best alternative
- Optimize the chosen design alternative through iterations of design
  simulation and refinement

Build Process Prototype
- Choose the primary process branch of the process management solution
- Develop business logic, component interfaces and web pages for the solution prototype

Complete Detailed Solution Design
- Update organizational design with revised roles and responsibilities
  in support of the process management solution
- Design detailed process flows for all possible branches of the process management solution
- Develop process solution technical model
- Complete functional design documents

Figure 10.6   Tasks for Phase 4 — Design.

The business change team has the responsibility for designing the solution. The approach for process design should include workshops with various business stakeholders to obtain their inputs. Once business inputs have been gathered, the business change team, led by the process design experts, should come up with alternative high-level process designs. The alternative design solutions are entered into the BPMS process designer and simulations are run to choose the best process alternative. The process alternative chosen is then the focus of further design activities. It has been remarked that processes are like onions, with layer upon layer of detail. The chosen process alternative should undergo cycles of refinement and simulation so it contains all the decision points, branches, and exceptions that are likely to be encountered in real life. Readers interested in knowing more about process design and analysis techniques might want to read books by Harmon and Burlton.[3,4]

The same time the process design is being refined, the organizational design experts should look at the current organization and determine what needs to be changed to take advantage of the process solution. Organizational changes might be as simple as updates to job descriptions or they might be as radical as creation and deletion of organizational units. The organizational design outputs from the design phase include descriptions for jobs, roles, activities, and work processes. The roles involved in the to-be business process and activities to be performed by each role should be finalized by the end of this phase.

To validate the feasibility of the to-be process solution, a prototype should be built. The prototype should cover the main processing branch of the process solution. If any applications are involved in the process solution, the prototype should include integration to at least one application. The prototype is a joint effort between the business change team and the development team. This provides the development team with a chance to see what the process solution looks like and what the level of development efforts might be. Traditional waterfall methodologies do not provide the development team the opportunity to be involved in the solution until after the functional team has completed detailed design. The inclusion of the prototype in the design phase should hopefully bring about a closer working relationship between the business change and development teams. The other benefit of the prototype is it serves to mitigate implementation risks. By engaging the development team during the design effort, the technical feasibility of the process solution can be determined. Sometimes functional teams would design elegant and highly complex solutions only to have the technical teams determine the solution is either impossible to build or cannot be implemented within the project timeframe. The prototyping effort makes sure the final process solution is technically feasible while still covering the main process requirements.

In building the prototype, the enterprise application architect works on designing a high-level process solution technical model. This model contains a data model and a component model. Traditional object-oriented design methodology usually contains state transition and sequence diagrams to capture changes in the object state and the flow of process activities. In the BPMS design approach, state transitions and process sequences are modeled graphically as part of the process design using the BPMS process designer. This has the advantage of integration between modeling and development, because the development is done by directly embedding logic into the process design. This also means the enterprise application architect can focus on designing the functions of each component without having to be bogged down by working on specific interactions of the components using Unified Modeling Language (UML)–like diagrams. Process sequences, thus component interactions, are handled in the BPMS process designer as part of the overall process design crafted by the process design experts. The enterprise application architect draws on the standard enterprise data model when building the process solution data model. This ensures the solution data model will be consistent with the enterprise data model. The other members of the technical team would also be involved in building the prototype. If there is no enterprise Web design style guide, the Web designer could come up with several Web page templates for the project team to choose. Web and application developers would be working closely with the process design experts from the business change team to make sure all the development items for the prototype are designed and developed.

One of the handicaps of IT–enabled process change methodologies has been a disconnect between functional design and the actual development output. In these methodologies, the functional design team gathers the business requirements. These requirements are translated into functional design documents. The functional design documents are handed to the technical analysts to convert to technical design specifications. These design specifications are given to programmers for development. The multiple layers of communication and translation of requirements usually leads to differences between the original requirements and the implemented solution. Using a BPMS designer and a project methodology can help alleviate the requirement-development gap. The BPMS process designer comes with a high-level process flow layer and a low-level business logic–scripting layer. The low-level business logic-scripting layer adds detail to the process flow. It is the layer integrating components (such as other applications) and Web services (such as component interfaces encapsulated as Web services). Process design experts who are technically savvy and are trained in the BPMS process designer should be able to design detailed process flows using the high-level graphical process flow layer of the BPMS process designer. The developers leverage on the process flow has already been completed for the process solution in building the low-level business logic script. Using the same environment for process flow and low-level business logic development should help reduce the chance for the functional–technical disconnect.

Aside from a BPMS process designer, methodology-related measures can be taken to foster the environment for close cross-team collaboration, thus reducing chances of functional–technical disconnect. The construction of a prototype is a good opportunity for close cross-team collaboration. It requires the business change and development teams to work together in building the prototype. Process design experts from the business change team create the process flow, and the development team has to develop business logic scripts and integration to the applications or services included in the prototype. Work on the design document provides another opportunity for fostering close cross-team collaboration. While the business change team has the primary responsibility for delivering the functional design documents, the business change team members should work closely with the development teams in completing these documents. It is a good idea to have a development team member shadow a process design expert during this phase. This approach enables the development team member to fully understand the rationale behind the process solution design. Even though most IT–enabled project methodologies stress the importance of a close working relationship between functional and technical project teams, the relationship, from this author's experience, has usually been uncomfortable. Functional team members are sometimes miffed about the length of development time and shortcomings they perceive of the developers' meeting design specifications. Technical team members are sometimes frustrated with changes to design requirements and what they perceive as unreasonable requests from functional team members. Not understanding each side's challenges might be the cause of most of the discomfort. This tension between functional and technical sides will probably never go away regardless of the methodology or tool. However, any opportunities to enhance understanding and bring collaboration between the business change and development team will ultimately help in the delivery of the process solution.

Phase 5: Implement

At the end of the design phase, the solution prototype has been built and the process solution has been deemed feasible to proceed with follow-on phases. The implement phase is when the rest of the solution development is performed. This phase leverages the solution prototype and functional design documents. Several activities happen during this phase:

1. Complete the technical design document
2. Develop the programs and the user interfaces needed for the process solution
3. Conduct a unit test of the individual programs
4. Conduct multiple iterations of integration tests involving all roles, components, and programs
5. Design training documents
6. Conduct user training
7. Create online help documents
8. Go live

Work on the technical design documents could actually start during the design phase. The technical design work has to be done to support prototype building. Any remaining technical design for the process solution that was not part of the prototype should be finished at the beginning of this phase. The enterprise application architect should have defined the high-level technical model for the process solution during the design phase. Once the high-level technical model has been refined to contain the information on individual interfaces, the developers are responsible for completing the technical design specifications. In the course of completing the technical design, the development team would have to engage in a series of team discussions and design walk-throughs to ensure that all the pieces fit together and form one coherent solution design. When the technical design has been finalized, technical team members start on the development items assigned to them. Unit testing follows completion of the development items. Unit test plans for each development item should be drafted and executed.

Unit tests are the first set of tests in the software testing cycle. The other sets are the integration tests. There should be at least two iterations of integration tests. Integration test is the end-to-end process management solution. Business scenarios make up each cycle of the integration test. Business processes is typically composed of multiple decision points and branches that a process instance can undertake. A scenario is one end-to-end path of a business process instance. The integration test scenario contains the activities performed by human and system participants for a business scenario. Each activity in the scenario has input test data and an expected output from the activity. When executing the integration test plan, the output should be compared to the expected output to determine whether there are any defects. There are several testing management tools in the marketplace, such as TestDirector from Mercury Interactive, Silk-Central from Segue Software, eTest from Empirix, etc. It is advisable to use a test management tool. Test plans for each scenario can be loaded into the test management tool and testers are assigned to each test plan. Defects encountered during test plan execution can be entered in the test management tool and assigned to the appropriate party for resolution. Once the defects are in the test management tool, the integration test manager can track them for resolution. A good integration test is one that uncovers and resolves a high number of defects. Defects should not be closed until all the test plan steps have been re-executed to ensure the defects have been resolved. The first cycle of integration testing should cover the main scenarios that account for 80 percent of business process instances. The second cycle of integration testing should cover as many other scenarios as possible. Typically, the scenarios in the second cycle are exception process paths, while the initial cycle covers the main process branches of the business processes in scope. During defect resolution, if a defect uncovered in the integration test has implications to other scenarios, all impacted scenarios should also be retested to make sure the changes do not negatively impact these scenarios.

The integration tests involve the process design experts from the business change team and the development team members. The core team members and the organizational design experts are responsible for creating the training documents. Care should be taken to make sure the changes resulting from the integration test defect resolution are communicated to the team members crafting the training documents. Effective training material usually involves computer interaction for the trainees. When the training documents are done, they can serve as the basis for online help documentation. To coordinate the training effort, there needs to be a training manager who handles the scheduling and coordination of the training sessions. It is important that sufficient resources and attention be devoted to the training effort. The most common complaint from users of IT–enabled business change projects is insufficient training. Properly trained users will help reduce support needs and help raise acceptance of the business process management solution.

The implement phase is the phase requiring the highest amount of involvement from the technology support team. Regardless of how well a project has been planned, the implement phase usually involves long working hours from team members. It is not inconceivable that work will be done 24 hours a day. It is critical to have timely support from the technology support team. In terms of project system landscape, the minimum requirements are to have development, quality assurance, training, and production environments available. Figure 10.7 shows the migration of the process management solution between the various environments.

The development environment is where process design experts do the development work and where the development team constructs the process management solution. The process management solution is promoted to the quality assurance environment after all the components in the process management have been unit tested. The integration tests are performed in the quality assurance environment. No development work should be done in the quality assurance environment. In fact, no development work should be done in any environment except the development environment. All defects are fixed and unit tested in the development environment and promoted to the quality assurance environment to retest the integration test scenarios. The training environment can be a copy of the quality assurance environment. After the training environment has been created, any defects fixed in the development environment should be promoted to both the quality assurance and the training environments. At the

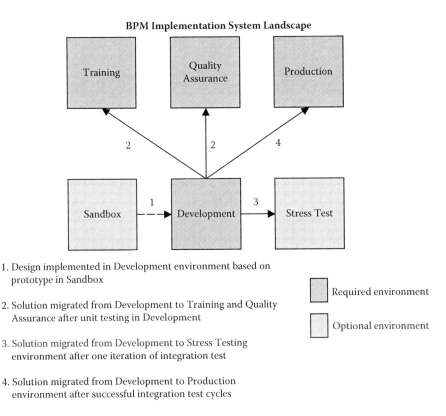

1. Design implemented in Development environment based on prototype in Sandbox

2. Solution migrated from Development to Training and Quality Assurance after unit testing in Development

3. Solution migrated from Development to Stress Testing environment after one iteration of integration test

4. Solution migrated from Development to Production environment after successful integration test cycles

Figure 10.7   Diagram of BPM System Landscape and Solution Migration Paths.

conclusion of the integration tests, the production environment should be built by promoting all tested components of the process management solution from development environment.

Other than the minimum required environments, it is very useful to have a sandbox environment. The sandbox environment is used to build the prototype and for the process design experts and developers to experiment with different alternatives before creating the desired alternative in the development environment. Another helpful environment is stress testing. For process management solutions expected to experience high throughput, stress testing is essential to make sure the solution, when put into the production environment, can handle the throughput with reasonable response times. During stress testing, process instances are created using an automated testing tool with test data from the integration test plans. Because of the high volume of process instances required for stress testing, it is not recommended to perform stress testing in the same environment and at the same time integration testing is taking place.

Go live is the last activity of the implement phase. Go live is when the users are allowed into the production environment to use the process management solution. It is the most exciting time of the project. This is the moment when the project team and the organization find out whether the process management solution is working or not. As the saying goes, this is when the rubber meets the road. Some project team members should be assigned to support groups of users. Those team members not assigned to specific users serve as the issue resolution team. Inevitably, users will encounter problems. An issues tracking tool should be used to capture all issues reported by users. Once issues have been reported, they should be assigned to issue resolution team members for resolution. Go-live support can last from two weeks to two months or longer. The end of go-live support marks the transition from project implementation to production support. This is when the support for the project management solution shifts from the project team to the process support office.

Phase 6: Support

The last phase of the BPM implementation methodology is the support phase. Where the previous three phases, analyze, design, and implement involve the process management project team, this phase involves the process support office. The process management organization units report to the process czar. The process implementation office is the unit that implements process management projects. The process management project team participating in the analyze, design, and implement phases comes under the auspices of the process implementation office. The process support office is the organizational unit that takes over support of process management solutions from the process management projects. The transition occurs during the go-live support period. Once project go-live support ends, some project team members (such as the change leaders and core team members) return to the business units and other project team members (such as the project manager, the organizational design experts, and the process design experts) prepare for the next process management project.

The process support office contains several support teams. Each of the process support teams is assigned business processes that it supports. Once the process management solution from the project team has been transitioned to the process support team, the support team is tasked with monitoring process performance, gathering process statistics, validating the process management solution design, and managing the process. Monitoring process performance and gathering process statistics can be done using the BPMS product. The process performance statistics can be used to determine whether the original design goals of the process management solution have been attained. If the goals have not been attained, the process data will help in diagnosing problems with the design and provide feedback to the process implementation office for future projects. In a process-oriented organization, process performance serves as a benchmark for employee rewards. The performance statistics gathered by the BPMS product serve as inputs for management and human relations (HR) to decide on employee rewards. Finally, the process support team resolves issues encountered with any process instances. Working with process managers, the process support team implements enhancements to the processes it is supporting. Enhancement opportunities that require a longer time frame and substantial resource involvements are submitted to the process implementation office. The project planning function of the process implementation office prioritizes, plans, and schedules process improvement opportunities for implementation.

Conclusion

In this chapter, we discussed a generic BPM implementation methodology. What we described here might not be 100 percent applicable to all organizations intent on pursuing BPM. It should serve as a high-level reference for most organizations. Hopefully, a BPM–bound organization will find this reference methodology useful in developing its own implementation approach. In this book, we discussed a wide range of topics regarding the BPM principles and technology. BPMS is a young and maturing technology. New products and enhancements for existing products are constantly being introduced. What we described in this book are ideal features we believe a BPMS product should possess. While the current offerings by product vendors still have room for improvement for effecting a process management solution, the products that are available by the time this book is published will undoubtedly be markedly improved. BPMS is a very exciting technology that promises benefits long desired by process-oriented organizations. The excitement also generated hype about what this new technology can do. This book takes a realistic approach in discussing what this technology can offer. Hopefully, readers will find the content of this book useful in your journey into BPM.

Notes

1. Markus, M. L. and Benjamin, R. I. 1997. The Magic Bullet Theory in IT-Enabled Transformation. *Sloan Management Review*. Winter: 55–68.
2. A good book on mindset is *Beyond Change Management* by D. Anderson and L. Anderson published by Jossey-Bass/Pfeiffer in 2001. In fact, Practicing Organization Development series by the same publisher contains good books on the subject.
3. Harmon, P. 2003. *Business Process Change: A Manager's Guide to Improving, Redesigning, and Automating Processes*. Morgan Kaufmann. San Francisco.
4. Burlton, R. T. 2001. *Business Process Management: Profiting From Process*. Sams Publishing. Indianapolis.

Index